D0857016

STEALING YOUR
VOTE

THE INSIDE STORY OF THE 2020 ELECTION
AND WHAT IT MEANS FOR 2024

CHRISTINA BOBB

INTRODUCTION BY STEVE BANNON

Skyhorse Publishing

Copyright © 2023 by Christina Bobb

All Rights Reserved. No part of this book may be reproduced in any manner without the express written consent of the publisher, except in the case of brief excerpts in critical reviews or articles. All inquiries should be addressed to Skyhorse Publishing, 307 West 36th Street, 11th Floor, New York, NY 10018.

Skyhorse Publishing books may be purchased in bulk at special discounts for sales promotion, corporate gifts, fund-raising, or educational purposes. Special editions can also be created to specifications. For details, contact the Special Sales Department, Skyhorse Publishing, 307 West 36th Street, 11th Floor, New York, NY 10018 or info@skyhorsepublishing.com.

Skyhorse® and Skyhorse Publishing® are registered trademarks of Skyhorse Publishing, Inc.®, a Delaware corporation.

Visit our website at www.skyhorsepublishing.com.

10 9 8 7 6 5 4 3 2 1

Library of Congress Cataloging-in-Publication Data is available on file.

Print ISBN: 978-1-5107-7669-2
eBook ISBN: 978-1-5107-7670-8

Cover design by Amber Colleran

Printed in the United States of America

This book is dedicated to:

The conspiracy theorists, election deniers, political prisoners, deplorables, and every American who dared to question The Narrative.

Contents

Introduction

by Steve Bannon

Christina Bobb is first of all a Marine. A Marine Corps Major, in fact. This is not something on the margins of her personhood. This fact, that she is part of the finest combat fighting force in the American military and arguably the world is central to who she is and how she comports herself.

Stealing Your Vote: The Inside Story of the 2020 Election and What It Means for 2024 reads like a combat memoir. Why? Because it is a combat memoir. The steel one would expect from an officer "from the Corps" comes through on every page, in every encounter. This is the story of how a Commander-in-Chief was thwarted, a coup was carried out, and an illegitimate President was installed. It is not a novel or some other work of fiction. It is a first-person, eyewitness account of a woman who saw her duty clearly, logically, and uncompromisingly. To Stop the Steal—and in doing so, save The Republic that she took an oath to defend—as an officer in the United States Marine Corps.

Stealing Your Vote focuses on the two central issues in the destruction of America's elections: Radical Democrats who game the System with illegal ballots and Gutless Republicans who are too intimidated to stop it.

Major Christina Bobb reveals the behind-the-scenes politicking that prohibited any real investigations in the moment when it mattered the most into the obvious theft of the 2020 presidential race.

The United States of America is the greatest nation ever to exist on earth, and yet it's under attack like never before in our nation's history. Since our foundation, we have proven to the world that a nation's greatness directly correlates to the level of freedom its people experience. We've been the freest nation on earth, and therefore, we prospered more than our peers. Since the 2020 election, we've watched America rapidly decline—putting us at risk to invasion through our southern border, economic collapse through reckless spending, and indoctrination in our education system, among other problems.

The Make America Great Again movement is about making America free. Freedom is our greatest weapon, the "secret sauce" that elevates us among the nations. Yet, an elitist cabal of globalists aim to syphon our freedoms to centralize it among a few. We vastly outnumber them, so they must use deception and convince us that centralizing their power is *our* idea. If they can convince us that their power grab was our choice, they can seize control of the freest nation ever to exist and strip us of our rights before we're wise enough to stop them. They're doing it through our elections.

The front line of this globalist takeover is the ballot box. If Americans believe we choose these leaders, then their power, policies, and decisions appear legitimate. The cabal has disguised their takeover by obscuring the election process.

November 2022

COVID accelerated the takeover of our elections by fundamentally changing the process. The establishment, both Democrats and Republicans, flooded our election system with mail-in ballots, drop boxes, and private organizations who took over the job of government officials. What they said was only a safety precaution for COVID became the norm for 2022.

Arizona stands out as the example of how elitists hide behind incompetence to seize control of an entire state, and ultimately our nation. Half of the voting machines in Maricopa County broke in the early morning of Election Day, forcing people to wait in line for hours (if they could) just to cast a ballot. When people couldn't cast ballots, the county had them use "door 3," which meant they dropped their ballots in a locked box, and the county promised voters officials would cast their ballots for them later. When door 3 filled up, voters were forced to cast their ballots into Rubbermaid bins and pray that some-one actually cast their votes.

The Maricopa County recorder stated, "the issue impacted less than 7 percent of Election Day voters (about 17,000 ballots)," which is coincidentally the margin of victory for the gubernatorial race, and much more than the margin of victory for the attorney general's race, if you believe the statistic.

Is it a coincidence that these problems occurred on Election Day when MAGA voters were all waiting until Election Day to cast their votes in person? Or, that the secretary of state running the election was the Democrat gubernatorial candidate who was declared the winner? Incompetence benefits Democrats, and the elitists hide behind it to manipulate our elections for their benefit.

Save Our Elections

Americans have a very small window, and it's rapidly closing, to save our elections and ensure the people actually elect their leaders. *Stealing Your Vote* pulls back the curtain and educates the reader on how public officials manipulate their votes. It's up to us to get involved and prevent the manipulation that is robbing us of our ability to self-govern. Major Bobb has compiled an infuriating compilation of stories that should provoke the reader to participate in the process.

The book explains the complex and often contradictory recommendations, the competing interests, and the hand-to-hand combat between the media, the campaigns, the political parties, elected officials, and law enforcement. *Stealing Your Vote* spares no one—including the author herself, in a riveting first-person account that "puts you in the room."

Bobb is a partisan and an advocate, and she writes from that perspective. However, the most unique aspect of the book is the unsparing take on the Republican Party and its failed responsibility to keep Radical Democrats like Marc Elias in check; to put "Election Integrity" at the top of the agenda and take the necessary actions to safeguard the "sacred vote" of the American People. The tragic collapse of our election system is changing America—*Stealing Your Vote* will make you angry. The test for Major Bobb is to see if the book makes you translate that anger into action.

America can be great, and free, again, but it will only happen if enough people are aware of the problem and work to correct it. It takes all of us. Get involved in your local precinct to volunteer or become a committeeman. Work for your county's elections office or join a grassroots effort. The only thing that has ever made any country great is its people. When people are empowered to live life to the fullest, a nation will prosper. We have two years until the next presidential election. What are you prepared to do about it?

CHAPTER 1

Election Day

This was the most secure election in U.S. history. Joe Biden is the most popular presidential candidate in American history.

—The Narrative

For more than two hundred years, the recipe for influence in Washington, DC, has been a potent cocktail of money, political power, and media. When Donald Trump won the presidency in 2016, he had all three. He was beholden to no one, and therefore, a threat to everyone.

The political elite were taken completely by surprise. "The swamp"[1] thought they controlled the narrative, the political parties, and the direction of the country. They thought they controlled elections too, but somehow they had lost. They were determined to never let that happen again.

November 3, 2020

For months, we had watched as President Donald Trump held multiple rallies a day, jam-packed with tens of thousands of people clamoring to see him. Meanwhile, Joe Biden had been unable to get even a hundred people to show up to his campaign rallies. The Biden-Harris campaign had resorted to drawing circles on the ground or renting cars to try to make it look like they had more support. By election night, there was no doubt in my mind that Donald Trump would set records with the number of voters showing up at the polls to support him. And he did. Trump received 11.2 million more votes[2] than any incumbent president in history . . . depending on how you count.

Chanel Rion and I were reporting from the White House on election night. As the chief White House correspondent for One America News, Chanel took the lead and handled most of the live hits. Between hits, we sat in the green tent on the North Lawn tracking the races and making predictions. It's freezing cold sitting outside for hours in Washington, DC, in November, so we took turns rotating from the space heater to the heated blanket as we chatted about the tight races.

While Chanel was reporting from the North Lawn, I moved to the plaza in front of St. John's Church to report on the people in front of the White House. DC had taken precautionary measures and boarded up windows all around the city, after 2020's "summer of love" had wreaked havoc on the city. Yet now, on election night, everything was pretty quiet outside the front of the White House. There were people in the street, but nothing threatening. As we edged closer to the results, I re-entered the White House compound and joined Chanel back in the tent.

"Looks to me like Trump has a really solid lead. What do you think?" I asked Chanel.

"Yeah. I'd say he has this pretty handily in the bag." Chanel nodded to her laptop as we followed the results across the states. "Florida's looking pretty solid Red. I think we can expect Trump to claim Florida here any minute."

Not long after President Trump won Florida, we saw Fox News call Arizona for Joe Biden. "Arizona?!" Chanel and I both questioned. "Wait. What?!" I looked at Chanel as if to say: why had Fox News skipped *the entire country* to call a West Coast state? Could they have done it simply to throw off Trump's momentum? We waited so long for Florida—on the East Coast—and then they called *Arizona*?!

Chanel looked just as confused as I. "Where are they getting their information from?" Chanel and I both started searching for a source and calling OAN headquarters to try to figure out what was going on with Arizona. Nothing. We couldn't find any legitimate reason to call Arizona for Joe Biden.

"You don't think they're going to cheat, do you?" I asked Chanel. I didn't really believe anyone would cheat in any significant way, but the move to call Arizona gave me pause. On our morning conference call for our daily reporting, our bureau chief had asked us each our predictions for the day. I said I thought President Trump would win decisively. I went so far as to say that despite COVID, I thought we'd have a result by the end of the night. Now . . . I wasn't so sure.

"I don't know what to think. But this is weird," said Chanel.

Our concerns intensified as we started hearing reports that battleground states were going to pause counting and resume in the morning. We both questioned whether anything like that had been done in the history of the country. States like Pennsylvania, Georgia, Wisconsin, and Michigan were reporting problems and saying they needed to pause and pick up the count the next day. President Trump was heading for victory in many states, and now they wanted to stop counting?! A little voice in my head raised a frightening idea: whoever was trying to get Trump out of office needed time to find more ballots. *A lot more ballots.*

I started tracking the secretary of state's website in Michigan and the vote tally was completely wrong. The numbers Secretary of State Jocelyn Benson was reporting did not match what was on the website, which didn't match what was being reported.

Chanel and I watched as states announced they would pause counting and resume in the morning, and no one in state leadership pushed back. Why were none of these states insisting that the vote count continue? We had counted through the night before, what was so different this time? Citizens needed their state leaders to step up and stop these rogue practices, yet no one did. Arizona, Wisconsin, Georgia, Pennsylvania, and Michigan all have *Republican* majority legislatures. Yet no one, on election night, successfully demanded a stop to the illegal practices of excluding Republicans from the process, accepting ballots after Election Day, and using unlawful mail-in ballots. Not one state legislator, governor, or elected official stood up and demanded that the law be followed. Like every other American, they all went to bed thinking we'd wake to the same America. We didn't.

Media's Response

Chanel and I recognized the problems and reached out to OAN headquarters to try to get more information. Maybe headquarters knew something we didn't. Why are they stopping the count? Why are Republicans being excluded from the process? We watched as President Trump's attorney, Pam Bondi, got a court order to be allowed inside the Philadelphia counting facility, but the sheriff refused to enforce the court order.

Judges and secretaries of state were laughing at Republicans as they were excluded from the election process, and no one stood up to protect our most sacred democratic process, our right to free and fair elections. Surely, Chanel and I weren't the only reporters questioning what was happening? OAN headquarters did not have any more information than we had, and shared our concerns. We looked to other networks to see how they were covering the strangeness.

Most major news networks didn't skip a beat. Even on election night, with plenty of videos of networks *subtracting* votes from Republican candidates, including President Trump, on live television, they all seemed to be acting like this was normal, nothing to worry about. But conservatives worried. Did we just witness an election heist?

As the media pushed forward, trying to ignore the avalanche of irregularities and inconsistencies, hoping Americans didn't have time to figure out what was going on, One America News dug deep to try to make sense of what had just happened. Nothing was as it seemed . . .

- Sheriffs ignored lawful court orders.
- Election officials blocked meaningful participation in the election process.
- Secretaries of state threatened and bullied local county canvassers and illegally declared elections certified that weren't.

This wasn't just bad, it was *un-American.*

America prides itself on free and fair elections. In fact, election integrity is so fundamental to our country that we insist on free and fair elections from our allies as well. The US State Department has decades-old procedures in place to ensure that when America runs elections overseas, like we did in Iraq in 2005, for example, we follow specific protocols to safeguard them as legitimate elections.[3] In 2009, the Obama administration published an assessment of how it determined the Ukraine elections were illegitimate. Specifically, the following six criteria qualified the Ukrainian election as rigged:[4]

1. Illegal use of absentee ballots,
2. Opposition observers were ejected from the counting process,
3. North Korean–style voter turnout,
4. Mobile ballot box fraud,
5. Computer data allegedly altered to favor a candidate, and
6. Reports of opposition fraud (stuffing the ballot box).

According to those very same guidelines, the 2020 US presidential election did not meet our own State Department standards for a legitimate election. **Serious and credible allegations of every single one of these six criteria were present in *our November 3 election*.** And the media were silent.

Worse than silent, the media tried to brainwash Americans into believing everything was as it should be. One anchor was even caught on a hot mic whining that people were protesting the election, saying "what is happening?! . . . we've called it!"[5] She seemed to believe she was endowed with some sort of divine authority to bestow power on elected offices. No rebuttals. Certainly, no objections allowed from the peasant class; us lowly commoners shouldn't have a voice.

Rudy Giuliani's Legal Team

In the days after the election, as questions continued to go unanswered, I was put in touch with Rudy Guiliani, and by mid-November 2020, I had volunteered to help Rudy's legal team investigate and challenge the results of the 2020 election. I was asked to focus on coordinating the litigation efforts in Arizona, Michigan, and New Mexico.

By the time I joined Rudy's legal team, most of the Republican establishment had checked out, and the campaign apparatus cut off funding to the legal team. Technically, the campaign was over. Support staff couldn't afford to stay and help the fight, because now that the election was over, the campaign funds were no longer available. Attorneys were left to do their own administrative work, which further ate into the time available to do substantive legal work. At first, we didn't even have access to PACER, the federal court case tracking system, which meant we couldn't follow our own federal cases without local counsel providing the documents. The establishment Republicans wanted nothing to do with a team of lawyers asking uncomfortable questions and digging up dirt on the 2020 election irregularities.

The election was already two weeks past and the establishment wanted to look ahead to 2022. The campaign headquarters building in Arlington, Virginia, was largely vacant, with a few loyal staffers sticking around, unpaid, to continue the work of cleaning up the mess of 2020. With few exceptions, the campaign lawyers hired and paid by the Trump campaign had moved on to other work. One senior attorney claimed any question of election fraud was a waste of time, and criticized the attorneys trying to fight for election integrity. Rudy Giuliani told me that attorney didn't want Trump in office, because he believed he could raise more money challenging a Democrat incumbent for president in 2024. To him, it was all about money, and Trump *out* of office raises more money than Trump *in* office.

Around the same time that I joined Mayor Giuliani's efforts, the big corporate litigation firms retained to defend President Trump were all quitting. Their other big corporate clients threatened to take their business elsewhere if their lawyers defended President Trump.[6] So, predictably, they all bailed.

We were left with a small handful of dedicated attorneys who had worked the campaign, and a few more attorneys, like myself, who simply cared about the mission and volunteered to investigate election fraud. With about a dozen attorneys and investigators, we got to work.

The Establishment Shuts Down Fraud Claims

A complaint over election irregularities in Pennsylvania had already been filed by the lawyers who quit, but Mayor Giuliani wanted to add some causes of action, so the lawyers began work on a First Amended Complaint. After a few days of drafting, revising, and perfecting the First Amended Complaint, the team sent it to local counsel in Pennsylvania and asked her to review and file it. If she had questions or suggestions, she should speak directly to Mayor Giuliani.

Early the next morning, I got a call from my friend, Matt Stroia. "Did you hear what happened to the Pennsylvania pleading?" Matt asked.

"No. What happened?" I asked.

"Local counsel filed the First Amended Complaint," Matt said slowly, leaving me anxious to know where he was going. "But she removed the cause of action for fraud before filing it. So, we don't allege fraud in the election *anywhere* in the Pennsylvania case."

"What?! That's the whole point of the case!" I shouted. It took me a second to process what happened. How could an attorney do something like that without first calling Mayor Giuliani? "Did she call the mayor first?" I asked. Surely, I was missing a crucial piece of information.

"Nope. None of us knew. We found out when we got the certified copy. No fraud alleged." Matt was matter-of-fact. He also seemed not to know what to make of it.

"I mean, that's malpractice if she did that without permission," I said, questioning how on earth that had happened. "How long before the mayor fires her?" I asked, dreading the search for a new lawyer.

"Well, I just emailed him the certified court copy. So, 3 . . . 2 . . . 1," Matt said, joking.

When we got to the conference room at the RNC headquarters, Rudy was already fired up and working to fix the mistake. One attorney was at the white board charting out the options to fix Pennsylvania and move forward in the other states. Rudy vigorously announced his frustration at the local counsel and her apparent incompetence.

The mayor threw the Pennsylvania court filing down on the table. "Damn it! This is the kind of case lawyers dream of! Our lawyers aren't fighting!"

Unbeknownst to the Giuliani legal team at the time, the Pennsylvania local counsel *had*, in fact, consulted the pre–Rudy Trump campaign legal team on what to do with the First Amended Complaint. Those lawyers instructed her to remove any reference to fraud in the election. From Giuliani's perspective, they had torpedoed the case.

Giuliani went to work to seek permission from the court to file a Second Amended Complaint so his legal team could actually argue fraud. But first, the court asked him to acknowledge that no fraud was alleged in the First Amended Complaint. He had to agree, conceding that the First Amended Complaint contained no allegation of fraud.

The media erupted with headlines saying, "Giuliani acknowledges there is no evidence of fraud!" This was just the beginning of a persistent, overwhelming media campaign to lie to the American people about the 2020 election fraud evidence. We didn't know it at the time, but we were about to face months of similar frustration, when the facts seemed clear, but the media intentionally distorted those facts to paint a very different picture.

When I read the coverage of the Pennsylvania case, I was angry. Those stories were completely untrue. Mayor Giuliani didn't say there was no evidence of fraud; he simply acknowledged to the court that the fraud allegation had been left out of the First Amended Complaint, and he would like to refile in order to allege fraud.

Rudy Guiliani received unprecedented criticism of his efforts to investigate the 2020 election. He was unfairly ridiculed and canceled, because he dared to question openly what everyone questioned privately: Was the election stolen? Critics claimed Guiliani was not an election law attorney, which is true. He is simply a dedicated American who stepped into a void no one else could fill, and he got canceled. It wasn't just for his dogged pursuit of truth surrounding the 2020 election. Don't forget that it was Rudy Guiliani who uncovered Hunter Biden's laptop. The Left was on a rampage to stop Rudy, and they did everything they could to destroy America's mayor simply because he did what he always does—tried to save America.

Let's Try the Legislatures

Problems were emerging in multiple state courts, largely because local counsel had a very small window to actually challenge the election results. Most states required that any challenge to the vote must be litigated within days, possibly weeks of the election. The timeline was nearly impossible to meet. We decided to try a different tactic and turned to the state legislatures.

As you probably recall from your high school civics class, our presidential elections use an electoral college system, meaning the popular vote in a given state determines which slate of electors will vote for president, and each state is awarded a certain number of electors based on population. Article 2, Section 1, Clause 2 of the United States Constitution vests the authority to select electors with state legislatures, ***and only state legislatures***. Most states delegate the responsibility to their secretary of state, but the authority to appoint electors lies solely with the state legislatures.

Our Founding Fathers believed state legislatures were the best defense against federal government overreach, and that state legislatures would defend and fight for the citizens of their states, because they are closer to the people. That's what we were counting on when we decided to contact the state legislatures.

Pennsylvania State Senator Doug Mastriano had already stepped up to the plate and agreed to hold an informal hearing to allow Mayor Giuliani to present evidence to state officials in Pennsylvania. I decided to reach out to state lawmakers in Arizona to see if Arizona would do the same.

My first call went to Arizona State Representative Mark Finchem. He was cautious, and asked me several identifying questions. After taking a few minutes to confirm my identity, he called me back.

"Ms. Bobb, what can I do to serve the people of Arizona? We all feel we got cheated, and my constituents want to know the truth."

Representative Finchem is a character with a passion for Arizona. He wears a cowboy hat and boots and sports a thick mustache. "It just so happens I have already been working on holding a public hearing on the election issue. This is fortuitous timing. I'd love to host Mayor Giuliani if he has evidence he'd like to present."

Over the next few days, Representative Finchem and I coordinated the hearing for Arizona, which took place in Phoenix on November 30, 2020. Arizona Speaker of the House Rusty Bowers—a Republican—blocked all attempts at holding the hearing and refused to allow it to take place at the Capitol. So Finchem held the hearing off site and on a voluntary basis, inviting any lawmakers who wanted to attend and consider any irregularities with the election. (Bowers eventually became a witness in Liz Cheney's show-trial January 6 hearings, demonstrating his contempt for his own constituents.)

The mayor's legal team held similar hearings in Pennsylvania, Arizona, Georgia (twice), and Michigan. These hearings allowed the public to learn about the hundreds of poll workers and volunteers who were excluded from meaningful participation, the bullying and physical removal of Republicans from the process, and a number of mathematical anomalies discussed by experts. One America News covered all of the hearings, but I had come down with COVID and was unable to attend any of the hearings.

Airing the hearings so the public could learn about some initial findings of fraud, mismanagement, and irregularities was a good start, but it wasn't enough to correct a stolen election. We needed more evidence, and that would take time and a lot of effort.

The Race to January 6

Investigating fraud often takes years, but we only had eight weeks until the January 6 deadline, when the election was due to be certified by the Senate. Not only did we need to investigate the fraud, but we needed to convince state and local leaders to use their constitutional authority to protect their states.

Most state and local leaders don't think of themselves as the backstop to runaway federal government . . . but they are. For far too long, state legislatures had ceded the responsibility for managing voting and vote counting to administrators and state executives, never worrying about what might happen if someone actually cheated. Now they were faced with evidence of cheating on a massive scale. Nothing like this had happened in our country before. State officials had no idea how to handle the situation.

I sat with Mayor Giuliani as he talked with state official after state official, and almost all of them expressed fear at the thought of standing up to The Narrative and using their authority to question the results. There were a few exceptions. Mark Finchem, Sonny Borrelli, and Leo Biasiucci of Arizona were ready and willing to take a stand. Burt Jones, Brandon Beach, and William Ligon of Georgia, and Doug Mastriano and Rob Kauffman of Pennsylvania were all willing to explore possible solutions to a fraud everyone suspected but couldn't yet prove beyond a reasonable doubt. Mayor Giuliani continued his fruitless efforts with Mike Pence all the way until the morning of January 6, 2021.

But as January 6 approached, we realized we couldn't assess the situation, gather all the evidence, investigate and confirm the fraud, and use the legal process to correct a stolen election in fewer than eight weeks. Despite media coverage to the contrary, we didn't lose the battle due to the facts. We simply ran out of time.

CHAPTER 2

January 6, 2021

And we fight. We fight like hell, and if you don't fight like hell, you're not going to have a country anymore . . . My fellow Americans, for our movement, for our children and for our beloved country, and I say this, despite all that's happened, the best is yet to come.
—President Donald J. Trump, January 6, 2021

It was early afternoon, and I was debating whether I should stay outside the Capitol and report what was happening on the ground, or move to a different location. One America News had reporters inside the major buildings, as well as on the roof overlooking the events, but we didn't have anyone reporting right outside the Capitol. I had just completed my report from the third-floor Rotunda in the Cannon Office Building, the same building where Congresswoman Alexandria Ocasio-Cortez has her office and later claimed she feared for her life. Absolutely nothing happened inside Cannon while I was there. It was so quiet that, as a reporter, I thought it was a bit boring and decided to leave to see what was happening out front.

A few protesters were making a lot of commotion as I walked through the crowd on the lawn of the Capitol. I stopped to watch, and saw what looked like a disturbance. There were a handful of unruly people, but there was a large police presence, so I figured the police would squelch any potential disturbance pretty quickly. One group of police officers had detained a Trump supporter, as his friends demanded they let him go. It struck me as odd, because he looked pretty benign, while others looked to be doing more damage to the actual Capitol building with batons, but the police completely ignored them. Why not focus their efforts on the individuals doing more damage? I zipped my coat up higher and turned to survey the crowd.

I wanted to interview the people out front and on the National Mall, so I called my videographer to tell him to leave Cannon so we could film outside.

"I can't leave," he said. "They moved all the press to the basement and made us leave our equipment in the Rotunda. I'm heading to the basement now and don't know if I'll have signal."

"Wait. What? Why are they sending you to the basement?!" I asked. It had only been a few minutes since I'd stepped outside and there were no indications of a need to evacuate. Cannon had been perfectly quiet, why would they make the press leave their equipment and move to the basement of the building?

"Security is saying there's a threat. They're sending us to the basement for precautionary measures." He was annoyed he'd be on lockdown for the near future, but was otherwise fine.

"*Is* there a security threat?!" I asked.

"I didn't see anything happen, but security says there is. So, we have to go." He was at the mercy of the Capitol Police.

Locking the press in the basement may have been an important safety procedure. It just so happens that it also prevented a dozen news networks inside the Cannon Rotunda from reporting that it was perfectly safe and quiet. Not every Capitol office building was put on lockdown; perhaps the Capitol Police in Cannon were simply more cautious than the others. It's still unclear.

I was lucky to have stepped out when I did, and just missed getting locked in the Cannon basement myself. But now I had no videographer and no way to broadcast what was happening, or conduct any on-camera interviews. Social media was the next best option. I posted a few clips of the crowd, chants, and some updates, then I pulled my coat above my ears and pushed against the crowd, making my way towards the Willard Hotel. Rudy Giuliani and some other members of the legal team were watching the events of the day unfold from his hotel room, so I went to join them.

January 6 Information War

When I arrived at the Willard, I found the team watching the events on television.

"They sent the press in Cannon to the basement!" I announced, thinking I'd be sharing news. They all looked at me unsurprised. What else was new?

"Didn't you walk here from the Capitol?" Someone asked, somewhat confused. "Didn't you see the commotion?!" They looked at me like I'd been completely oblivious to reality.

I *had* walked from the lawn of the Capitol down Constitution Avenue and then down Pennsylvania Avenue to get to the Willard. Every street was jam packed with people marching to the Capitol. But I hadn't seen any commotion. Just the initial little tussle, but surely the cops got that under control, right? "What commotion? There's nothing happening there."

"Look at the TV!" One of the Trump attorneys yelled. He was mad and pointed with both hands to the TV. "This is so bad. Why are people going inside the Capitol?!" He was genuinely upset and felt that the disrespect of the Capitol reflected badly on the Trump crowd. "The media will blame Trump supporters! We'll lose popular support to continue to look into the election fraud."

I watched the TV and heard the anchor talking about a riot at the Capitol, but it didn't make any sense. I was just there, and it was *overwhelmingly peaceful.* I watched as they showed pictures of people filing into the Capitol and walking around. The news portrayed the rioters as Trump supporters and declaring that Trump protesters were assaulting the Capitol.

Rudy interrupted and yelled at the TV. "Those aren't our people!" he protested. "Our people are farmers from Ohio, and plumbers in Missouri. They don't do parkour off the Capitol building!" He said, pointing to the rioters in black climbing the walls of the Capitol and scaling the building. The mayor was protesting the description by the media. "Our people don't scale walls! That's ANTIFA!"

We watched as the media looped the same damaging footage of smoke grenades and batons beating the Capitol windows. They didn't show the Trump supporters yelling at the police to help,[1] or the police moving barricades and shuttling the people into the Capitol *at the direction of the police.*[2]

The media served up a convenient Narrative: *Trump supporters are bad and evil and are assaulting the Capitol.* Never mind that we had just lived through "the summer of love" with ANTIFA and Black Lives Matter destroying businesses and buildings in virtually every major Democrat-run metropolitan city in the country. Never mind that Trump rallies produced larger turnouts than any ANTIFA or BLM event and had *never* had a significant violent incident. We were now being fed The Narrative, which we must accept or be deemed a conspiracy theorist, insurrectionist, or national security threat.

Mike Pence and the Great Republican Compromise

As we watched the TV and saw what was happening *outside* the Capitol, we discussed what was taking place *inside*. Congress was involved in a solemn duty. Every four years, Congress receives all of the electors submitted by the states, counts them, and ultimately the president of the Senate signs to certify the final vote count. The vice president serves as the president of the Senate, so the authority to certify the 2020 final vote tally belonged to Republican Vice President Mike Pence.

There were a lot of questions over the integrity of the election, and Pence needed to make a weighty decision determining the fate of the nation.

Two days earlier, Vice President Pence had met with constitutional law scholar John Eastman[3] in the Oval Office, along with President Trump, Pence's chief of staff Marc Short, and Pence's attorney, Greg Jacob. State legislators from four of the seven contested states had sent letters to Pence asking him to return their electors slate back to the states so they could reconsider. Eastman was there to discuss the options. Arizona, Wisconsin, Pennsylvania, and Georgia[4] had all sent letters asking Mike Pence to return the votes to the states for reconsideration. The question was *would he do it?*

Democrats claimed Pence had no authority other than to certify the results before Congress. Republicans were arguing that the United States Constitution gives the president of the Senate the authority to take any action deemed necessary to ensure an accurate vote count. Both sides argued over the implications of the Electoral Count Act of 1887, which was passed by Congress after the 1876 election, when several states issued competing sets of electors and Congress was unable to determine who won the election for several weeks.[5] The ensuing presidential elections were also very close, causing concern in Congress about the procedure for counting votes. Without a consistent way to count the votes, different counting procedures could change the outcome of an election in a very close race. In an effort to prevent that from happening, they passed the Electoral Count Act.

Interestingly, the two parties had been on opposite sides twenty years earlier. During the 2000 *Bush v. Gore* election and the years that followed, those opposing Bush's victory opined that the Electoral Count Act was unconstitutional.[6] Al Gore was the vice president and president of the Senate at the time, and would have benefited from the view that he had full authority to resolve any disputed electors, if the issue arose.[7]

In 2020, the tables were turned, and now Democrats aggressively wanted limits on the president of the Senate, while conservative lawyers were arguing that Pence had the power to decide whether to send the electors back to the states. The constitutionality of the Electoral Count Act has never been litigated, so this was the perfect opportunity.

Cowardice and Corruption

The legal issue in question was complicated, but it comes down to whether Mike Pence had the constitutional authority to allow the contested states to reconsider the slate of electors they had sent to Congress to be certified. Constitutional law scholar John Eastman advised Mike Pence that he did have the constitutional authority, and there were plenty of Democrat opinions from about twenty years ago to support that position.[8] The states had asked for a second chance to review. We should have given it to them.

However, on January 6, President of the Senate Mike Pence ignored their requests and certified a Biden victory despite the concerns over the accuracy of the election. Pence refused to give the states a second chance.

Worse than that, Pence manipulated the public by saying "some believed that as vice president, I should be able to accept or reject votes unilaterally."[9] Pence went on to defend himself for not unilaterally exchanging the electors and awarding Trump electors. *That was never the question.* The lawyers never asked Pence to swap out electors and award the election to Trump. While Pence would claim President Trump wanted him to unilaterally change the electors, that was never the crux of the discussion. In fact, Eastman advised him *against* awarding Trump electors. Pence was simply asked to honor the states' request to allow them to reconsider which slate of electors they wanted to certify. Rudy Giuliani had sought meetings with Pence to discuss the issue, and Pence refused to take or return the mayor's phone calls. He would not meet with Rudy.

Teams of lawyers were ready, armed with constitutional arguments to defend his decision. Scholars have debated for one hundred years whether the Electoral Count Act is constitutional. Let's finally put it to the test. To do so, Republicans needed a fighter. Mike Pence wasn't it.

Pence boasted of his integrity for resisting the lust for power of unilaterally exchanging electors. In reality, he capitulated to Democrat demands and did what the Republican establishment always does. He folded.

Thomas Jefferson set a historic precedent in the election of 1800 when Georgia's electoral vote failed to comply with constitutional requirements.[10] Jefferson "used his authority as Senate president to exclude his Federalist competitors, restricting the runoff to a two-man race between himself and Aaron Burr."[11] Jefferson used his authority as the president of the Senate to determine whether or not to count the electoral votes from Georgia.

President Trump has long admired Jefferson's courage to make that decision in the face of opposition. After Pence buckled under pressure, President Trump told him "you're no Jefferson." The Republican establishment has a habit of pretending to take the high road, but actually refusing to fight when challenged. The Republican establishment is the embodiment of *cowardice.*

The "Insurrection"

The Narrative tells us that a group of rogue, angry Trump supporters, incited by Trump's patriotic speech, stormed the Capitol to commit violence, but the evidence doesn't support The Narrative. The evidence *does* support the idea that a group of malicious actors coordinated with Capitol Police to initiate what appeared to be a violent break-in of the Capitol, and innocent protestors got swept up in the scheme. America-loving Trump supporters simply followed the cues of the Capitol Police who waved them inside and directed them throughout the building.

Should they have gone into the building? No. Was it reasonable for them to believe that if the police were waiving them inside and directing them where to go, then it may have been legal to be there? Yes.

Those who hate Trump and wanted to see him impeached knew hundreds of thousands, if not more, would be marching the streets of Washington, DC, and would end at the Capitol to protest certifying the votes on January 6. They took advantage of their First Amendment right to protest and used it to frame Trump and his supporters.

They also refused, for months, to release the identity of the police officer who murdered Ashli Babbitt, an Air Force Veteran. After an "internal investigation," *not released to the public,* they exonerated him. Liberals had cried to "DEFUND THE POLICE" for over a year, and suddenly, on January 6, they decide to do a private investigation and protect the police officer who killed a Trump supporter. After his name became public, we learned this officer had a history of poor weapons handling and had even left his firearm in a Capitol bathroom.[12]

Democrats had been using every opportunity to protest police brutality, yet not a word of protest over the murder of Ashli Babbitt. Suddenly police were their allies, at least if it furthered the narrative that Trump supporters invaded the Capitol.

Why would anyone arrange such a destructive and bizarre event? Two reasons. First, it was another opportunity to frame Trump and impeach him so he couldn't run again in 2024. Second, the establishment knew about the legal efforts to persuade Mike Pence to honor the states' requests and return the electors to the states to decide. If Pence heeded the states' requests, the states might switch electors and award them to Trump, giving Trump his second term. Rather than allow Mike Pence the opportunity to stand firm, causing chaos and mayhem would keep him in line and ensure he certified the election for Biden, which he did.

Lying to the American people, staging a fake insurrection, and tricking innocent Americans to break the law all for political gain falls squarely within the Democrat establishment's standard operating procedures. The Democrat establishment is the embodiment of *corruption*.

CHAPTER 3

No Checks and No Balances

Wherever law ends, tyranny begins.

—John Locke

In many ways, the 2020 election turned into a fiasco because those who should have been minding the store abdicated their leadership roles. The henhouse was unpatrolled, and the fox marched right in. Whether it was state legislatures failing to rein in their governors and secretaries of state, or the Republican establishment folding under pressure instead of demanding answers, the sentinels who should have been keeping our elections safe abandoned their posts—and let democracy be overrun.

Yielding Power

At the state level, the problem began when state legislatures and courts failed to rein in their state's executive branch concerning elections. State legislatures are responsible for making laws in each state, including election laws. Only the state legislature can change the laws in a state. None of the contested state legislatures changed their state voting laws due to the COVID-19 pandemic. So how did we have a tidal wave of new voting procedures, rules, and policies? The governors and secretaries of state in Pennsylvania, Michigan, Wisconsin, Georgia, Nevada, and Arizona simply used the COVID-19 crisis as an excuse to break the law.

Every state has laws in place that dictate absentee or mail-in ballot requirements. Mail-in voting is particularly ripe for fraud, so it's up to each state legislature to balance the convenience of mail-in voting versus the integrity of the election. The laws in each state vary slightly, but the gist is that legal mail-in ballots must be requested from a registered voter for a lawful purpose. Once the request is received, the county election officials must verify the information and note it in order to process an absentee ballot. The point of these laws is to make sure that each ballot mailed out is going to a registered voter who requested it at a specific address.

In 2020, Democrat secretaries of state decided to disregard the law and mail ballots out to everyone regardless of whether that person wanted a mail-in ballot, intended to vote, or even lived in the state anymore. Doing so created a massive influx of "extra" ballots. These rogue secretaries of state also disregarded the law by registering people outside of the legal guidelines, mostly past the lawful voter registration date. All of these secretaries of state who disregarded the law are Democrats, with the exception of Georgia, who had a Republican secretary of state . . . who also violated the law.

The new COVID rules, simply made up by government officials, *not the legislature*, were filled with ways to cheat. Expert witnesses testified that no one conducted signature verification,[1] meaning the mail-in ballots could have been filled out by anyone. Without verifying the signature, and without the voter being present (because the ballot was mailed in), how could election officials know it was cast by a real-life legal voter? They couldn't.

Ballot drop boxes were another weak link in the chain that is supposed to protect voting integrity. Mark Zuckerberg, founder and

CEO of Facebook, donated $350 million[2] to a non-profit organization called Center for Tech and Civic Life. As you will read in future chapters, the Center for Tech and Civic Life was active in the 2020 election and worked in key swing states to "help" their elections. The organization has not disclosed a lot of its activities or how the money was spent, but we do know at least some of the money was spent on drop boxes.

These drop boxes look like oversized mailboxes and are simply a place where voters can deposit their ballots and someone else will pick them up and deliver them to the polls to be counted. It's basically a government-sanctioned form of ballot harvesting, which is illegal in many states. Very few security measures can protect against any rogue individuals discarding or replacing ballots once they've picked them up from the drop boxes. Drop boxes also make "ballot stuffing" easier. Any volunteer or election worker could add additional ballots to the count and no one would know the difference, especially since no one checked the signatures or voter IDs.

Some of the efforts funded by Zuckerberg include targeting Indian reservations and hiring workers to establish early voting on the Indian reservations in Arizona. Historically unprecedented, critics claim that the efforts influenced voting on the Indian reservation and unlawfully aimed to produce Biden votes among the Native American population.

Another maneuver that opened the door to fraud came in the form of refusing to consider a voter's ID. Mail-in ballots, or ballots dropped off at the COVID drop boxes, were received without the benefit of having the voter standing there to confirm the ballot is a legal vote. Without signature verification and without enforcing voter ID requirements in many of these states, how could election workers verify that the ballot they had in front of them was legally cast from a legal voter? They couldn't.

Democrats claimed it was the compassionate thing to do, making sure that everyone had a chance to vote whether they legally registered or not, and whether they had a legal ballot or not. Some courts, like Arizona, ruled that the practice was illegal and must be stopped. That ruling came after 150,000 people had been illegally registered. Other courts, like Pennsylvania, shrugged their shoulders at the fact that the executive branch had illegally overruled the legislative branch. Hundreds of thousands of ballots were affected in Pennsylvania, and the court didn't care.

Some have argued that the executive branches in these states did not overstep their authority; pointing out that most state legislatures have passed laws *allowing* the secretaries of state and governors to have certain authority as it pertains to elections. There are a number of reasons for state legislatures to delegate responsibility to the secretaries of state or governors. From a practical standpoint, it's easier to have the executive branch manage and control the operations for elections. They are set up to *execute* the laws, so it makes sense to have them run elections. Also, many state legislatures are part-time legislatures, meaning the individual legislators have other jobs and only legislate when they are in session. Some of the state legislatures are not actually in session during the month of November, which would make it impossible for the legislature to run the elections. **But remember, this authority is to run the *operations* of the elections—to make sure the rules are followed—*not to change the rules*. That power belongs to the legislature, and the legislature alone.**

The fact that the state legislatures delegated their authority to the executive branch is not surprising. What *was* surprising was their response when so many people pointed out that governors and secretaries of state had overstepped their authority, forced through rule changes that violated the law, and conducted elections "operations" in ways that seemed to invite fraud.

Most of them did nothing.

To be fair, it was a bizarre time, and I think many of the legislators were shocked and surprised at what appeared to be a fraudulent election. They needed to get their bearings and figure out what they could do. Sadly, after months of waiting, it became apparent most of the Republican state legislatures either went into vapor lock, unable to figure out how to solve the problem, or they simply didn't care.

Mayor Giuliani called several Republican state legislators to discuss the options. Most were apologetic, saying, "I'm sorry, but there's nothing I can do." That of course wasn't true, but most were in denial, unprepared, unwilling, or simply too scared.

DHS Folds

Unfortunately, the abdication at the federal level was even worse.

The Department of Homeland Security, where I served as the executive secretary during the Trump administration, is the federal agency that has some jurisdiction to assist in securing our elections. Senior executives that work there will tell you "it's complicated," because each state is responsible for their own elections. With thousands of counties across the country, each independently running separate elections, the differences in so many counties create a sufficient obstacle to prevent widespread fraud. In theory, that's true. In practice, states have adopted similar procedures, often using the same companies, and have a network in place to report election results faster than any lone county can check their work. The counties use enough similarities in practice that the safeguard does not actually work.

The Cybersecurity and Infrastructure Security Agency (CISA) is the agency within the Department of Homeland Security that focuses on election security, among other things. CISA has an advisory board with experts in the community to help the director make key decisions. The director of CISA is a presidential appointee confirmed by the US

Senate. The advisory committee, at the time of the 2020 election, was made up of representatives from four of the major election software and management companies involved in the 2020 election.

Specifically, the members of the advisory committee, known as the Election Infrastructure and Sector Coordinating Council (SCC), included Chair of the Council Brian Hancock (Unisyn Voting Solutions), Vice Chair Sam Derheimer (Hart InterCivic), Chris Wlaschin (Election Systems & Software), Ericka Haas (Electronic Registration Information Center), and Maria Bianchi (Democracy Works). Every single one of those companies played a role in the 2020 election, and would have a specific and financial interest to ensure the public believes their companies made sure the election was secure.

On November 12, 2020, the director of CISA, a Republican Trump appointee, issued a statement in conjunction with the advisory board saying, "The November 3 election was the most secure election in American history."[3] The statement was pure propaganda. CISA hadn't conducted an investigation and actually had no information upon which to base the statement. It simply fit The Narrative.

The statement released disclosed the fact that each of the SCC members, and all of the election companies represented, contributed to the statement, but most of *the media* failed to inform the public. The Narrative said this was the most secure election in US history, and they used election companies, with a vested interested in that narrative, to fool the public into believing President Trump's own administration had investigated and made that determination. That was never true. Unfortunately, the leaders at the Department of Homeland Security never addressed the misinformation.

Shredded Ballots?

On one specific occasion, Rudy's legal team had learned through sources on the ground that a federal investigator had received a call from a shredding company in Georgia. The shredding company stated that it had been contacted by a suspicious group claiming to be a trucking company looking to shred four thousand pounds of paper quickly. The shredding company has a shredder inside their truck, like a garbage truck, and typically does an initial shred on-site when they pick up a load of paper. Then they move the shredded paper to another facility and turn the shredded paper into powder. After initially accepting this particular job and taking custody of the documents, the shredding company called the federal investigators. They were concerned the documents might be ballots from the Georgia election, and they were worried they had just run them through a shredder.

We could not confirm whether they were ballots or not without an investigation. The senior executives at DHS said they didn't have authority to do anything, and asked the FBI to take custody. The four thousand pounds of shredded paper may or may not have been ballots. I don't know. The point is that no one on President Trump's team, with authority to do so, bothered to figure it out.

The Department of Justice Folds

The Department of Justice (DOJ), which includes the FBI, would lead any criminal investigation, should DOJ choose to investigate allegations of fraud in the 2020 election. Bill Barr was the attorney general at the time and responsible for initiating any criminal investigation. If there was ever any hope that Bill Barr had the backbone to stand up to the establishment, it evaporated when he stated that the Department of Justice had no evidence that there was any fraud in the 2020 election.

Barr failed to make clear that the Department of Justice and FBI had not actually *looked* for evidence of fraud in the 2020 election. He never opened an investigation, never issued subpoenas, never contacted state officials to coordinate resources, never interviewed any of the hundreds of witnesses that provided affidavits, nothing. He never contacted Rudy Giuliani or the lawyers working the case to see what information we had gathered.

I distinctly remember one evening when Rudy and about half a dozen lawyers were strategizing what we could do before January 6. Rudy had reached out to Barr to try to coordinate efforts. He was told Barr was on vacation and not to be bothered. Bill Barr refused to help the investigation and any legal efforts. Neither DHS nor DOJ, the most crucial agencies in the executive branch after the election, was willing to use their authority to investigate the 2020 election. The Republican establishment folded.

The Two-Party Balance of Power

It's worth noting that—although the parties have changed over the centuries—we effectively have had a two-party political system since the birth of our nation. For the last 150+ years, it's been Democrats versus Republicans battling and bartering to have their party's policies implemented. Just like our three branches of government, the two parties serve as a natural check and balance for each other.

Democrats tend to have an emotion-centered ideology, claiming to care for the population in a sentimental or humanitarian way. Republican ideologies tend to be more logical and pragmatic, and the policies usually have a clearly defined method of implementation. Both ideologies are needed to create a balanced society that *functions efficiently* (Republican efforts) and *operates with empathy* (Democrat efforts). Too much Republicanism and our society will function, but it may seem devoid of institutionalized compassion. Too much Democratic ideology and the culture will feel warm and fuzzy, yet it will cease to function properly, depriving everyone of a working society.

For most of our nation's existence, we have balanced the two parties appropriately, allowing us to grow into the most powerful, wealthy nation on earth where people can prosper.

Most people paying attention today, however, would say something is wrong with our government. And they'd be right. But the problem is not our political ideology or difference of opinion. The problem is that our two-party system has failed. More specifically, the Republican establishment has let go of their end of the rope, causing the checks and balances system to collapse.

Tension and Compression

Imagine the Golden Gate Bridge in San Francisco, or the Brooklyn Bridge in New York, with their magnificent cables and artistic towers suspended above the city, bearing the load of the masses. These suspension bridges hang majestically over their cities while carrying thousands of pounds of weight per foot, allowing their travelers to efficiently get to their destination. Millions of tons of traffic cross these bridges every day, yet the bridges remain stalwart in their purpose, unmoving. How do these stately structures carry so much weight while seeming to float in midair? The combination of *tension* and *compression*.

These two competing forces make suspension bridges possible. The structure of the bridge that cars drive on presses down, exerting force in the form of compression. The cables, or suspenders, respond to the compression with the opposite force of tension, which disperses the weight of the structure onto the towers, which transfers it to the earth, making the bridge drivable and sturdy.

If a suspension bridge suddenly lost its tension, it would collapse. Similarly, if one political ideology stops pulling its weight, government fails everyone. The cultural collapse we're seeing today is the result of the Republican Party retreating to cowardice and refusing to fight for conservative values.

Democrats haven't had to fight Republicans in any meaningful way on policy grounds for years. So, it should come as no surprise that rather than demanding an explanation for the irregularities that took place, the Republican establishment just said, "okay fine, you can have the 2020 election," and moved onto raising money for future elections.

That's also what happened in Michigan, Pennsylvania, Georgia, Wisconsin, and Arizona—all Republican majority legislatures. Republican state legislatures abdicated their responsibility to ensure fair, secure, and transparent elections by giving so much power to governors and secretaries of state, and failing to oversee them or rein them in *for years*.

Over the next several months, citizens across the country were still convinced that the 2020 election was riddled with fraud. Brave patriots united together to uncover the truth and figure out exactly what happened during the election. It turned out to be harder than we ever imagined. Citizens hired their own experts, investigated in their own time, and even went to court to try to get access to more information. As you'll see in the following chapters, it turned out that Republicans were the greatest obstacles to the election investigations that unfolded after November 3.

CHAPTER 4

The Battle for Arizona

When elections aren't conducted according to the rules and electors block efforts to perform an audit, it's very hard for people to accept the results.

—Karen Fann, Arizona Senate President

"Motion denied."

A wave of relief and fear came over me all at once. "Hurry up and adjourn the hearing!" I silently pleaded. After months of court battles, multiple hearings, filings, and challenges, the Arizona Senate had just won the last and most important battle.

The judge rapped his gavel to adjourn the hearing, and with that the power elite's relentless campaign to derail an investigation into the Arizona election was finally tabled. The Maricopa County Board of Supervisors, the Arizona Democrat Party, the secretary of state, and the lone Democrat on the Maricopa County Board of Supervisors had sued the Arizona state legislature *three times*, seeking to prevent any post-election audits into what transpired in Maricopa County during the 2020 election. And they had lost every time.

Finally, the Arizona Senate was free to begin their audit.

The Long and Winding Road

It had taken five months just to clear a path to *start* an investigation into what had gone wrong in Maricopa County. It had been a long and arduous road. At every turn, the establishment politicos had put up roadblocks and minefields. They tried every trick in the book, from delays to threats to wild accusations, and when they couldn't deter the investigators, they turned to the courts.

Their first request for an injunction came in December 2020, following a December 15 subpoena issued by the Arizona Senate to Maricopa County. The subpoena ordered the county to turn over the ballots, machines, and a number of other election-related items in order to enable the Senate to audit and investigate irregularities surrounding the election.[1]

The Maricopa County Board of Supervisors, made up of four Republicans and one Democrat, refused to cooperate. They went so far as to file a request for a restraining order against the Republican Senate. That's right, Republican county supervisors filed a request for a restraining order against the Republican-led Senate, because they did not want to comply with their Senate's lawful subpoena.

The United States Constitution vests authority to oversee elections with the state legislatures, and *only* the state legislatures. Arizona law gives subpoena power to the presiding officer of either chamber (House or Senate). Thus, President of the Senate Karen Fann had issued a lawful subpoena to Maricopa County for their election evidence, and the county simply said "no." In a bizarre but unsurprising twist of events, the Republican county supervisors actually sided with the Arizona Democrat Party, supporting their suit to prevent the Senate from conducting a forensic audit. But the lawsuit failed. The judge ruled that the subpoena was legal, the audit could proceed, and instructed the county to cooperate.

Undeterred, the county supervisors[2] then focused on making examination of those machines and ballots as cumbersome and expensive as possible. They refused to allow the Senate's auditors to use county facilities, which would have made the most sense. The ballots and machines were still in the county's possession, and the auditors could have easily used the county's facilities to simply audit the ballots and machines on-site. Nope.

The county demanded that the auditors remove the ballots and machines from the county's facilities and audit them in a separate location. Of course, that move increased costs, logistics, and the likelihood of problems, but that appeared to be the county's goal. Obstruct. Make transparency as difficult as possible. The Senate's auditors were forced to lease another location and decided on the Veterans Memorial Coliseum, which became the landmark for the audit.

If at First You Don't Succeed, Sue, Sue Again

Back in the courts, after losing their first request for an injunction in December 2020, the Board of Supervisors sued again in February 2021. Multiple parties filed similar suits, creating a number of cases, so the court consolidated all of the cases into one. Spearheaded by Maricopa County, the plaintiffs once again sought relief from the court, asking for an injunction or restraining order to prevent the Arizona Senate from investigating. They lost again.

The Arizona Senate proceeded to bid and select the Cyber Ninjas to run the state audit. They agreed to conduct the audit at the Veterans Memorial Coliseum and to begin the week of April 26, 2021, with the auditors moving the equipment on-site the week before.

Meanwhile, there were still more attempts to shut down the audit before it could begin. The "Protect Democracy Project" tried to intimidate the audit team. (The Protect Democracy Project is a far-Left liberal non-profit that attacks conservative initiatives, despite calling themselves "non-partisan.") They hired the long-established Democrat law firm Perkins Coie to send a letter to the auditors and their subcontractors threatening a lawsuit if the auditors completed their contractually obligated duties to audit Arizona. The letter was signed by four different attorneys, representing four different organizations. I'm told there are about seventy attorneys working at those organizations combined. I believe this is where the rumor originated that "Perkins Coie sends seventy lawyers to Arizona to stop the audit."[3]

The auditors were in place, Veterans Memorial Coliseum was leased, and the bills were piling up. In an effort to obstruct and delay the audit *one more time*, the Arizona Democrat Party filed their third request for an injunction on April 22, 2021. By delaying until the auditors were literally moving into the Coliseum, the Democrats managed to cause the biggest possible logistical challenge. They knew full well that the longer this dragged out, the more expensive the audit became and the probability of completing it plummeted. Judge Christopher Coury even acknowledged that the doctrine of laches (or unreasonable delay) could apply, although he never made that ruling. The Democrats could have brought their claim again in February or March, but specifically waited until the Cyber Ninjas had incurred costs and expenses to launch their final assault.

The $1 Million Question

On Friday, April 23, 2021, the Honorable Christopher Coury heard this third request for an injunction. Coury was appointed to the bench in Arizona by Republican Governor Jan Brewer in 2010. He won a retention vote in 2012 with 71 percent of the vote. In October 2020, the Maricopa County Democrat Party had campaigned against Coury to try to get him off the bench due to his conservative rulings on an education ballot proposition.[4] Coury won retention in 2020, despite the Democrats' efforts to remove him. He was considered a favorable judge for a Republican Senate.

The Democrats' grounds for requesting this latest injunction was their accusation that the Cyber Ninjas were interfering with voting rights, disenfranchising voters, and that the auditors' activity was illegal and must be stopped. The allegations were outrageous. One attorney representing the Arizona Democrat Party, Ms. Roopali Desai, actually hypothesized that the auditors could be using volunteers from the FBI's Most Wanted List. She provided no evidence to support her wild hypothesis, but told the court that since the Arizona Democrat Party had not approved of the auditors or the volunteers, then the audit should not be permitted to go forward. The Democrats were sure the auditors were doing illegal, dangerous things that must be stopped.

Judge Coury ruled that he would issue a stay, meaning the auditors could not continue any work on the audit until the judge made his final ruling at the next hearing on the following Monday. However, Judge Coury also expressed concerns over whether the Democrat Party was coming to the hearing "with clean hands," a legal phrase effectively meaning they weren't being totally honest. In order to protect against any gamesmanship, Judge Coury added an interesting condition: He ordered that the stay would only take effect if the Arizona Democrat Party posted a $1 million bond. If the Arizona Democrat Party was able to prove their claims of erratic illegal behavior on the part of the Cyber Ninjas, they'd get their money back. But if they failed, their $1 million would go to fund the audit.

It was one of the most crafty and masterful pieces of judicial work I have personally witnessed. He was giving the Democrats what they wanted, but he was calling their bluff . . . if they were bluffing. The accusations they had made were quite severe, and if true, must be addressed. So, Judge Coury gave the Democrats seventy-two hours to produce evidence to support their claims. He even ordered the Cyber Ninjas to turn over documents that could potentially corroborate the Democrats' theories.

It was noon. Democrats had until 5 p.m. to post the bond. I watched the clock and prayed they didn't post it.

The press immediately went to work claiming a Democrat victory, saying the judge ordered a stop to the audit. Many conservatives I spoke with were concerned, wondering how a judge could possibly do such a thing and stop the audit?! I was thrilled. Judge Coury was exposing the Arizona Democrat Party for the liars they were. He was forcing them to put up or shut up.

Did the Democrats believe in their claims enough to post the bond and risk funding the audit? No. They never posted the bond and the audit proceeded as planned over the weekend. The final hearing on Monday would be the decisive blow . . . or so I thought.

The Arizona Democrat Party didn't believe their own arguments enough to put their money where their mouth was. But the media weren't deterred. While they had to acknowledge the Democrats' refusal to post the bond, they heralded it as a success, saying the court still required the auditors to comply with all applicable voting laws while conducting the audit.[5] That was not news; *of course* the auditors had to comply with voting laws, that was never at issue.

It was a sneaky parlor trick of wordsmithing to obscure the truth. Democrats sued, saying Cyber Ninjas were breaking the law. The Cyber Ninjas explained how they were following the law. The Judge gave the Democrats seventy-two hours to provide proof the Cyber Ninjas were violating voting laws. Democrats provided no evidence whatsoever of illegal activity. The judge effectively said, "Okay, as long as the Cyber Ninjas continue to follow the law, the audit can go forward." The liberal media used that to say, "the judge ordered the auditors to comply with the law!" A more correct headline would be, "Judge denied Democrats request for an injunction. No evidence of illegal activity found." But that wasn't The Narrative.

By refusing to post bond, the Arizona Democrat Party effectively acknowledged to the court that they did not believe they would prevail on their legal claims. To this day, they still have not produced any tangible evidence to support their concerns of erratic illegal activity on the part of the auditors. "Maybe the volunteers are on the FBI's Most Wanted List!" Any proof? Nope. None. As Monday approached, the Senate just needed the court to enter the final order denying the motion for an injunction and the case would be closed.

Switching Judges

On Sunday night I got an angry call. "What the fuck happened, Christina?!" I received a colorful phone call from a colleague angry about something I knew nothing about yet.

"What?!" I had no idea what he was talking about.

"Judge Coury recused himself! Why?! What happened?!"

Oh no. Judge Coury was a great judge for the Senate. He had just masterfully forced the Democrats to reveal they knew they didn't have a case, and now he's recused himself? Would the next judge be as fair and impartial? The Senate had good success in court up until this point. Would they lose their winning streak right at the finish line?!

"I hadn't heard that yet. Let me look into it. I'll call you back." I had been on the ground in Arizona since the day before the ballots arrived at Veterans Memorial Coliseum. Many of my friends and colleagues, particularly those that live in Washington, DC, or really anywhere outside Arizona, would call me for "on the ground" information. But this was information I did not yet have. I made some calls and dug into the court filings, desperate to find out what had happened.

I discovered Coury had recused himself because a new attorney from the firm for the Cyber Ninjas had made an appearance on the case, and that attorney had clerked for Judge Coury in the past. Coury believed he could no longer impartially oversee the case, because his former clerk was now listed on the pleadings as a member of the firm representing the Cyber Ninjas. Less than twenty-four hours before what appeared to be the decisive hearing, we were about to get a new judge.

My phone was blowing up from *everyone* who knew I was covering the story in Arizona. Most folks I had worked with on Rudy's team were calling to figure out what was going on. We were all anxious; on Friday it looked like the audit would go forward, and now it could all be derailed. Worse, there was nothing any of us could do about it but wait. I told my colleagues the recusal was a result of a new name being added to the list of attorneys representing the Cyber Ninjas.

"What the fuck?! Why did they add a new attorney now?!" was the typical response I got.

"I have no idea. I don't know if it was intentional or not. The attorney works at the firm, but I don't think he's actually on this case. Maybe he did join this case, or maybe they accidentally used the wrong pleading template when filing their documents over the weekend. I can't tell if they intentionally added his name to the pleadings or not. I really don't know what happened."

Tensions were high and everyone was upset. "That was so stupid! This judge was great for us!" My colleagues expressed their anger and everyone was frustrated.

The next morning, we learned Judge Daniel Martin was assigned to the case. Judge Martin had been appointed to the bench in 2007 by Democrat Governor Janet Napolitano. Local attorneys I had talked to told me Judge Martin has the reputation of being a fair judge, but is a Democrat. On Monday morning, Judge Martin postponed the original hearing set by Judge Coury for twenty-four hours. Now the hearing to decide the injunction would be on Tuesday. It felt like it would never end.

The hearing opened on Tuesday morning, and the attorneys recorded their appearances. The attorney for the Cyber Ninjas, Alexander Kolodin, informed the court that he could no longer continue representing the Cyber Ninjas and needed to withdraw. He then asked the court for a continuance to allow the Cyber Ninjas' new counsel time to prepare. The court explained to Kolodin that with-drawing at this point could severely disadvantage the Cyber Ninjas and he should continue as co-counsel with the new law firm for the remain-der of the day. Kolodin politely declined the suggestion and withdrew from the hearing. Judge Martin proceeded with the hearing, request for continuance denied.

I was very nervous. From my perspective, this hearing was enor-mously significant, not just for Arizona, but constitutionally. The judge's ruling would determine whether the Senate maintained its constitutionally bestowed authority to oversee elections in the State of Arizona, and act as a check in the balancing act of power.

After summarizing the history of the case and hearing arguments, Judge Martin articulated his findings and confirmed what we knew to be true: the Arizona Senate has authority to investigate and oversee elections in the state, and they can lawfully subpoena information to do so. Nothing about the subpoena or the audit was illegal.

Motion denied.

CHAPTER 5

The Arizona Audit Begins

Justice Department, you need to stay in your lane. Do not touch Arizona ballots or machines unless you want to spend time in an Arizona prison.

—Wendy Rogers, Arizona State Senator

Ken Bennett couldn't wait to hold a press conference. The former secretary of state for Arizona and initial spokesperson for the Arizona Senate was eager to be the face of the audit, and mistakenly believed a press conference would go well. He invited the media to the audit floor the day before the audit started. All of the equipment was in place and the media could get a demonstration of how the audit would work and ask any procedural questions. I attended with my videographer on behalf of One America News.

Most of the press attending the event had been to Veterans Memorial Coliseum earlier that week to report on the delivery of the machines and ballots. We all, myself included, went through the same press entrance we had entered earlier in the week. Turns out, that wasn't the right entrance for this event. Immediately, a dozen or so liberal reporters started tweeting, filming, and writing that the facility wasn't secure. Of course, they failed to mention that the head of security corralled us and escorted us to the correct entrance where they conducted security sweeps. The media claimed there *could have been* a security breach, much the same way the auditors *could have* selected their volunteers from the FBI's Most Wanted List. There wasn't. They didn't.

Bennett had very good information to offer, and was prepared to explain the whole process, but he hadn't taken the hecklers into account. One or two reporters in the group actually made it difficult for him to speak. They also attacked Doug Logan, the CEO of Cyber Ninjas. Logan held his own, explaining the review process and how the ballots and machines would be handled—and as soon as the presser was over, he swore off all future press events, except for public hearings with the Senate. Ken Bennett wanted to do them every day but was shut down by the Senate. I'm told Bennett was repeatedly reprimanded for leaking information and giving CNN a behind-the-scenes tour.

Not So Fast

On paper, the schedule for the Arizona Audit looked great. The hand recount would synchronize perfectly with the paper examination and the machine forensic evaluation. Everything would be wrapped up by May 15, when the auditors had to be out of the Coliseum to make room for high school graduations. Unfortunately, the subcontractor responsible for providing the labor underestimated, *by a lot*. They had miscalculated how long it would take to process each ballot for the hand recount, and were off by about 400 percent. Beta tests, I'm told, projected the hand recount would take about three seconds per ballot. But that didn't account for how long challenges and questions in the recount would take. In reality, each ballot took twelve seconds. Which meant, rather than the audit taking three weeks, at the rate they were going it would take twelve.

Doug Logan jumped into action. He negotiated a way for the audit to pause, vacate the premises for the graduation ceremonies, then resume again on Monday, May 24, 2021. The ballots and equipment could move to an on-site storage facility for a week, and then move back into the Coliseum after graduations. Of course, the move and the increase in time meant a drastic increase in expenses. We needed to raise more funds to ensure the audit completed in its entirety.

Voices and Votes

The Senate had approved a budget of $150,000 to conduct the audit. The auditors and the Senate quickly realized the costs would be substantially higher. But $150,000 was as much as the Senate was prepared to spend. The public would have to contribute if they wanted to complete something of this scale. From my coverage of election issues and my involvement on Rudy's legal team, I knew what all the powerful opponents of audits knew: even if Democrats lose in the courtroom, even if they can't intimidate the state Senate, they can shut down an audit by simply choking off the money.

So, I made the bold decision to start my own non-profit, Voices and Votes, to help ensure that legal audits were not starved to death. Chanel Rion, chief White House correspondent for One America News, also wanted to be involved, and said she could help keep our donors informed with emails and marketing materials. Done. We officially formed in March 2021 and started fundraising for the Arizona Audit in April.

I had never been involved in any campaign, political or otherwise. Neither Chanel nor I had any idea how to raise millions of dollars in a few months. One America News was exceptionally gracious to me with my efforts for Voices and Votes. The Herring family, the owners and principal executives of One America News, is as patriotic as they come and could not have been any more supportive of my efforts. They allowed me to mention Voices and Votes on air, frequently, and to ask for donations from viewers. We raised our first $150,000 in a day or two.

Naturally, the Left howled over a supposed "conflict of interest," claiming that a reporter can't also be involved in philanthropic activities. Notice how they never worry about "activist journalists" when those activities promote a leftwing agenda? I was completely transparent with my involvement in helping fund the audit. But my goal was never about The Narrative or the outcome—I wanted to ensure transparency and integrity for all elections. Something you'd think reporters on both sides of the aisle would support.

One America News viewers certainly thought election integrity was a worthwhile goal. They were generous with their donations and support. I'm humbled and honored to have been entrusted by so many Americans with their resources to help fight this fight.

Voices and Votes was not the only organization helping fund the audit. In fact, without other organizations, the effort would have failed. Many other non-profits and philanthropists donated to the Arizona Audit, much more than Voices and Votes. On at least one occasion, donors single-handedly saved the Arizona Audit from having to shut down due to a lack of funding. At one point, payroll was due on Monday, and increased expenses had eaten away at the resources. The auditors worried that if they didn't make payroll, the audit employees would walk out and the audit would come to a screeching halt. Private donors stepped in and wired the money on Friday, ensuring the auditors could continue their work.

Sneaking in a Spy

Meanwhile, there were plenty of people making the audit as difficult as possible. Arizona Secretary of State Katie Hobbs initially seemed to pretend that the Senate wasn't even conducting an audit. She seemed to be under the impression that if she ignored it, the rest of the country would too. Once she realized that wasn't working, someone from her team tried to sneak into the audit.

The story, as told to me by security at the audit, goes like this. Security became suspicious when a man tried to gain access to the audit as a member of the press, but showed up without any camera equipment. They asked for his media credentials, and he pulled out what appeared to be either a fake ID or a fake network. Security asked him to pull up the network's website or confirm the network was real and that he was who he said he was. He opted instead to leave.

The next day, Secretary of State Hobbs told security officials that she was sending a representative to the audit. Security waited to give special access and privilege to this representative from Katie Hobbs' office. Who was this representative? The same man who'd tried to get in with a fake press ID! Only this time he identified himself as a representative of Katie Hobbs's office. Security promptly turned him away, and notified Hobbs's office that she was welcome to send a representative who hadn't lied to them the day before.

Unable to stop the audit, Hobbs demanded to have her own set of observers on the audit floor—lawyers with notepads, writing down all the activity of the audit. President Fann kindly obliged. Hobbs partnered with The Brennan Center, a radical leftist organization in Washington, DC, to send staff attorneys to the audit to roam the floor and note all discrepancies and raise them to the auditors as they happened. The entire audit was color coded; each job had a specific color so everyone else on the floor knew which job each person performed. The auditors decided to put the observers from the secretary of state's office in pink shirts, bright pink fuchsia shirts.

Democrats also tried to discredit the audit by claiming that the Cyber Ninjas were not "certified forensic auditors." The truth is there's no such thing. The US Election Assistance Commission ("EAC") certifies voting equipment and test laboratories for equipment *to be used in an election.* They do not certify auditors. Their ninety-nine-page Testing and Certification Program Manual only uses the word "audit" five times, and does not even attempt to cover the scope of work conducted on the Maricopa County forensic audit. Any attempt to portray the EAC as a body governing forensic audits is intentionally misleading and untrue. There is no such thing as a certified forensic auditor for elections in the United States.

Arizona Unimpressed with DOJ Threats

The next anti-audit tactic was the Department of Justice's Civil Rights Division sending a "letter of concern" to President Fann, in what appeared to be an attempt to intimidate her into limiting the audit. They clearly underestimated Karen Fann. Every concern raised in the letter had previously been addressed in court, on at least two occasions, and every time the court ruled in favor of the Senate. Fann was on solid legal ground to ignore the letter, and she did.

Once the Department of Justice realized their letter hadn't worked, they raised the stakes. Biden's attorney general, Merrick Garland, publicly rebuked the Arizona Audit, calling it "based on disinformation," and promised to double the number of voting rights attorneys at the Department of Justice. His actions were a not-so-subtle threat to Arizona suggesting the DOJ might intervene in their efforts to double check the election results.

That didn't go over well in Arizona. Arizona Senator Wendy Rogers summed up the sentiment best when she told Merrick Garland: "Justice Department, you need to stay in your lane. Do not touch Arizona ballots or machines unless you want to spend time in an Arizona prison." Senator Rogers shot to superstar status as a beloved representative of the people. Rogers, a retired Air Force pilot, is tiny but packs a punch. I spent a lot of time talking with Senator Rogers and she is a true patriot. Humble and honored to serve, Rogers is determined to represent the will of the people of Arizona. Her constituents are telling her they want full transparency, and she'll stop at nothing to give it to them.

Arizona's attorney general Mark Brnovich also stepped up and voiced a strong opinion in response to the Department of Justice. He wrote a letter to the Department, telling Merrick Garland that the DOJ had displayed "an alarming disdain for state sovereignty." He stated, "Arizona will not sit back and let the Biden administration abuse its authority, refuse to uphold laws, or attempt to commandeer our state's sovereignty." Arizona's attorney general put Biden's attorney general on notice that his "office is not amused by the DOJ's posturing and will not tolerate any effort to undermine or interfere with our state Senate's audit to reassure Arizonans of the accuracy of our elections. We stand ready to defend federalism and state sovereignty against any partisan attacks or federal overreach." Brnovich added that the DOJ "letter appeared more interested in supporting the hysterical outcries of leftist pundits on cable television, rather than the rule of law." The message was clear. Stay out of Arizona.

Carnivals and Cartels

The media had been blasting reports that the audit venue was unsecure and could easily be infiltrated by bad actors. In reality, Veterans Memorial Coliseum was extremely quiet and felt remote despite being in downtown Phoenix. The parking lot was massive, extending for an entire city mile, which provided a secluded feeling.

It appeared the audit would come and go from Veterans Memorial Coliseum with little to no fanfare . . . until the carnival showed up.

Literally. A traveling carnival had rented space and set up camp in the west side of the Coliseum parking lot. At first, we were concerned the carnival would be an unnecessary nuisance. As time went by, we realized it wasn't going to be an issue. The audit was as peaceful as could be, and the carnival provided comic relief at times, seemingly appropriate for our collective experience.

In fact, it was a little strange for things to be so quiet. ANTIFA and BLM were nowhere to be found. Why? Liberal corporate media was doing everything it could to stop, stall, or shut down the audit. Why hadn't the liberal rioters arrived?

The nation had just watched for nearly an entire year as BLM and ANTIFA destroyed cities across the country for political reasons. Senate President Fann had certainly expected protesters and perhaps even violence. She had reached out to Governor Doug Ducey's office on multiple occasions asking for law enforcement support for the audit. Ducey didn't respond to her requests. Fann also sent a letter to Democrat Sheriff Paul Penzone asking for law enforcement assistance with the audit. He too ignored her requests.

Just like the private funds that helped pay for the audit, it took private citizens to provide a safety patrol. Enter the Arizona Rangers, an all-volunteer law enforcement organization. They are armed and lawfully allowed to assist local law enforcement to keep the peace and security of any event for which they are needed. True to their western roots, they dress the part in western-style uniforms. After covering the audit for over two months, I got to know a few of the Rangers and am better for it. The men that I met are dedicated patriots who love their country, their state, and their freedoms. They all sacrificed their time, a lot of it, to make sure the people of Arizona got the audit they demanded, and that it was conducted safely.

The Rangers pulled more than their fair share of security duty, but the truth is there were no security breaches, not even any attempts. Rumors had swirled that rioters from Portland would be flown in. It would only take one rogue actor to break through security and light the ballots on fire, and everything would be over. Yet no one tried.

Some people believed that Arizona's open carry laws prohibited cowardly rioters from messing with the audit and risking a bunch of armed cowboys showing up for a real fight. Possibly. But a larger group believed the explanation lay in the fact that Veterans Memorial Coliseum was right in the middle of drug-smuggling territory for the cartels. The prevailing theory was that since the cartels did not want law enforcement presence in the area, they had pressured Governor Ducey to pull all law enforcement support. To give Ducey cover, the theory continued, the cartels would ensure there was no disruption, and therefore no need for law enforcement. No one ever produced any real evidence, but it was a pervasive belief among those at the audit and in the area. I was surprised to learn that was a plausible reason, but it certainly could explain why Ducey, a Republican governor, refused law enforcement support for the Republican Senate.

Myths in Montana

Once the media realized they weren't going to be able to shut down the audit simply by calling people conspiracy theorists or racists, they switched tactics. After weeks of railing about how the audit lacked security and was too accessible, CNN decided to say the exact opposite. Maybe they could get viewers to believe the audit was secretive and lacked transparency, despite the fact that every table had cameras on it that were live streaming the contents of the audit non-stop.

The auditors had set up cameras covering every possible angle of the audit so that the public could view and see the audit twenty-four hours a day. The cameras served a dual purpose. Everything was broadcast live, but also recorded for potential litigation. If anyone challenged the results of the audit and challenged the auditors' handling of the ballots, machines, or any aspect of the audit, the auditors had it all on tape. They can identify the tape down to the ballot and table, as well as the machines. Any challenges to their handling of the evidence are available on tape for all to see.

Nevertheless, CNN claimed the audit was secretive and started a rumor that the auditors shipped the evidence to a secret remote lab in Montana where no one would be able to know what the auditors were doing with the evidence. They sent a reporter to a remote location in Montana, standing in front of a No Trespassing sign, showing how secretive the location was. The report was intentionally misleading.

It would be easy to miss that the reporter said "copies" of the hard drives were analyzed in Montana, sparking a rumor that the ballots and machines were now in Montana. No machines, ballots, or any other original evidence from Arizona ever left the state. The auditors maintained the chain of custody for all original machines, ballots, and every piece of evidence turned over by Maricopa County.

So why Montana? Because the Cyber Ninjas, the lead auditors, had subcontracted with CyFIR, a forensics company based in Montana, for the purpose of conducting the cyber forensic analysis on the evidence.

Ben Cotton, CyFIR's CEO, was present in Phoenix when the audit began and the machines arrived for analysis. He worked with his team to make exact replicas of the hard drives, and any other equipment necessary. The replicas were shipped via secure carrier, maintaining the chain of custody, to CyFIR's lab in Montana where they conducted the forensic examination of the replica hard drives. At no point did any ballots get copied or sent out of the state. Any objection to CyFIR's analysis can be run against the original.

The real story was that the Arizona Senate had hired a firm from Montana to analyze their equipment. There was nothing sensational or particularly newsworthy about the story, but corporate media went wild trying to sow doubt about the validity of the audit.

Lies about Special Privileges

The liberal press seemed intent on claiming that One America News had special privileges or special access to the audit. We didn't. They lied.

For example, they charged that OAN had special access for streaming the audit, which is why only OAN continuously streamed the audit live on our network and website. Nonsense. Any network could have streamed the audit live, and every network had exactly the same access to the auditors' camera feeds.

Here's the real story: Doug Logan was determined the entire audit be accessible to the public. So a few weeks before the audit began, he mentioned to me that he needed a little help figuring out how to stream all of the cameras live. I told him, OAN knows how to do that, maybe we have someone who could help him.

The Herring Family strongly supports election transparency and were happy to help make the information freely available to the public . . . *including to other news networks at no cost*. One America News *never* provided any type of physical assistance with the audit. They didn't own the cameras, didn't install them, and never touched the equipment. OAN simply allowed the auditors to run their streaming cameras through OAN's KlowdTV, which they made freely available on www.AZAudit.org. At all times, the feeds were available to every network to air, at no cost, and freely available to the public to view. OAN chose to air the entire audit live in the bottom corner of the screen on their news channel. Any other network could have done the same. They simply chose not to.

Corporate media also had been complaining from the start of the audit that I had special privileges and exclusive access to the audit. I didn't. I had the same access—about three times a week—as dozens of other reporters from a wide range of media outlets, including CNN. But that didn't stop the liberal press from claiming I was allowed to report from the audit floor every day. I did request more access—I thought the public would want to know everything that was going on in Arizona—and eventually the auditors agreed to allow daily coverage. It wasn't just me. Jordan Conradson from *The Gateway Pundit* was there nearly every day as well. *The Arizona Republic* was in the press box about half the time. Other reporters stopped in for an hour or so. But the liberal press seemed more interested in covering my "special access" than they were in covering the audit itself.

CHAPTER 6

Following the Evidence

We must give voters the confidence that their ballot was counted and cast by supporting mandatory, statistically meaningful post-election audits and full transparency of all election results and data.

—Page 56 of the 2020 Democrat Party Platform

The audit was going fine until Mike Roman called me on May 11. "We've got a problem." Roman ran Election Day operations for Republicans in Pennsylvania and was a consultant to the Cyber Ninjas on how to handle and manage ballots.

"What kind of problem?" I responded. By this point, Mike and I had solved many "problems" together and I was sure we'd solve this one. I just wondered how painful it would be.

"The records, including the ballots, the county turned over to us are a mess and we can't be confident that at least some of them have not been tampered with." The auditors had completed their initial inventory and discovered that evidence seals on some of the ballot boxes had been cut, some of the boxes were missing ballots, some of the boxes had extra ballots, and the chain of custody logs were inconclusive or even missing.

"Okay. That's not that bad. Just put it in the report. It just goes to show a level of incompetence on the part of the county. You can still evaluate the ballots and machines, right?" I was relieved the problem didn't seem insurmountable.

"Yeah. Of course. That's not the problem. The problem is that we need to leave the Coliseum for the high school graduations. If we move these ballots *at all*, then the county will say the auditors broke the chain of custody and messed it all up in the transition to the storage facility. We have to get the information out that the chain of custody was messed up by the county before we move out."

Well that was a problem. The auditors were all subject to non-disclosure agreements and unable to talk to the press. Only the Senate can approve release of information like this, and the Senate wanted to hold all information until the final report was written in August, three months away.

"The auditors are all under NDAs," I replied. "I can't report on this unless they get permission. President Fann will need to approve the release of the info."

Over the next twenty-four hours or so, I waited as Doug Logan worked with President Fann and their legal teams to issue a letter documenting the discrepancies. I wanted to report the letter's contents to OAN viewers immediately upon its release. The next afternoon, I received a head's up from Mike that the letter would be coming out that day, May 12, 2021. I scheduled with our newsroom to go live at 6 p.m. to make the announcement. By 5:30, I still hadn't received the letter and was getting nervous, wondering if I'd have to cancel the announcement. About 5:55 p.m., the letter hit my inbox with President Fann's signature. I had five minutes to read and digest it before the cameras were live.

President Fann's May 12 Letter

President Fann addressed the county in a professional and collegial way, clearly intent on working together to get to the bottom of elections in

Maricopa County. Never once in the letter, nor since, did she accuse the county of any misconduct or wrongdoing.

Fann first addressed the fact that the county remained non-compliant with a lawful legislative subpoena. The subpoena demanded production of the routers, administrative passwords, and splunk logs associated with the machines used for the November 3, 2020 election. Splunk logs are "a software mainly used for searching, monitoring, and examining machine-generated Big Data through a web-style interface. Splunk performs capturing, indexing, and correlating the real-time data in a searchable container from which it can produce graphs, reports, alerts, dashboards, and visualizations."[1] These logs would have given the auditors the real-time information of what was happening with each machine as it happened.

The county claimed the routers contained sensitive law enforcement data and couldn't turn them over. The court disagreed and said the county was obliged to turn over the information, but the county disobeyed the legislative subpoena *and* the court, and refused to hand over the routers. As for the splunk logs, they didn't even bother giving a good explanation for refusing to turn them over; they simply said no.

But the administrative passwords to the voting machines were the real kicker. The county claimed *they never had the administrative passwords* to the voting machines! Only Dominion, the private company contracted to run the machines for the election, had access to the administrative portion of the machines, according to the county. What?! Maricopa County turned over the administration of their elections to a private company, and didn't maintain the ability to check their work? According to Arizona Secretary of State Katie Hobbs, it's totally appropriate for the county to have zero control over what the machines spit out on election night, and Arizonans just need to accept that.

Fann's letter also revealed the information Mike had called me about: that the records were sloppily maintained. Ballots were missing in some boxes, while others had more. The precincts were out of order and mixed together. Chain-of-custody documents were incomplete and, in some cases, missing all together. Evidence seals on the ballot boxes had been cut with no record of who accessed the ballots. Lastly, the letter addressed the fact that machine databases had been intentionally deleted, and the Senate wanted to know why.

The Senate invited county officials to a public hearing on May 18, 2021, where the citizens of Arizona, and the nation, could watch and evaluate the questions and answers for themselves. No one from the County Board of Supervisors showed up. The Senate proceeded with the hearing, walking through all the discrepancies. The Senate again publicly requested the county to cooperate with the audit and help them understand what took place during the election. They never cooperated.

The Will of the People

It's worth noting that when Fox News called Arizona for Joe Biden on election night with only 75 percent of the vote in, Arizonans were *mad*. Trump had won Arizona in 2016 by more than 91,000 votes over Hillary Clinton. Despite rarely leaving his basement, Joe Biden earned a total of 1,040,774 votes in Maricopa County, AZ (Phoenix). That's 508,490 more votes than Obama earned in 2012 (532,284), nearly doubling Obama's 2012 performance in the key swing state. Arizonans wanted an explanation.

During his four years in office, President Trump had corrected their border crisis and shut down much of the human and drug trafficking coming into the state. Arizona is Trump country. Many locals believe there is no way he lost their state, and they weren't going to let Biden take it without a fight. They showed up in mass numbers.

Arizonans protested all over the state—including out front of Speaker of the House Rusty Bowers's and President of the Senate Karen

Fann's homes. State elected officials had been thrust into the fight for our nation's survival. Most couldn't handle the pressure.

Republican Speaker of the House Rusty Bowers folded like a cheap lawn chair. He refused to even acknowledge any problem with the Arizona election. At one point, after the audit had begun, I went to the Arizona House of Representatives to interview members on a number of issues. I was told I was not allowed to conduct interviews on the audit inside the House of Representatives, because Republican Speaker Bowers didn't want it to look like he had anything to do with the audit. I could interview members on the border crisis or any other issue, but not the audit. If officials wanted to talk to the press about the audit, Bowers made sure it had to be outside . . . in Phoenix in the summer. In my view, Bowers is a coward and retreated to the known Republican safe space of business as usual.

In contrast, President of the Arizona Senate Karen Fann is a tough woman. She spent much of her career in the roadway construction industry in Arizona and was used to working around rough men and running the show. Fann launched Arizona Highway Safety Specialists, Inc. in 1984 with only $500, and developed a successful career installing roadway guardrails and signage. She and her husband Jim McKown were ranchers and worked closely with local 4-H clubs and sponsored community events. Karen Fann will not be pushed around.

Fann openly admits she wasn't planning on ordering an audit at all, and had no intention to challenge the result of the election. But her constituents demanded it, showing up at her house for days on end until she delivered. She's committed to serving her citizens. The people wanted an audit, so she gave them one.

Preliminary Findings

By July, the public was hungry for some results. The counting stopped June 28, the auditors had moved out of the Coliseum, and people wanted to know the results. The Senate agreed to hold a hearing and allow the auditors to disclose some preliminary findings, understanding that they needed to complete more work before making conclusions.

The July hearing revealed some startling results. The margin of victory in Arizona between Joe Biden and Donald Trump had been just 10,457 votes. Yet, the hearing showed that 74,243 mail-in ballots had been received by the county without any record of them ever having been mailed out. The county later claimed these were in-person early voters, which is why there was no record of the ballots having been mailed.

168,000 ballots were printed on non-secure paper that did not meet the county's requirements. The auditors believed these were ballots printed at polling locations by the county, which would mean the county failed to comply with Arizona standards. 11,362 people were not on the November 7, 2020, voter rolls, but appeared on the December 4, 2020, voter rolls and were marked as having voted in the November 3, 2020, election. Almost 18,000 voters who voted in the election show as removed from the voter rolls soon after the election. The election server was hacked during the election, and remote access was available. All access logs to the machines were wiped in March 2021 (after the subpoena was issued). Original and duplicate ballots were not properly marked with serial numbers and cannot be verified. There is no way of knowing how many times a ballot was duplicated. The number of votes certified did not match the number of ballots sent to the audit.

These were just the initial findings, and already there were enough discrepancies to change the outcome of the election several times over. While the auditors completed their analysis for actual fraud, the Senate went to work and issued another subpoena to Maricopa County and the private company administering the machines, demanding they turn over the routers, splunk logs, and administrative passwords. Both the county and the company[2] refused to comply. *Republican* County

Chairman Jack Sellers explained in his letter to the Senate: "the Board has real work to do" and referred to the Senate's audit as "Never Land."[3]

The Senate's Response

By the time the Senate issued second subpoenas, Senate President Karen Fann had been ambushed by CNN in the parking lot, bashed and berated across all media platforms, picketed at her home by angry Arizonans who wanted an audit, and accused of trying to steal an election that happened ten months earlier, despite her *repeated* statements that she had no desire to overturn the election. Now her longtime friend and colleague, Republican County Chairman Jack Sellers, had sent an arrogant, disrespectful letter to her after failing to comply with her lawful subpoena. President Fann was fed up. Senate Majority Whip Sonny Borrelli, a retired Marine Corps gunnery sergeant, had been champing at the bit to put the overconfident and insolent county in place. Fann was now ready to let him. Send in the Marine!

Sonny Borrelli served twenty-two years in the United States Marine Corps and retired as a gunnery sergeant. For those who have never had the privilege of serving in the Marine Corps, gunnery sergeants are a special breed. Known for their tenacity, bullishness, and quick-wit humor that humiliates anyone subject to it, gunnies embody the Marine Corps reputation of "no better friend, no worse enemy." They seemingly have a divinely bestowed ability, given to anyone who attains the rank, to simultaneously solve all your problems while being the biggest pain in the ass. Experts in their field, they have the know-how to accomplish the mission, years-in-service to be crusty and intolerant of incompetence, and the dedication to find solutions. Senator Sonny Borrelli fits that bill. In addition to his military career, Borrelli is a Bronco-riding rodeo cowboy. He was inducted into the Military Rodeo Hall of Fame in 2020 for his achievements in Bronco riding and Leadership as the Commissioner of the Rodeo Cowboys Association from 1988–1999. He's tough, and he doesn't mess around.

For eight months, Republican Maricopa County did everything in its power to obstruct the Republican Senate from conducting a thorough audit and investigation into the 2020 election. Senator Borrelli, like the good Marine that he is, was at the tip of the spear fighting back. He had worked with Arizona State Representative Mark Finchem to coordinate the Arizona hearing back in November 2020. That hearing gave President Trump's attorney, Rudy Giuliani, the opportunity to present the case to the Arizona Legislature, in attendance, and expose for the first time the concerns over the Arizona election. Borrelli heard the evidence and supported the constituents in their efforts for more transparency in the election. When President Fann initiated the audit, he supported her and is largely responsible for whipping it up and getting a consensus for it.

Maricopa County had now rebuffed the Senate's *second* subpoena, and written a nasty letter to President Fann, which amounted to a personal slap in the face as well as an open rejection of the Senate's authority. Gunnery Sergeant Borrelli wasn't having it. Citizens of Arizona had complained for months that there were no consequences for corrupt or cowardly officials who disregard the law at the expense of the citizens. Borrelli referred the county's contempt of the Senate's subpoena to the Arizona attorney general's office.

"What do you think Brnovich will do?" I asked Borrelli, referencing Arizona's Attorney General Mark Brnovich. Brnovich had sent a strong letter to the DOJ getting them to back off of Arizona, but that was all he had done. He refused to do any type of in-depth investigation and spent little to no effort on election integrity. He prosecuted a couple low-hanging-fruit cases, but refused to criminally investigate any corruption by state officials.

"He needs to put the county on notice that they are in contempt of the Senate's subpoena and give them thirty days to comply." He responded.

"Thirty days!" I responded, frustrated that they'd just keep running out the clock. "That's terrible! He needs to just open a criminal investigation already!"

"Christina." Senator Borrelli was frustrated with my insistence on a more drastic course of action. "We don't want Brnovich to open a criminal investigation yet. We have to finish our audit first. The Senate has done a great job of allowing the auditors to investigate and we need to let them finish. If Brnovich opens a criminal investigation before our auditors can complete their work, the bureaucrats in the AG's office could sit on this investigation for *years* without disclosing any information. If we want real results in a timely manner, we have to allow the Senate to complete this work. We just want Attorney General Brnovich to force the county to comply with our subpoena."

I knew he was right. In my time on Rudy's legal team, I had worked Arizona and investigated much of the evidence. I tangentially came across the Election Integrity Unit of the Arizona attorney general's office. To say they were less than helpful would be an understatement. They demonstrated zero interest in actually investigating the election fraud of 2020. Giving this case to them would have killed it. Arizonans needed Attorney General Mark Brnovich to exert his weight to make the county comply, but not so much so that he took over the case. Borrelli was threading the needle, and we just held our breath to see what Brnovich would do.

"What happens if the county doesn't comply within thirty days?" I asked.

"The Attorney General can turn off a percentage of state funding to the county until they comply. That's a budget of about $61 million.

They'll comply real fast when the citizens of Phoenix start complaining their county resources have been shut off." Borrelli responded.

I didn't love the idea that no one was getting charged criminally, or that we'd have to wait another thirty days for any type of result, but I knew Borrelli was right and would get the job done. We just needed to wait and see what Attorney General Mark Brnovich would do.

Unfortunately, he did just enough to say he tried, but not enough to actually force action. Republican Arizona Attorney General Mark Brnovich firmly sided with the establishment, failing to compel the county to comply with the subpoena, and refusing to investigate his colleagues.

The people of Arizona were sick of the political games and sick of do-nothing RINOs corrupting their state. In August 2022, Arizona held its primary elections. Mark Brnovich was on the ballot running to become the Republican nominee for the US Senate seat held by Democrat Mark Kelly. Brnovich lost decisively to Blake Masters, a Trump-endorsed patriot who campaigned on America First policies, including election integrity. It wasn't even close. Masters won 40.2 percent of the vote and Brnovich garnered a measly 17.7 percent.[4]

Rusty Bowers, the RINO Speaker of the House who opposed Karen Fann's audit efforts, met a similar fate. He ran for an open state Senate seat because he was termed out in the House, and he also lost to a Trump-endorsed America First candidate, David Farnsworth. Bowers made a name for himself as a witness in the hoax January 6 hearings chaired by RINO Liz Cheney, who also lost her re-election bid in August 2022. Arizona voters spoke clearly. No more RINOs.

Why the Republican Interference?

Throughout the process, I couldn't help but wonder why on earth so many Republicans were working overtime to block the efforts of their fellow Republicans to investigate election fraud. What on earth did the Republican Maricopa County supervisors get out of obstructing justice, violating court orders, disregarding a lawful Senate subpoena, and ignoring the will of their constituents?

None of it made sense until Jordan Conradson of *The Gateway Pundit* published his story of leaked audio he received from a private Maricopa County Board of Supervisors meeting.[5] In a heated exchange, Steve Chucri, a Republican, chastised fellow Board members for falsely claiming that prior audits had been conducted. The Board had said the county already conducted an audit and the Senate's audit was unnecessary. Chucri called the county's sham effort "bullshit."[6]

He went further to point out that the other county supervisors were nervous that their own races were so close, and *that* was the real reason they didn't want an audit or any extra scrutiny.[7] **They were afraid they didn't win their own races**.[8] Clearly the "winners" of elections should not be the ones auditing elections or declaring them legitimate without any oversight. There's an inherent conflict of interest. Which we will see manifest itself again when we consider what happened in Georgia.

CHAPTER 7

Georgia's Republican Roadblocks

Trust but verify.
—Ronald Reagan, Fortieth President of the United States

It took six months to uncover detailed evidence of fraud and corruption in Arizona's election; in Georgia, the proof was at hand almost immediately.

At approximately 10 p.m. on November 3, 2020, election workers at the State Farm Arena in Atlanta announced that they were shutting down the counting for the evening and that the observers should return in the morning.[1] The Republican observers had been kept off to the side of the room for the entire day, throughout the counting process, away from where the actual counting was taking place, and prevented from participating in the counting process.

Nevertheless, according to their signed affidavits, the Republican observers believed the election worker when she told them they were stopping the counting and would resume the next day. They were told to come back at 8 a.m. the next morning. So, they left.

But the counting did not stop. Surveillance video from election night shows that after all the observers and challengers were escorted out, Democrat election workers continued to work the tabulation room, despite everyone else being removed. It's at this point that "Suitcase Gate" started. At about 11 p.m., after the tabulation room was cleared of Republican observers and the press, the surveillance video shows four women pull ballots out from under the table, in what looked like a suitcase, and run them through the tabulators.

The video clearly shows the women waiting for everyone else to leave the tabulation room, sitting patiently, acting as if they are not doing anything, and then, once the area is clear, begin counting the ballots pulled from under the table. In response to the video, Democrats claimed that the ballots were not stored in a suitcase, but in ballot containers on wheels, and that the procedure seen in the surveillance video is completely normal. However, at no other point on the surveillance camera video, during normal operations, do we see workers pulling ballots out from under the table the same way they did after the room was cleared.[2] Not only was it *not* normal, *it wasn't legal*. Georgia law says each party is entitled to have observers present to monitor the counting process, and Republicans were excluded from the process through deceit—they had been told the counting was stopped and they had been sent home.

The first time *anyone* had a chance to see the above-mentioned surveillance video was on December 3, 2020, when Rudy Giuliani held a hearing in Georgia to present the available evidence. An attorney played the surveillance video for the legislators, noting that the legal team had just obtained it the prior evening from State Farm Arena, and had not yet released it to the public or media.

Democrat Georgia Senator Elena Parent pushed back immediately, regurgitating The Narrative. As the hearing went on, she adamantly insisted that the video had already been debunked and wasn't worthy of attention. Republican Georgia Senator Steve Gooch asked Parent how the video could possibly have "already been debunked" when no one had ever seen it before?[3]

Senator Parent stumbled over her words, stuttering to cover the error she'd made, and eventually responded: "These very allegations came up right after the election, almost a month ago, and were repeatedly discussed by the secretary of state's office, including everything that we're seeing here." Her statement is not true. No one had made similar allegations of ballots being pulled from under the table until the video was made public at the hearing.

The liberal press went to work and quickly issued reports saying the video was debunked. It has never been debunked. What is seen on the surveillance video is a depiction of exactly what the witnesses said it is. Republicans were removed from the counting room so Democrats could add hidden ballots to the tally. Some later claimed that the ballots were legitimate. Reports surfaced that Georgia's Bureau of Investigation looked into the matter and said the ballots were legitimate. Then why were Republicans excluded and opposing counsel was never allowed to examine the ballots? Why was everyone sent home? Why did officials lie and say that the counting has stopped? Georgia officials insisted nothing untoward had happened, and simply demanded the public take their word for it.

Another oddity surrounding the Fulton County, Georgia, election was that on Election Day in Atlanta, staff working at the State Farm Arena complained of a water leak in the tabulation room where they were counting absentee ballots.[4] Early reports of the incident called it a "pipe burst," and Republican observers, along with the press, were ushered out of the tabulation room. Fulton County used this pipe bursting as a reason to delay the vote tally, saying that they needed extra time to tally the vote because they were required to evacuate the building. Most people believed *everyone* was being evacuated for safety concerns, but witnesses later stated that Republicans were removed and Democrats were allowed to stay. This is the same night that the surveillance camera showed Republican observers and press being told to leave, while four women were allowed to stay and count secret ballots they had pulled from under the table.

Republicans versus Republicans

Despite the media's attempts to bury this evidence of election tampering, Republican voters in Georgia were raising their voices and demanding answers.

Like Arizona, at the time of the 2020 election, Georgia had a Republican majority legislature, a Republican governor, Brian Kemp, and Fulton County had Republican commissioners. Unlike Arizona, Georgia *also* had a Republican secretary of state, Brad Raffensperger. Georgia, by all accounts, was a Republican state and the most Republican of the contested states. Voters wanted a full audit, not just a recount, of the 2020 election. With Republicans in charge in every aspect of the election, getting an audit should have been an easy win. It wasn't. Republicans in elected positions with the authority to provide the voters with what they wanted put up roadblocks. Just like in Arizona, Wisconsin, Pennsylvania, and Michigan, Georgia Republicans proved to be the biggest obstacle to election transparency.

Republican Secretary of State Brad Raffensperger refused to give Georgia the audit they wanted, but instead conducted a *recount*. The main difference between a recount and an audit is that a recount simply recounts all of the same ballots. An audit inspects the ballots, chain-of-custody documents, and logbooks, and determines whether the ballots were cast *legally*. If fraudulent ballots are cast, a recount will simply recount the same fraudulent ballots and come up with the same fraudulent results, which is exactly what happened.

Brian Kemp, Georgia's Republican governor during the 2020 election, had served as the secretary of state until beating Stacey Abrams to win the gubernatorial race in 2018.[5]

Fair Fight Action, a group backing Stacey Abrams, filed a lawsuit against Kemp, claiming that he used his powers as the secretary of state to benefit himself and manipulate the outcome of the 2018 governor's race by restricting 50,000 voter registrations in Democrat neighborhoods, among other claims. Kemp won the race with 50.3 percent of the vote, more than any gubernatorial candidate in state history.[6]

Claims of election misconduct in the lawsuit against Kemp from 2018 include: misuse or abuse of the provisional ballot process, misuse or abuse of absentee ballots, and failure to allow voters to cure their ballots. The complaint specifically states, "[Kemp] knowingly left Georgia's voting infrastructure vulnerable to hacking. Georgia maintains one of the least secure voting systems in the country. Despite being aware of these vulnerabilities for years, the secretary of state and Election Board rejected and rebuffed attempts to improve data security of the Georgia database of voters."[7]

The complaint also states, "[Kemp uses] election technology that is vulnerable to hacking and manipulation."[8] These are the same complaints Republicans made after the 2020 election. Apparently when Stacy Abrams makes them, the media takes them seriously, but when Republicans do, they are labeled conspiracy theorists.

By November 2020, both Democrats *and* Republicans demanded transparency in Georgia, but Kemp blocked every attempt to check his work. On September 30, 2022, the case was finally resolved in favor of Kemp, ruling that the state's election practices do not violate constitutional rights.[9]

With both parties upset at how Kemp and the secretary of state's office handles elections in Georgia, it's unclear who in the Georgia legislature was in favor of maintaining such fallible voting procedures. Giving the voters transparency into how elections are run in Georgia would give both Republicans and Democrats the information they need to have confidence in Georgia elections . . . assuming election officials properly manage the elections. Interestingly, on March 14, 2019, *Esquire* published an excerpt from the *Atlanta Journal-Constitution* (an article which the *Atlanta Journal-Constitution* has since removed from its website). The excerpt says:

> Democrats said the switch to ballot-marking devices is a costly waste of taxpayer money that will benefit well-connected voting companies at the expense of voters. They repeatedly pointed out that Kemp hired a lobbyist for voting company ES&S, former state Rep. Chuck Harper, as his deputy chief of staff. And they said it was suspicious that voting companies' estimates for the cost of ballot-marking devices, roughly $150 million to $200 million plus annual fees and additional equipment costs, didn't come to light from the Secretary of State's Office until Tuesday. When Kemp was secretary of state last year, his office refused to release the companies' pricing information.

Governor Brian Kemp and Secretary of State Brad Raffensperger have consistently stated there was no fraud in the 2020 election, but have refused to turn over any of the evidence and refused to allow Georgia voters to audit the vote independent of the secretary of state. Clearly, any election audit should be conducted by someone *other than* the official who ran the election.

Audits are designed to check the work of the officials who ran the election and determine if they were run properly. Elected officials should not be allowed to check their own work without outside oversight. Imagine the IRS trying to audit a business, and the business simply says, "Don't worry about it. We audited ourselves and we did everything legally." That would never suffice when it comes to paying taxes. It shouldn't suffice when it comes to our elections.

Secretary of State Brad Raffensperger spoke to many national news outlets claiming that he was under pressure from Republicans, including President Trump, to investigate the fraud and find that the Georgia election was stolen. He leaked his phone call with President Trump, which had so many people on the call, myself included, that it's hard to call it a private conversation. The call didn't contain anything substantial other than confirming President Trump wanted the fraud investigated. That didn't stop Raffensperger from pretending he was somehow a martyr and was standing up for Georgians by refusing to investigate, which is exactly the opposite of what Georgia voters have been demanding for years.

Raffensperger stood firmly by Governor Kemp's side and helped him block any attempts at a real audit. After multiple demands for an audit, Raffensperger continued to simply conduct recounts, which he claims all proved Biden won the election. The recounts were conducted by Raffensperger's team, and were all done outside the view of the public. No one questioned the validity of the ballots or the chain of custody, which has proven to be a problem for Raffensperger. Several grassroots efforts have shown large discrepancies, enough to change the outcome of the election. One group found that 35,000 voters had moved out of the county prior to the election, but still cast a ballot. Of those 35,000, 10,300 *also* cast ballots in the county where they currently reside.[10] Raffensperger simply ignores those findings. The margin of victory in Georgia was 11,779.

Mystery Ballots and Drop Box Miracles

Laura Baigert, journalist for Georgia Star News, got to work investigating the questions that Brad Raffensperger and Brian Kemp refused to answer. Through diligent Freedom of Information Act requests and open records requests, Baigert discovered that Fulton County, Georgia, the home of Atlanta, was missing chain-of-custody documents for 18,901 ballots.

Prior to the 2020 election, Republican Secretary of State Brad Raffensperger decided alone, without the legislature, to mail out absentee ballots to all Georgia residents, regardless if they had requested a ballot. Nothing in the Georgia's election laws permitted such a mailing, and the legislature did not approve the measure, but like many other secretaries of state during COVID, Raffensperger defied the law.

In July 2020, the Georgia State Election Board, not the state legislature, approved the use of drop boxes, claiming an emergency rule was needed due to COVID. Like others in state government, they decided that COVID was an excuse to disregard the law. These drop boxes were glorified mailboxes manufactured specifically for ballots.

Anyone can drop ballots into the drop boxes, making voter ID virtually non-existent. No one checks the ID of anyone dropping ballots in the drop boxes. The only way election officials claim to maintain a chain of custody on these drop box ballots is to require a log from every individual that collects the ballots from these boxes. Two people are required to collect the ballots, and both are required to sign the chain-of-custody forms. Those two individuals then turn the document over to the election officials who sign that they received those ballots from the two identified individuals. Laura Baigert confirmed that those chain-of-custody documents were missing for 18,901 ballots.

Georgia Public Broadcasting jumped to the defense of Fulton County, claiming the documents were not missing, but failed to produce the missing documents. Dispute arose between Georgia Star News and Georgia Public Broadcasting as to whether the chain-of-custody documents were, in fact, missing. According to Baigert, Georgia Public Broadcasting eventually turned over *some* chain-of-custody documents to Baigert that Fulton County never claimed to have had. How did GPB get election documents that Fulton County never had? Or, why did Fulton County not turn them over? Did they lose them? And then how did GPB find them? The whole situation was very weird and never sufficiently explained to show a proper chain of custody. Baigert still does not have all of the chain-of-custody documents, which likely means neither does Fulton County.

Ballot harvesting is a practice where someone collects ballots from voters and turns those ballots in on behalf of the voter, without the voter being present at the polling location. Ballot harvesting is expressly *illegal* in Georgia. Effectively, the secretary of state and Georgia Election Board decided to allow a massive ballot-harvesting scheme by approving these drop boxes, all in the name of public safety.

The drop boxes were disproportionately placed in Democrat neighborhoods,[11] making it more convenient for Democrats to vote. Anyone with access to ballots could have stuffed hundreds or thousands of ballots into the drop boxes, and no one would know, because no one checks ID. Voter roll bloat allows election workers to assign unidentified ballots to voters who have not yet cast a ballot in the election.

Critics claim that doing so is illegal and election workers would never do such a thing, but we know that they did from witness statements and testimony. In reality, election workers could assign ballots to voters innocently, without realizing they are helping to cast fake votes. If someone casts a fake vote and used a stolen voter ID number, the election worker is unlikely to throw the ballot out. The first assumption is that there's a *mistake,* not that the vote is fake. According to witnesses, the workers then assign an unused voter ID to the ballot and allow the ballot to be counted.

Hypothetically, if election workers were to remove all of the observers from the process, as they did at State Farm Arena, and run hidden ballots through the machines, as we saw on the surveillance video, they could simply assign those votes to unused voters on the voter roll.

Although it's unlikely most Election Day workers maliciously would cheat, we know they are more inclined to consider any problem *a mistake* rather than *possible fraud*, due to the percentage of rejected ballots. The 2020 election saw a huge influx of absentee ballots, which should have led to a greater rejection rate, as election officials would need to be more scrupulous in their acceptance of possibly fake ballots. But that didn't happen.

In 2016, the rejection rate of absentee ballots in Georgia was 3 percent. In 2018, it rose to 4 percent. In 2020, with the greatest possibility of fraud by absentee ballots, the rejection rate plummeted to 0.6 percent.[12] *The Atlanta Journal-Constitution* credits the installation of drop boxes for decreasing the rejection rate, claiming that most ballots are rejected because they are received after Election Day. Drop boxes, according to *The Atlanta Journal-Constitution*, encouraged people to drop their ballots off sooner, and thus nearly eliminated ballot rejections. That's one possibility.

The Carter Jones Report

Fulton County, Georgia, home to Atlanta, had problems with their election before Election Day even arrived.[13] Days before the election began, "election materials were not being delivered to polling precincts in a timely manner (or at all) . . . ,"[14] according to the State Election Board Report dated November 13, 2020. Precincts were missing poll pads, the machines that voters use to cast their votes, and the logs misplaced where the poll pads were actually allocated.[15]

Logs showing poll pads were delivered still had them stored in a warehouse, clearly not delivered. The northern part of Fulton County suffered from the worst error, where many of the machines for Election Day were never delivered at all, making it very difficult for residents in those areas to cast their votes. North Fulton County is a conservative part of the county, meaning conservatives had a harder time voting.[16]

John Solomon, with *Just the News*, broke the story of the report drafted by Carter Jones, the Election Day inspector assigned by Georgia Secretary of State Brad Raffensperger to inspect the operations of the 2020 election as they happened.[17] The twenty-nine-page Jones report details operations filled with avoidable errors, and documents the astonishing ineptness with which Fulton County ran their elections. Even Secretary of State Raffensperger is recorded as saying, "Fulton can't get anything right,"[18] yet publicly he told the world the election was "safe and secure" on *60 Minutes*.[19]

He said that, despite knowing that ballots had been left open and unsecured, the chain-of-custody documents for ballots and equipment were missing or wrong, poll pads had been left unsupervised on loading docks, and they had more ballots than secure black boxes . . . just to name a few problems.[20]

According to the Jones report, bags of poll pads and other election material were not picked up to deliver to the precincts and the paperwork did not match.[21] The shipping company called and canceled the shipment on November 2, the day before the election, expounding upon Fulton's problems.[22] Page two of the report states that "all this chaos with the poll pads was caused by getting a flawed file from the secretary of state's office" that failed to remove anyone who had voted during early voting.[23] Election workers had to update the books the morning of Election Day, because the secretary of state's office had failed to do so.[24] Needless to say, records didn't match in many areas of the election.[25]

Jones reports that he overheard a discussion among poll watchers. One party poll watcher asked another if the second poll watcher was ready for a long night. "The second replied that, 'yeah. I'm ready to f*ck sh*t up.'"[26] As it turns out, Fulton County was already doing a good job of that all by itself. Who was vetting these special interest groups to determine how they were vetting their volunteers? How could anyone with such a perspective be considered an appropriate volunteer for election work?

It also just goes to show that these special interest groups had an agenda. They were not innocent volunteers helping to facilitate an election. They were activists there with a purpose . . . "to f*ck sh*t up."[27]

Georgia Findings

Bryan Geels is a certified public accountant, a professional auditor, and was hired as an expert witness in the post-election lawsuit *Trump v. Raffensperger* by the Trump campaign. He was retained to examine the publicly available voter files, and other data, from the November 3, 2020, election and provide his expert opinion on the validity of the votes cast, and look for irregularities.[28] Here are a few of his findings, keeping in mind the margin of victory is only 11,779:

- At least **18,325** individuals voted in the Contested Election who were registered using residential addresses that are listed as "vacant" by the USPS.
- At least **86,880** individuals voted in the Contested Election who the State lists in its 2020 Voter Registration File as having registered prior to the 2016 General Election, but who are not listed in the State's 2016 Voter Registration File. If a voter was not registered to vote in the last election, he or she should not show a registration date that is prior to the last election.
- At least **907** individuals voted in the Contested Election who were registered using residential addresses that are, in fact, PO boxes.
- At least **2,326** individuals who voted absentee by mail-in the Contested Election used mailing addresses that are listed as "vacant" by the USPS.

- At least **1,377** individuals voted in the Contested Election who were registered using courthouses, churches, or hotels as their permanent residential address.
- At least **4,502** individuals voted in the Contested Election who do not appear in the State's 2020 Voter Registration File.
- At least **2,525** individuals voted in the Contested Election whose birth years were different in the State's 2016 Voter Registration File than the State's 2020 Voter Registration File.
- At least **2,047** individuals voted in the Contested Election who, according to the State's records, were registered to vote prior to their seventeenth birthday, below the minimum age permitted under the Election Code.

Favorito versus Fulton County

The Republican Senate in Georgia does not have subpoena power the way the Arizona Senate does, and could not simply issue subpoenas for the evidence. The legislature was told they needed to go through the courts, or rely on the governor and secretary of state to provide the transparency the voters demanded. So, on December 23, 2020, voters sued.

According to the complaint, Garland Favorito is a resident of Fulton County, Georgia, who voted in the 2020 election, and whose vote was not counted in the Official Statement of Votes Cast or the published hand-count audit results or the recount results. Favorito, who volunteered at the election, claims that he witnessed a 20,000-vote increase for Joe Biden and an abnormal reduction in the number of votes for Donald Trump. Favorito reported the drastic change, and it was ignored.

Half a dozen other Georgia residents joined Favorito to sue Fulton County, Georgia, and the election officials, claiming a number of anomalies contributed to manufacturing a Joe Biden victory. Favorito and the other plaintiffs, through discovery, obtained copies of 147,000+ ballot *images* and had a team of experts examine the images for potential problems.

These images are pictures of the ballots that the machines keep after the ballots are scanned through the machines. They are very good evidence, but someone could argue that the images were manipulated, so any findings must be confirmed with the actual ballots. After several months, the plaintiffs claimed they found several anomalies in the images and needed access to the actual ballots to confirm their findings. None of the experts announced their findings because they wanted to verify them with the actual ballots first. The judge in the case, Judge Amero, granted motion after motion by the defendants allowing them to stall.

By October 2021, after litigating the case for ten months, Judge Amero ruled to dismiss the case based on standing, a procedural claim that is usually argued at the onset of the case. The fact that the judge allowed the plaintiffs to argue the case for ten months and then decided they did not have standing to bring the lawsuit in the first place is an unusual process for standing arguments to be decided. Regardless, he dismissed the case and said the plaintiffs had not plead any injury that would lead to an equal protection or due process violation. Case dismissed.

Conclusions in Georgia

Georgia's 2018 and 2020 elections, coupled with the Republican leadership's backwards, and flat-out weird, response, leads to an obvious conclusion. Government officials should not be auditing themselves. It's a massive conflict of interest to give complete control for checking elections to the very people who may have cheated, or may simply be nervous that they didn't actually win. The American people should have easy access to check their work, regardless of party, and see for ourselves who actually won.

Brian Kemp and Brad Raffensperger blocked both Democrats and Republicans from confirming that Georgia's elections were honest and fair. Why? Are they afraid people will learn that they didn't actually win their own races? Will America find out they cheated? Or, that they'll be removed from office if they're honest?

We need another mechanism in place to confirm election results. Government officials have proven they cannot be trusted to check their own work.

CHAPTER 8

Stealing Votes in Pennsylvania

Pennsylvania voters had good reason to the skeptical that the 2020 election had been a model of integrity and efficiency.

The counting facility in Philadelphia was massive, possibly over 100,000 square feet, with different corridors sectioned off for different election-related purposes.[1] Philadelphia had prepared the large room as a central count facility for the election, with areas sectioned off for different responsibilities.[2] Under normal circumstances, poll workers from each party would work side by side to process all of the ballots, but 2020 wasn't normal circumstances. Republican poll watchers arrived on Election Day to gates and fences blocking off sections of the massive warehouse-like room, and were told they needed to stay behind the fence.[3]

Republican poll watchers[4] who arrived to observe the count realized they had to stand behind fencing, anywhere from 10 feet away to more than 200 feet away.[5] It was impossible for any Republican observers to see anything.[6] Republicans were segregated and not allowed to participate. Some tried to use binoculars, but they were so far away that even binoculars were not particularly useful.[7] Throughout Election Day and the days that followed, Philadelphia managed to count their mail-in ballots away from any Republican observers and without any Republican oversight.[8]

I had heard reports of Republicans not getting to watch the process, and knew it was taking place in states across the country. Pennsylvania was especially concerning, because President Trump had such a massive lead. Who would believe that Joe Biden could make up a 700,000-vote deficit when most of the vote had already been counted?![9] They'd have to cheat.

By November 5, crowds gathered outside the counting facility in Philadelphia to protest the odd behavior of election officials and their removal of Republicans from the process.[10] Officials blamed COVID for the odd behavior, saying the strict distancing protocols were for safety reasons.[11] In what other election have you seen rules that require people to stand 200 feet away?! What's the point? They claimed safety protocol from the virus,[12] but it appeared they were using it as an excuse to cheat.

MAGA patriots showed up to protest Republicans getting blocked from the process, and others showed up to watch and see if we'd ever get observers back inside.[13] Emotions were high, but the crowd was peaceful and calm.[14] Why wouldn't the election officials allow conservatives to observe how they were counting the votes? What were they hiding?

Republicans had been escorted out of the counting facility and blocked from meaningful participation in the process.[15] Someone inside the Philadelphia counting facility was wearing a badge, although he was not law enforcement, and he would keep Republicans away from the counting.[16] Republicans did not have representation in the facility and did not have an opportunity to observe the vote tally.[17] Pennsylvania law says each candidate must be allowed to have observers, or watchers, present during the counting process.[18] Once it was clear that Philadelphia had excluded Trump observers, the President's lawyers went to work.[19]

Early on November 5, 2020, Trump attorney Pam Bondi obtained a court order allowing immediate access to the facility.[20] It was a great court victory and Republicans were eager to get a team of fifteen observers inside the facility.[21] Bondi held a brief press conference out front of the facility where she explained the process and court ruling before announcing that her team would now head inside the facility to watch how Philadelphia was counting their votes.[22]

Several hours later, on the evening of November 5, 2020, Bondi held another press conference to provide an update. They still could not get into the facility to observe the process.[23] The sheriff refused to enforce the court order and the election workers in Philadelphia simply ignored it.[24] They continued to count the votes, and as Bondi stated, they allowed any ballots coming in to be counted without regard to whether they were legal votes or not.[25]

Days later, after they'd manufactured enough Biden votes to close the massive lead President Trump had, Democrat officials in Philadelphia held a press conference to update the public.[26] They stated that the election was not over, and they still had over 40,000 ballots to count, which they hoped to finalize soon.[27] They claimed a victory for democracy and called on President Trump to concede before they'd even finished the count . . . days after the election was over.[28]

For the next few days and weeks, the Trump Ccmpaign gathered over three hundred affidavits from Republican poll workers who had been excluded or precluded from meaningful participation in the process.

Kelly versus Pennsylvania

Pennsylvania has very strict voting laws, requiring strict compliance for in-person voting and limited-excuse voting for absentee voters.[29] The only way to change Pennsylvania's voting laws and allow for mail-in ballots is through a constitutional amendment, according to the Constitution of the Commonwealth of Pennsylvania.[30] In 2019, Pennsylvania's General Assembly introduced a joint resolution to amend the Commonwealth's Constitution to allow for no-excuse mail-in ballots.[31] The resolution never completed the process.[32]

Constitutional amendments in Pennsylvania require multiple sessions to vote on the proposed change and then require the electors of Pennsylvania to vote to pass the constitutional amendment.[33] That means it would take multiple years and multiple elections to pass the resolution to allow no-excuse absentee ballots in Pennsylvania.[34] It could not happen lawfully before the 2020 election.

The resolution, even when passed by a majority of the House and Senate, still needed to be passed by a majority of the House and Senate in the 2020 session, and then placed on the ballot for the 2021 election to be approved by the Pennsylvania electors.[35] Pennsylvania could not lawfully use mail-in ballots for the 2020 election. The Democrat governor and secretary of state did it anyway.

In October 2019, Governor Wolf signed Act 77 into law, which attempted to legislate the use of mail-in ballots for the 2020 election, and not go through the required process of a constitutional amendment.[36] Legislation gave the new procedures "color of law," meaning it appeared to be a legally appropriate procedure and authorized conduct, but in fact it was not.

The Democrat governor and secretary of state for Pennsylvania disregarded the Pennsylvania Constitution and mailed out no-excuse absentee ballots. Those ballots changed the outcome of the election for multiple races in the state, and it changed the results of the presidential race too.[37] President Trump was winning by over 700,000 votes, until Pennsylvania added another 1.4 million mail-in ballots to the tally.[38] Suddenly, the result flipped.

Pennsylvania Congressman Mike Kelly called foul and filed a lawsuit asking for an injunction from the court, ordering that Pennsylvania only certify *legal* votes.[39] The roughly 3 million[40] votes casts illegally by mail cannot lawfully be counted, because they are not lawfully cast, according to Kelly's lawsuit.[41] Millions of votes were cast illegally, and the governor and secretary of state approved of the illegal activity. It's convenient that the illegal votes they counted changed the outcome of the election in favor of the candidate from their party.

On November 25, 2020, the Commonwealth Court of Pennsylvania agreed with Congressman Kelly and ordered a stop to the certification process.[42] The court ruled in accordance with the Commonwealth's constitution, and put a stop to the illegal process.[43] Specifically, the opinion stated that the petitioners *would likely win* their constitutional claim, and went ahead and issued a stay.[44]

The Democrat executive branch immediately appealed to the Pennsylvania Supreme Court, which has a reputation of being a crooked liberal court.[45] On November 28, 2020, the liberal Supreme Court of Pennsylvania dismissed the lawsuit on procedural grounds.[46] According to the Pennsylvania Supreme Court, Kelly filed the case too late. They never addressed the merits of the case, but simply threw it out on timing.

McLinko versus Pennsylvania

In January 2022, in *McLinko v. Pennsylvania*,[47] the Pennsylvania Commonwealth Court again ruled that Act 77, the universal mail-in ballot legislation, was unconstitutional and mail-in ballots cannot be used for future elections.[48] So the ballots were illegal in 2019, before the 2020 election, and are illegal after the 2020 election, for the 2022 election. That means mail-in ballots were only allowed for the 2020 election? How convenient.

If mail-in ballots are illegal for the 2022 elections, they were illegal for 2020. The liberal hacks on the Pennsylvania Supreme Court knew that the ballots were illegal, so they couldn't rule on the merits of the case. They cowered and abandoned their positions as the third branch of government to reach their political objectives. They got the result they wanted by disposing of the case on procedural grounds.

Democrats wanted President Trump out of office so badly that they were willing to break the law and look the other way when others broke the law. How's that working out for America? Democrats immediately appealed the 2022 ruling to the Pennsylvania Supreme Court. Pennsylvania Democrat Governor Tom Wolf requested the State Supreme Court to order that Act 77, the allowing universal mail-in ballots that a Pennsylvania court had just ruled was unconstitutional, remain in place until the conclusion of the litigation.[49] On March 1, 2022, the high court issued a one-paragraph order saying that despite the lower court's ruling, the law would remain in effect until the case completes litigation.[50]

Again, the court did not address the merits of the case, nor the fact that the law blatantly violates the Pennsylvania Constitution, but allowed the Democrats to continue their illegal practice until some undetermined future date.

Secretary of State Steps Down

The election problems in Pennsylvania were so bad that the secretary of state was forced to resign. Kathy Boockvar, Pennsylvania's secretary of state during the 2020 presidential election, resigned in February 2021 due to egregious mistakes made during the election.[51]

Officially, the mistake which forced her resignation was her failure to advertise an amendment to the Commonwealth's constitution that would allow a two-year window for victims of childhood sexual assault to litigate their case after they age out of the statute of limitations.[52] Pennsylvania law requires an advertisement before the amendment can be added to the ballot, and Boockvar forgot. Her mistake means victims of childhood sexual assault will have to wait another election cycle before getting their day in court.[53]

Boockvar acknowledged the mistake and stepped down, effective February 5, 2021.[54] The real story is that Democrats needed a scapegoat to take the blame for the botched 2020 election. Looking at the Pennsylvania election as a whole, there were many errors that Democrats didn't want to have to explain. Depriving Pennsylvanians of their right to a free and fair election is one example. Forcing Boockvar to resign gave Democrats a clean slate to pretend that no one currently in power is responsible for any of the problems. That of course isn't true, but liberal operatives don't care about the truth.

The 2020 election in Pennsylvania was so poorly managed that it appeared at times to be criminal in its operation, considering how they excluded Republicans and conducted the count in secret. Pennsylvania's election was so badly run, and had so many obvious signs of questionable activity, that 138 members of Congress and seven senators objected to Pennsylvania's certification on January 6, 2020.[55] That's more than any other objections in history.[56]

Imagine that. One hundred thirty-eight members of Congress were willing to acknowledge the problems with Pennsylvania's election when Congress was voting to certify the results of the 2020 presidential election. That means nearly one-third of the House of Representatives[57] had serious enough concerns over the conduct of the Pennsylvania election that they objected to the results. More Republicans were willing to object, but dropped their objection after the incident at the Capitol.[58]

Where Did All Those Votes Come From?

Despite Congress's failure to act, Pennsylvania could well go down as the worst case of election theft in our country's history. When election officials halted the count on election night, President Trump was ahead by 700,000 votes. But three days later, they declared that Joe Biden had won. President Trump was winning by the greatest margin on election night, that I believe Democrats were convinced they couldn't catch him. So, Democrats stopped the counting,[59] blocked Republicans from even entering the building, and then somehow counted an alleged 1.4 additional million ballots[60] without oversight. That gave the race to Biden . . . three days later on November 7.[61]

Pennsylvania voters wanted an explanation for how Joe Biden made up a 700,000-vote deficit with no oversight, and then won the state by 80,555 votes.[62]

So, where did the votes come from? Traditional Democrat areas like Philadelphia didn't have enough of a margin to make up nearly three quarters of a million votes. Philadelphia only had about 700,000 votes cast total,[63] so they needed to make up the difference in other counties.

Since the election, an independent analysis and canvass of the voter roll by Audit the Vote PA has revealed several concerns in multiple counties.[64] They canvassed multiple counties, both Democrat and Republican areas, and made some disturbing findings. In Allegheny County, a Democrat stronghold and home to Pittsburgh, Audit the Vote PA knocked on five hundred doors and collected 185 responses. They made the following findings:[65]

- 78.6 percent of houses had some election anomaly, meaning the residents' understanding of who voted from their addresses did not match official records.
- 69.7 percent of houses had some registration-count discrepancy, meaning the official record of registered voters at the residence did not match the residents' knowledge.
- 64.8 percent had phantom registrations associated with their address, meaning the residents were unaware of additional voters being registered at their home.
- 4.8 percent had fewer registered voters on record than the resident stated.

- 42.5 percent of addresses had a different number of votes on record for 2020 than residents stated.
- 29.2 percent had phantom votes.
- 13.2 percent had missing votes.

Montgomery County, PA, is known for being a Democrat stronghold too, and the official results of the 2020 election say that Biden won 62 percent of the roughly 500,000 votes cast in the 2020 election.[66] Biden claims to have won 319,511 votes to President Trump's 185,460.[67] Audit the Vote PA knocked on 548 doors and 183 voters responded to their questions, creating the following findings:[68]

- 77 addresses had a registration-count discrepancy (42.1 percent).
- 42 addresses had phantom registrations (23 percent).
- 35 addresses were missing registrations (19.1 percent).
- 66 addresses had a vote-count discrepancy (36.1 percent).
- 24 addresses show phantom votes (13.1 percent).
- 42 addresses show missing votes (23 percent).

The results of the canvass in Democrat areas is mind-boggling. How could there be such a high rate of error?! Even despite all of the discrepancies in Democrat counties, they *still* didn't have enough to overcome the massive lead President Trump had in the state. They *had* to manipulate Republican counties too.

In Lancaster County, a conservative county that President Trump won, the group knocked on doors for 411 houses and successfully completed 256 surveys. Their findings showed:[69]

- 37 percent of houses had some election anomaly, meaning the residents' understanding of who voted from their address did not match official records.

- 29.73 percent had some registration-count discrepancy, meaning the official record of registered voters at the residence did not match the residents' knowledge.
- 21.17 percent had phantom registrations associated with their address, meaning the residents were unaware of additional voters being registered at their home.
- 8.56 percent had fewer registered voters on record than the resident stated.
- 26.39 percent of addresses had a different number of votes on record for 2020 than residents stated.
- 17.13 percent had phantom votes.
- 9.3 percent were missing votes.

Lancaster County is a conservative county where President Trump won 57 percent of the vote. Over 275,000 ballots were cast in Lancaster.[70] However, a 37 percent anomaly rate, if carried throughout the entire county, could mean that over 100,000 votes were impacted. Audit the Vote PA has canvassed multiple counties in Pennsylvania[71] and made similar findings in multiple counties.[72]

These findings show a shocking disregard for accuracy in our most important democratic process, our elections. While a very small fraction of error is expected, a 37 percent anomaly rate is entirely too high. 52 percent is mind-boggling. We'll always have some margin of error, but it should be very low. In order to have confidence in the process, voters must know that their elections are conducted fairly and that the people are actually electing their leaders.

CHAPTER 9

The Fight in Harrisburg

The people of our Commonwealth should have confidence that their vote counts.
                    —Doug Mastriano, Pennsylvania State Senator

If Pennsylvania voters were going to get any answers to what really happened in November 2020, they'd need an audit. Unfortunately, as you are about to read, it was Pennsylvania Republicans who prevented that from happening, despite the efforts of some courageous patriots who tried to follow Arizona's example.

When the Arizona Audit paused to make way for high school graduation ceremonies in mid-May 2021, I went home to Washington, DC, from Phoenix. Chanel Rion, OAN's chief White House correspondent, was on the road interviewing President Trump in New York and Governor Ron DeSantis in Florida, so I spent the week covering for her at the White House. As I sat in the OAN green tent on the North Lawn, I wondered if other states would follow Arizona's example.

Pennsylvania State Senator Doug Mastriano had been a strong proponent of election transparency immediately following the 2020 election. Mastriano had been the first state legislator in the country in November 2020 to host Rudy Giuliani and his legal team, inviting them to Gettysburg, his home district, to brief legislators on election irregularities and to explain why the legislature needed to investigate.

Senator Mastriano is a retired Army colonel with a few decades of combat experience. He served in West Germany during the Cold War, Iraq for Operation Desert Storm, and Afghanistan after September 11. He's led troops, planned operations, and directed NATO's Joint Intelligence Center in Afghanistan. Mastriano is a committed American patriot and dedicated to protecting democracy. I thought I'd give him a call.

"Hi, Sir!" I said. Mastriano was in the car with his wife driving some distance, so I had a captive audience. We chatted for a few minutes and then I asked him: "Is Pennsylvania considering doing anything like what Arizona is doing to audit their election?"

"I would *love* to do what Arizona is doing. We just don't have the pathway to do something like that." Mastriano sounded like he was eager to conduct an audit, but was getting some push-back.

I wasn't sure why Pennsylvania couldn't do what Arizona was doing. "Don't you have subpoena power in the Senate in Pennsylvania?" I asked.

The senator was quiet for a minute as he thought about it. "Why don't you walk me through what's happening in Arizona. Maybe I don't understand it as well as I thought I did. I thought they went through the courts."

As I began to explain the subpoena process and legal challenges in Arizona, Senator Mastriano stopped me. "Where are you right now?" he asked.

"The North Lawn of the White House. Why?" I said.

"What you're telling me is very detailed and specific. I'd like to sit down with you to talk about this. Can you get up to Chambersburg this week to sit down with me and some of my staff to walk us through this?" Mastriano was clearly trying to understand what I was telling him, and this needed to be an in-person conversation.

"I can come up Friday afternoon. I'll have to do a report from the White House in the morning, and then I'll hit the road. Could we aim for 2 or 3 o'clock on Friday?" I asked.

"Perfect. That'll give me time to do a little research as well. See you then."

Pennsylvania Bound

Mike Roman was such a big help operating the Arizona Audit, and he's from Philadelphia. He had also gone home for the "pause week" and I hoped he'd want to meet me in Chambersburg. When I called to invite him to the meeting with Senator Mastriano, he jumped at the chance. Chambersburg is a charming borough in southern Pennsylvania, about thirty minutes west of Gettysburg. It's filled with history, and driving through the downtown district looks like a step back in time. The city center boasts red brick buildings, a local theater, and the courthouse with its clock tower. We met in the senator's office, right above the local radio station.

Senator Mastriano had also invited Representative Rob Kauffman, his counterpart in the Pennsylvania House of Representatives who, I would learn, is every bit the fighter Mastriano is and just as committed to protecting American freedoms. They had a few staff members with them, and we all converged in the conference room looking out on downtown Chambersburg. Senator Mastriano kicked off the discussion.

"I've looked into some of the information you gave me earlier this week. Turns out, that Senate committee chairs do have subpoena power, but it's rarely used. In the past thirty years, I could only find *three* that have been issued, and none for situations like this." He went on to suggest that this subpoena would be scrutinized and challenged more than any subpoena in decades.

The other problem was that he did not anticipate support from a risk-averse Senate president pro tempore, Jake Corman. Mastriano initiated an effort the year before to subpoena the Wolf Administration to access the process that determined what businesses were exempt from the unconstitutional 2020 COVID closures. Senator Corman was not enthusiastic about this and delayed offering support on this for several weeks and then inexplicitly decided to have another committee chair issue the subpoena. The subpoena on business closure should have been easy, but it wasn't. It became clear with a lack of exercising their subpoena powers, and a lack of political will, Mastriano would not have broad support in Harrisburg.

There was clearly a lack of political will by the leadership in the Pennsylvania General Assembly to exercise oversight and address the concerns of the citizens. By now, eight months had passed since the November 2020 election, other than holding a few hearings, very little had been done to get answers or to move legislation that would tackle this issue. The daily thrashing of the Arizona Audit by the mainstream media added to the hesitance in Harrisburg. Issuing a subpoena in Pennsylvania would likewise garner significant national attention and the sort of pressure and attention that most politicians loathed to garner.

I began to realize, as you'll see in Wisconsin too, that a big problem with state legislatures wasn't an unwillingness to do the right thing, but rather, *a complete lack of knowledge and backbone*. For decades, state legislatures have failed to use their authority to check the power of the executive branch, and now *no one knows how*. Mastriano was willing to change that.

"It would be nice if you had a recent example to follow," I acknowledged.

"We definitely don't have that," said Mastriano. "However, the law is still valid, and we can use it. Walk us through exactly what's happening in Arizona."

Mike and I spent the next couple hours explaining the process. I detailed the legal process, hurdles, and court challenges in Arizona. Mike laid out the operational procedures and how the audit actually would work in Pennsylvania. Both Mastriano and Kauffman were very curious about the possibility of replicating Arizona in Pennsylvania. We answered all the questions we could, and directed them to their legislative counsel to see how Pennsylvania law would help or hinder the process. Everything needed to be done legally, and they'd need the Senate's attorney to sign off on it.

"What about Corman?" Mike asked. "Would he be on board?" We all knew Jake Corman, the president of the Senate in Pennsylvania, a Republican, was staunchly against any effort to investigate the 2020 election. Corman was first elected to the Pennsylvania Senate in 1998, and is part of the problem. He's among the breed of Republicans that repeatedly sacrifice the sacred ground his constituents want to defend, like election integrity, in order to gain something smaller and less meaningful, but easier to win. Corman appears all too willing to allow corrupt officials to cheat and get away with it, because he refuses to engage in the fight.

"He's not with us," Mastriano said directly.

"Is that going to be a problem?" I asked.

"Probably, eventually. He doesn't have to authorize the subpoenas, which is good, but he will do everything in his power to stop me." We all realized Corman would be a roadblock. We just didn't know *when* he'd be a roadblock, or *if* the Pennsylvania Senate would be able to work around him.

"We can deal with Corman when he becomes a problem. What do you need right now to answer your questions and give you what you need to investigate the election fraud in Pennsylvania?" I asked.

"Aside from Corman, my biggest concern is that I don't feel like I have a great grasp of how all this is going to work," Mastriano was honest.

"Why don't you come to Arizona?" I asked. "If you are serious about trying to audit Pennsylvania, you need to see what's happening in Arizona."

Mike jumped in, "The auditors will give you a tour. They can explain everything to you, and answer every possible question you could have. If you want to have a better idea of how to look into election transparency, there's no better place to do it than Phoenix. You don't have to do exactly what they're doing, but it'll give you an idea of what you'd like to look into in Pennsylvania. I'm sure the Arizona legislators would meet with you and answer your questions too."

"That would be great!" Mastriano was thinking about it. "I just don't know how we'd pay for it. Corman certainly wouldn't allow us to use Senate funds."

"No problem," I said. "Voices and Votes will pay for your trip. If you, as a state senator, want to educate yourself on what's happening in Arizona, for the purpose of possibly replicating it in Pennsylvania, there's no better way to do it than to get a front-row seat. All it will cost you is your time." I added that Voices and Votes would pay for as many state legislators to come to Arizona as were interested in the issue. Turns out there were only three.

Mastriano thought about it for a long second, looked at Representative Kauffman, and said, "I think we need to go to Arizona."

Pennsylvania's Road Trip to Phoenix

Senator Mastriano asked me not to report on the fact that they were coming to Arizona until they were wheels up from Pennsylvania. He was concerned if Republican President of the Senate Jake Corman caught wind of it, he would try to stop them from going. I waited until I had confirmation they had taken off, then I broke the story on June 1, 2021, that a Pennsylvania delegation was on its way to Arizona and would tour the audit the next day. Big corporate media had a meltdown, and it got people's attention.

A small delegation of six officials from Pennsylvania arrived at the audit site the next day. The delegation was made up of Senator Mastriano, Representative Rob Kauffman, and Senator Cris Dush, along with a staff member each. They met with Arizona legislators in the morning, and then went to tour the audit afterwards. They spent the better part of the day asking every question they could think of, getting a presentation on how the volunteer coordination works, the use of live-stream cameras, and the process of the investigation.

After touring the audit floor, I asked them to come to the press box for interviews, which they did. All three of the elected officials gave me an interview, with the rest of the members of the press standing around us like pigeons at a park bench. Some of the legislators gave interviews to other members of the press, some didn't. Once they were done with the media, the tour was over, and they headed back to Pennsylvania with a better understanding of what could happen in the Commonwealth—if Republican leadership would allow it.

Republicans versus Republicans

A few weeks passed after the Pennsylvania trip and it didn't seem like much was happening. I reached out to Senator Mastriano to ask how things were going.

"Not as well as I'd like, unfortunately." Mastriano was a bit disappointed he hadn't made more progress. He had spoken with Senate President Jake Corman, who didn't like the idea, didn't support it, and encouraged Senator Mastriano to drop it. Corman did not have to sign off on the subpoena, so Mastriano could do it without his blessing, but he needed other senators on his committee to vote for it. Since Corman appoints the committee chairmen, and he could strip Mastriano of his committee chair anytime he wished.

Republican Senator David Argall, the chairman of the State
Government Committee, had issued statements saying they needed to
conduct an audit. Just the day before, he had come on One America
News demanding that Pennsylvania conduct an audit. He's lucky I
didn't interview him. I knew he had the authority to issue a subpoena
and conduct the audit, but he was too chicken to do it. Perhaps he
feared Jake Corman stripping him of his title as chairman of the State
Government Committee; in any case, he just talked about it on TV
rather than actually doing something about it. Doug Mastriano was
alone in this fight.

"What needs to happen to actually issue a subpoena in
Pennsylvania?" I asked Senator Mastriano.

"We just need to vote on it, but Corman is holding me up. He
doesn't want to vote on the subpoena until after the budget. Corman
thinks an audit is too contentious and if we vote before the budget
passes then he'll never get the budget passed." But Mastriano knew
that the budget is usually the leverage everyone uses to get their initiatives passed. The risk in waiting was that once the budget passes, the
session is usually over and all the legislators leave to go back to their
districts.

The whole thing sounded fishy to me. Telling Senator Mastriano
to wait until after the budget passes is like telling a golfer you'll let him
play on the nineteenth hole. "It sounds like he's lying to you, don't you
think?" I asked. "I mean, if you wait until after the budget, and everyone leaves, you'll be stuck. You won't have a quorum to vote. What
happens then?" I asked.

"He may be insincere, but he won't give me a conference room,
so I can't hold the vote now anyway. I can't issue a notice of the vote
without a conference room listed due to our state's Sunshine Law that
requires public notice and public access. If he won't give me the room,
I can't hold the vote. He's telling me he'll approve it after the budget is

passed." Mastriano sounded really frustrated, but like he was hoping for the best.

Predictably, after the Pennsylvania Senate passed their budget, Republican Senate President Jake Corman adjourned the session for the summer and sent everyone home. There was no one left in Harrisburg to vote on Mastriano's subpoena.

One More Shot

Senator Mastriano was determined to give the people of Pennsylvania what they were demanding. He received thousands of calls and emails each week from constituents demanding election transparency, and he was on a mission to deliver it. Mastriano had support from the Republican members of the committee to send a letter to three counties on July 7 that they intended to audit: Tioga, York, and Philadelphia. The letter asked for the counties to voluntarily submit their evidence to his committee for an audit. Mastriano knew the counties probably wouldn't comply without a subpoena, but it was a first step from a legal perspective to making the audit discussion public in Pennsylvania.

The letters to the counties gave them until July 30, 2021, to respond. Philadelphia County ignored the letter altogether, while the two Republican counties responded to Senator Mastriano and let him know they would need him to subpoena the evidence in order for them to turn it over.

The acting secretary of the Commonwealth[1] of Pennsylvania, Veronica Degraffenreid, was apparently so threatened by Senator Mastriano's actions that she issued a directive[2] to all of the counties telling them not to comply with any attempts to audit elections in Pennsylvania. This is particularly noteworthy, because the *acting* secretary of the Commonwealth is not even an elected official. She stepped in to fill the vacancy left when the appointed secretary of the Commonwealth stepped down after getting caught in the mire of an election scandal and her botched handling of the 2020 election. Degraffenreid is a government bureaucrat with no accountability to the people whatsoever.

The office of the secretary of the Commonwealth is a part of the executive branch, just like the governor, and they ran the elections for the Commonwealth of Pennsylvania in 2020. As we'd seen before, although the United States Constitution vests the power of choosing the electors to the state legislatures, most state legislatures have delegated that authority to the secretary of state for ease of operations. It's still the legislatures' authority and responsibility to protect elections in the state. Now, the acting secretary of state in Pennsylvania (executive branch) was directing the counties to ignore the law and refuse to cooperate with the state legislature. She seemed intent on doing everything in her power to ensure that the legislative branch couldn't check the work of the executive branch.

In addition to instructing counties not to comply with lawful subpoenas, Degraffenreid also turned her attention on Fulton County. Fulton County, Pennsylvania, had audited their election earlier in the year, confirming that Donald Trump had won 85 percent of the county's votes and that "the election was well run."[3]

Now the *acting*, unelected and unaccountable, secretary of the Commonwealth was decommissioning Fulton County's machines. She demanded that Fulton County purchase all new election equipment to be used in the next election. Fulton County is very small, with a population of only about fifteen thousand people, even fewer voters. Purchasing new election equipment would be a huge burden on a small county. Fulton County Commissioner Stuart Ulsh pushed back, rightfully demanding Degraffenreid back off of Fulton County. It was the county commissioner's responsibility to determine if and when they needed new election equipment, and Fulton County did not want new election equipment.

Degraffenreid then went a step further and issued a directive that *any* county in the entire Commonwealth that dared to audit its elections would be penalized and forced to purchase all new election equipment. This is blatant overreach on the part of the executive branch, but the legislative branch wasn't providing the check and balance to prevent the executive branch from acting like a dictator. So, she did.

July 30, 2021, arrived, and the three counties failed to accommodate Senator Mastriano's request in his letter. They did not turn over the evidence. Meanwhile, during the three weeks leading up to the deadline, Senator Mastriano had worked hard to ensure that the Republicans on his committee were available to come to Harrisburg for a vote on a subpoena to conduct a forensic investigation of the 2020 election. He had the quorum he needed. Mastriano only needed Jake Corman to assign him a conference room so he could properly notice the hearing.

Not only did Corman refuse to give Senator Mastriano a room to hold his hearing, he did everything he could to torpedo the subpoena. Corman demanded Mastriano jump through a dozen hoops to satisfy him. He asked for the details of what would be subpoenaed, who the experts would be, how the audit would be funded, which lawyers would work the case, and a litany of other questions. Mastriano was prepared and answered all of Corman's questions with as much precision as a NATO planning officer during combat operations could provide. Corman refused to allow Senator Mastriano to use the attorney of his choice and refused any reasonable accommodations Mastriano needed to conduct the audit. Even worse, Corman personally called all of the Republican senators on Mastriano's committee and told them that the vote had been canceled. Mastriano hadn't canceled anything.

Once Corman realized he was unable to deter Mastriano, he played his final card. Republican President of the Pennsylvania Senate Jake Corman stripped Mastriano of his committee chairmanship and fired all of Mastriano's committee staff, leaving him without authority and without assistance. Corman single-handedly killed any ability to audit the 2020 election in Pennsylvania. The Republican Senate never had the chance to challenge Democrats in Pennsylvania because they couldn't get past the Republican Senate president.

Corman's Charade

Corman then replaced Senator Mastriano with Senator Cris Dush as the committee chairman, and he removed Mastriano from the Republican Caucus. Cris Dush was the only other Pennsylvania State Senator to visit the Arizona Audit, and he did so at the invitation of Mastriano.

Corman claimed that Cris Dush was responsible for leading the fact-finding trip to Arizona,[4] but that was not true. I had the receipts for the flights and hotels that my organization purchased for them, and I confirmed with the Arizona senators that they had not been working with Pennsylvania senators until *after* I invited them to Arizona. Doug Mastriano led the delegation from Pennsylvania, but Corman said it was Dush. To what gain?

Cris Dush apparently worked better with Jake Corman, and also was *not* rumored to be running for governor, so any publicity he might receive would not detract from Corman's campaign, or Mastriano's, for that matter. Jake Corman announced his bid for governor in November 2021. Doug Mastriano announced his bid for governor in January 2022.

By removing Doug Mastriano from the committee chair and replacing him with Cris Dush, Jake Corman made a calculated decision. Corman knew that he would eventually be running against Doug Mastriano for the Republican nomination for governor. Mastriano's superstar status increased the longer he was in the forefront of the election integrity fight. Corman needed to end that if he wanted a chance at beating Mastriano for governor.

By placing Cris Dush in charge, Corman established that he was taking the investigation in a different direction. It may have been a good political move, but at the expense of the people of Pennsylvania.

In September 2021, the Pennsylvania Senate, approved by Jake Corman, issued subpoenas seeking voter information. The information sought would help verify each voter on the voter roll in order to confirm that the voters on the role are legitimate legal voters. However, Corman used a different tactic than Mastriano had planned, and the subpoenas were quickly jammed up in court.

Almost immediately, Pennsylvania Democrat Attorney General Josh Shapiro filed a lawsuit challenging the Senate's ability to receive the information sought in the subpoena. The crux of the claim is that the Senate doesn't have the authority to seek private personal information of voters and the state (i.e., attorney general) wants to protect private information of Pennsylvania voters.[5]

As of January 2023, Pennsylvania voters are still waiting for transparency. Interestingly, though, in November 2022, just days before the midterm election, the Pennsylvania Supreme Court ruled that mail-in ballots with incorrect dates cannot be counted.[6] Funny that undated or incorrectly dated ballots were only allowed in 2020.

When I tell people this story, every once in a while someone asks, "If so many Republicans were against investigating, do you think it's possible no one *should* be investigating the election?" I always respond that elected officials are elected to do the will of the people and honor their constituents. What did the people of Pennsylvania want?

We do have one indication of what the citizens of Pennsylvania want: Mastriano overwhelmingly defeated Corman in the 2022 Republican primary. The Pennsylvania Republican gubernatorial race had nine candidates. Doug Mastriano decisively defeated all nine with 591,240 votes, and 43.82 percent of the votes.[7] Jake Corman only received 26,091 votes and came in seventh place out of nine candidates,[8] and that was as the sitting president of the Pennsylvania Senate. Yikes. Republican voters in Pennsylvania made their voices heard. They wanted election transparency, and they wanted Doug Mastriano.

CHAPTER 10

Wisconsin Fights Back

One would think that if [the Governor] is so confident there were no issues [with the election], he would be more than willing to show it. What are they hiding?
—Rep. Janel Brandtjen, Wisconsin Assembly Elections
Committee Chairwoman

Once Arizona and Pennsylvania began publicly pursuing audits, more and more people across the country were paying attention and taking the process seriously. To make these efforts worth anything, however, we needed more than Arizona and Pennsylvania. I started reaching out to other states.

Wisconsin seemed to have a grassroots movement demanding election transparency, but I didn't know anyone in the state legislature. A friend mentioned that he knew Representative Janel Brandtjen and connected me to her. I nearly jumped for joy when I looked her up and realized she was the chairwoman of the Assembly Elections Committee. She had authority. I hoped she'd use it.

Each state legislature handles subpoena power slightly differently, but state legislatures all have investigative power. Some leave it up to the president of the Senate or the Speaker of the House, others give subpoena power to the committee chairpersons. I didn't yet know if Representative Brandtjen would have subpoena power, but as the committee chairwoman, she'd at least have influence. I decided to call her.

Representative Brandtjen is one of the most humble, kind, and attentive public officials I have ever spoken with. She takes her duty as a public servant very seriously and is dedicated to doing the will of the people of Wisconsin. Brandtjen listened to me as I explained the Pennsylvania visit and invited her to come to the Arizona Audit.

"I've heard it's just a circus out there and that it's a complete mess. What good would it do if I came to see it?" she asked sincerely.

"Who told you it's a circus?!" I asked, surprised to think anyone who had actually seen it would describe it that way. "It's amazing! The level of detail they're using is really impressive."

"I've just heard on the news that it's not going well and that the Arizona legislature regrets doing the audit at all."

"Oh!" I laughed, relieved that her impression was based solely on what she'd read in the press. "You can't believe the reports in the press," I said. "Especially the local Arizona press, they are extremely liberal. They've been badmouthing the audit since before it even began." She was listening, so I continued. "Come see it for yourself. What's the harm? Voices and Votes will pay for you and your fellow legislators to come take a look at what's happening in Arizona. If you like it, you can take what you like back to Wisconsin. If you don't like it, at least you'll know for yourself. You need to get the media out of the middle. Just come see for yourself."

After some discussion, Brandtjen said she was interested in coming to Phoenix and she would check with her colleagues to see if anyone else wanted to come with her. She called me back a few days later with the list of names, and we booked their trip to Phoenix.

A Different Perspective

I met the Wisconsin delegation at Veterans Memorial Coliseum on a Saturday in June 2021, just after they toured the Arizona Audit. As a member of the press, I wasn't allowed behind the scenes, so I met them after their tour just outside the press box near the exit. We huddled in a corner near an inoperable burger stand, away from the other members of the press.

"That was amazing!" Janel said, and the others agreed. "I had no idea the level of detail and scrutiny they were conducting. I'm honestly blown away." The entire delegation was in shock over the details, telling me about the recount teams, ballot counting, and the cyber exam. "We need this in Wisconsin!"

"Was your experience a little different than what you read about in the papers back in Wisconsin?" I joked, knowing the press had been lying about the audit.

"Unbelievable!" Representative Brandtjen was incredulous. "They are lying! I knew the press was bad, but I had no idea that they are blatantly making up lies about what is happening out here!" Brandtjen was in disbelief over the media's dishonesty, and the others agreed.

An Imaginary Audit

A week or so after the Wisconsin legislators toured the Arizona Audit, I reached out to Representative Brandtjen to learn what, if any, steps the Wisconsin legislature would take to audit the state.

"Christina, it's crazy. I'm having a hard time getting anywhere. The Speaker of the Assembly, Robin Vos, is insisting that he's already doing a full forensic audit."

Robin Vos is a Republican and has worked in Wisconsin State politics for decades. He was elected to the Racine County Board of Supervisors in 1994 and has worked in politics ever since. In 2005, he won his election to become a member of the Assembly, and became the

Speaker in 2013. The Wisconsin Assembly is what many states, and the federal government, refer to as The House of Representatives. Rather than the title of Speaker of the House, Robin Vos is the Speaker of the Assembly. Same thing.

"What?" I was confused. "What do you mean? There's nothing happening in Wisconsin. How can he say that?" I asked.

"It's really weird. He says there is already an audit happening." She was as confused as I was. Back in February 2021, Wisconsin had announced that they would audit the 2020 election and everyone cheered. It was now July and nothing had happened. "Vos insists that he's got everything under control and is looking into everything. He says we just need to sit down and wait for him to finish his audit."

"What audit?!" I demanded. "There's *nothing* happening in Wisconsin! Who are the auditors? Which counties are they auditing? What exactly are they looking at? Are they examining the ballots, the machines, or both? Where is the audit taking place?" I ran off a list of questions that Brandtjen couldn't answer.

After more back and forth, Representative Brandtjen and I concluded that Republican Robin Vos seemed to be hoping the election integrity concerns would all just go away. Back in February, the Wisconsin legislature had indeed announced they were launching an audit, but nothing seemed to be happening. Vos had appointed a few investigators, but he never gave them the tools they'd need to actually do a full forensic audit. Arizona had over one thousand people working on the audit. Vos had appointed two, neither of whom had any cyber experience, and I was told they both quit. It was hard to know for sure what was going on.

For weeks, Representative Brandtjen and I tried to figure out what type of audit the Wisconsin legislature was doing. She was unable to determine which counties they were looking into, whether the investigators were looking at 100 percent of the election or just auditing a sample, whether anyone was examining the machines, and whether they were examining the ballots or the ballot images (saved images of the scanned ballots that went through a machine).

Quite frankly, Brandtjen was unable to discover *any* meaningful information about the so-called audit, and *she's the chairwoman of the Election Committee!* If Brandtjen couldn't find the information, the people of Wisconsin didn't stand a chance. It seemed Vos and his fellow Republicans expected to do some type of perfunctory audit, all behind closed doors, with undisclosed personnel, and zero transparency into the process. They planned to just release a report and expected everyone to believe it. Nope. Not on this topic. The people of Wisconsin wanted to see the receipts.

Nothing to See Here, Folks!

One of the most troubling signs of potential fraud in Wisconsin involved the role of far-Left operatives in managing the election. Prior to the 2020 election, the City of Green Bay, Wisconsin, received a $1.6 million grant from the Center for Tech and Civic Life, the leftist activist organization that received $350 million from Facebook, for the purpose of helping to run the election. A condition for the grant was that liberal non-profits have unrestricted access to run elections for the City of Green Bay.

Michael Spitzer-Rubenstein is a Democrat political operative based in New York. As a result of this arrangement, Spitzer-Rubenstein, a resident of New York, was given a City of Green Bay employee ID, keys to the central counting room on election night, and passwords to the election's electronic databases. To be clear, Spitzer-Rubenstein *never worked for the City of Green Bay*, yet was given a city ID in order to ensure he had unrestricted access on election night. When confronted with this information, the mayor of Green Bay, Eric Genrich, simply said "oops." He acknowledged it was a mistake, and everyone looked the other way.

Claire Woodall-Vogg is the executive director for the Milwaukee Election Commission. Ryan Chew is a representative from The Elections Group, a liberal non-profit that collaborates with the Center for Tech and Civic Life, the Facebook-funded group sponsoring Michael Spitzer-Rubenstein. In the early morning hours of November 4, 2020, in other words *election night*, Woodall-Vogg received an email from Chew saying:

> Damn, Claire, you have a flair for drama, delivering just the margin needed at 3:00 a.m. I bet you had those votes counted at midnight, and just wanted to keep the world waiting!

Woodall-Vogg responded to Chew's email at 4:17 a.m.:

> Lol. I just wanted to wait to say I had been awake for a full 24 hours!

The email communications between the Milwaukee Election Commission Executive Director (Woodall-Vogg) and the special interest group partnering with Facebook money clearly suggests an organized effort to manufacture a Biden victory. Chew's phrase "delivering just the margin needed at 3:00 a.m." can be reasonably interpreted as fabricating a Biden victory that would not have otherwise occurred. When confronted with this information, the Milwaukee Election Commission ignored it.

Indefinitely Confined Voters

Another irregularity that alarmed Wisconsin citizens was the conduct of "indefinitely confined voters" in the state. Indefinitely confined voters are not required to show ID when they cast a ballot, so the legislature limited that privilege to a very small group of people. Wisconsin has some of the strictest, most expressly prohibitive laws in the country for absentee voting. Every state legislature, in all fifty states, is responsible for making laws that reflect the will of the people of that state. The executive branch executes and enforces those laws, and the judicial branch interprets the law in the case of a disagreement over meaning. Wisconsin's legislature was extremely clear in their written intent for absentee ballots. Wis. Stat. 6.84 states:

> The legislature finds that voting is a constitutional right, the vigorous exercise of which should be strongly encouraged. In contrast, voting by absentee ballot is a privilege exercised wholly outside the traditional safeguards of the polling place. The legislature finds that the *privilege of voting by absentee ballot must be carefully regulated to prevent the potential for fraud or abuse* . . . [emphasis added]

The law is clear. Voting must be done in person, with very limited exceptions. In 2020, the executive branch, namely the Dane and Milwaukee County clerks and Wisconsin Election Commission, decided to disregard the law, and encouraged Wisconsin citizens to do the same. They issued guidance to their residents to declare themselves "indefinitely confined" and request an absentee ballot, as a result of COVID, despite the fact that the law defines "indefinitely confined" as a result of age, infirmity, or physical illness.

Across Wisconsin, approximately 265,000 voters[1]—the vast majority likely healthy, able-bodied citizens—declared themselves to be "indefinitely confined." That's nearly four times higher than 2016. The margin of victory for Joe Biden in 2020 was only 20,682. In 2020, there were enough indefinitely confined votes to change the outcome of the election ten times.

Wisconsin law stipulates that absentee ballots by indefinitely confined voters who are not *actually* indefinitely confined shall not count in the tally. The rationale is that Wisconsin so values the sanctity of the vote, they protect it by requiring voters to vote in person, unless absolutely impossible. Absentee ballots are ripe for fraud and prone to abuse by election workers.

Shortly after the election, President Trump's legal team filed suit challenging the wrongfully obtained absentee ballots. Wisconsin law says they should not be counted. In a 4–3 decision, the Wisconsin Supreme Court decided the case was brought too late, and should have been raised *before* the election. Three liberal judges and one conservative judge ruled to refuse to allow the inquiry to go further. They never ruled on the merits of the case.

Voting by mail, as we've already seen, is wrought with potential fraud. 2020 saw late-night drop-offs by questionable characters, and concerns in many states that bad actors had "stuffed the ballot box" with mail-in ballots. Mail-in ballots are prone to abuse by overzealous individuals with personal interests. Wisconsin's "indefinitely confined" debacle created a big problem. Wisconsin election officials had encouraged legitimate voters to violate the law. Doing so gave election officials room to cheat by potentially mixing in fraudulent absentee ballots (i.e., ballots filled out by someone other than the registered voter) with legitimate votes. It would be extremely difficult, if not impossible, to separate legitimate votes from fraudulent votes—a scenario that only benefits cheaters. Even if no cheating took place, the people of Wisconsin would have no way to confirm that under the conditions created by county officials.

Independent groups like the Wisconsin Institute for Law and Liberty (WILL) investigated through open records requests. WILL found that 54,259 of the indefinitely confined voters had *never* shown ID. Not in any prior election and not while registering to vote.[2] Also, 23,361 voters were allowed to cast a ballot "despite failing their DMV check this year, meaning their name, address, and/or birthdate doesn't match what is on file with the DMV.["3] WILL's analysis also found that "31,664 Wisconsin voters were in the National Change of Address Database.["4] Again, the margin of victory was only 20,682.

Did the abuse of "indefinitely confined" absentee ballots change the outcome of the election in Wisconsin? Did Green Bay and Milwaukee have personnel cheat to produce an artificial Biden victory? Only an audit could provide the answers.

Blow the Dust off the Subpoena Process (Again)

Chairwoman Brandtjen and I had discussed the possibility of issuing subpoenas to a couple Wisconsin counties to get the process started. I got some feedback from the Arizona team, pulled the Arizona subpoena, and offered suggestions to Brandtjen.

"Christina, I've done my research. My lawyers have done their research. The Wisconsin Assembly has not issued a subpoena for *anything* substantial in forty years." Brandtjen expressed her frustration that this process would not be easy. Although Pennsylvania had a similar problem, at least there had been three subpoenas issued which could serve somewhat as an example. The Wisconsin Assembly hasn't substantially investigated *anything* in forty years.

Janel Brandtjen needed to get to work to reconstruct the pathway of accountability, and re-establish the Wisconsin Legislature as the meaningful second branch of government. Unfortunately, this was a problem I noticed throughout the country. State legislatures have neglected their responsibility to act as a check in the checks and balances of our government.

Not only have the legislatures not been exerting *their own* authority, they haven't even been pushing back on the executive branch when it overstepped *its* authority. By 2020, we had executive branches in many states completely disregarding the law and creating new laws as governors or secretaries of state. That's not legal, and the legislatures weren't doing anything about it. An overpowering executive branch becomes a dictator. Our founding fathers gave us legislatures to protect against that. The legislatures need to step up. They are failing us.

"Forty years is a long time," I sympathized with Janel. "That's way too long for a legislature to go without holding anyone accountable," I added.

"It's way too long. The legislature, as a body, hasn't been doing its job," Janel admitted.

It was the end of July, and Wisconsin citizens were losing patience with the lack of progress on the legislature's supposed audit. Probably in response to pressure, Vos appointed retired Wisconsin Supreme Court Judge Michael Gableman to investigate. However, Vos had not funded Gableman's investigation. Surely Gableman alone couldn't conduct an audit without additional resources. Gableman, once appointed without funding, was effectively sidelined until further notice. Chairwoman Brandtjen had had enough.

"I'm issuing subpoenas to Brown and Milwaukee counties," Brandtjen told me matter-of-factly on August 5. Brown County is home to Green Bay.

"That's great! When?" I asked.

"Tomorrow. I'm having the county clerks personally served in the morning."

"Oh wow! That's fast. Okay." I held my breath and hoped for the best. Considering no one had done that in forty years, we weren't exactly sure what the reaction would be . . . especially from Republicans.

The press and Democrat politicians in the area went crazy. When asked if he thought the counties should comply with the lawful subpoena, Wisconsin's Democrat Governor Tony Evers, a Democrat, responded "hell no!" The governor had apparently become so accustomed to disregarding the law and dictating from the executive branch, that he didn't even think twice about telling counties to *disregard the law*. Political sides can hold differing opinions, but when our elected leaders intentionally disregard the law and encourage others to do so, our nation quickly descends into lawlessness.

After the initial shock wave and temper tantrum, Democrats challenged the subpoenas in the press, claiming they were not valid without Speaker of the Assembly Robin Vos approving them. Vos had been stonewalling every effort at election transparency, but that had all been in secret without anyone knowing he was stalling. Janel Brandtjen had just blown the doors off his hideout and caught him in the light of day. Would Robin Vos support the subpoenas and approve of Chairwoman Janel Brandtjen's audit efforts? Or would he single-handedly shut down Wisconsin's audit efforts, just as Jake Corman had done in Pennsylvania? The nation waited to see.

CHAPTER 11

Wisconsin Steps Up

It just so happens this statute is called "Election Fraud." We're stating that the rules weren't followed . . .
—Lt. Michael Luell, Racine County Sheriff's Office

In August 2021, President Trump held a rally in Cullman, Alabama, to support US Senate candidate Mo Brooks. Due to security procedures, my camera crew and I had to be there eight hours in advance to have our equipment checked and set up. We spent most of the time trying to stay out of the rain between live hits.

President Trump arrived to the rally later in the evening, after we had a full day in the rain. Despite being sufficiently drenched, I was grateful that he offered me a brief one-on-one interview moments before he took the stage to address the crowd. His communications team ushered me and my videographer to the tent in the back. We waited until President Trump finished his receiving line and then they directed us to him, giving me five minutes to interview him.

Once we finished the interview, President Trump asked us to turn the camera off and chatted with me off camera. Liz Harrington,

President Trump's spokeswoman, joined us. We briefly spoke about the efforts to push the legislatures to conduct audits in Pennsylvania and Wisconsin. I told him that Rep. Janel Brandtjen had issued subpoenas, but was getting blocked by Speaker Vos. He asked me if I thought Vos would help us. I honestly answered no.

With a smile, President Trump said, "you'll never guess who's here right now."

"Who?" It sounded like he meant Vos, but that was impossible.

"Robin Vos," President Trump smiled.

"Robin Vos?!" I questioned.

"Yeah. Vos," Trump persisted.

"What's he doing in Alabama?!" I was shocked. Vos did not act like a Trump supporter and had not supported *anything* President Trump wanted to do with election integrity. Why on earth would he be at a Trump rally in Cullman, Alabama?!

"He wanted a meeting with me to discuss the Wisconsin audit. The only time I had available was my flight to Alabama. So, I invited him to join me on my flight. We had a very good conversation. In fact, you should talk to him," said Trump.

I was stunned. I'd been trying to get a hold of Robin Vos for *months!* He didn't return my calls to his office or my emails. I'd been working every contact I had in Wisconsin, and couldn't get Vos to talk to me. Now, President Trump was going to introduce us in person! It seemed so simple I almost laughed. President Trump turned and asked someone to grab Vos for him. Then he turned to me.

"He's just over in the other tent. He should really talk to you."

"Yes. I would love to talk to him. I have a lot of questions about an audit in Wisconsin, and I'd love to know what he plans on doing about it," I said as Speaker Vos walked up.

President Trump greeted him warmly and said, "Robin, I've got someone I'd like to introduce you to. She's an excellent reporter from

One America News, and has followed the election cases very closely. I think it'd be great if you connected with her."

Speaker Vos was kind and shook my hand saying hello. I don't know if he'd ever seen any of my reporting or not, but based on things I've heard from people in Wisconsin, I believed he did not like my perspective. If he *was* familiar with my efforts, I was probably the last person he wanted to meet.

"Sir, it's a pleasure to meet you. I've reached out and haven't been able to connect. I'm so glad we could connect here," I said, trying to be as friendly as I could.

"You should let her interview you!" President Trump weighed in.

"I would love that! I would come to Madison to have a sit-down discussion with you. I can coordinate it with your staff and make it very simple for you," I chimed in. Maybe that was a bit pushy, but I was eager to lock him in. Who knows if I'd ever talk to him again if he didn't promise anything in front of President Trump.

"That would be great. I'd love to do an interview with you," Speaker Vos said. We went on to discuss details and I pushed him a little bit on his audit efforts. He maintained that he *was* conducting a full forensic audit, but wouldn't give me the details, citing legal restrictions. He gave a few details of an investigation he stated he was opening, but was fairly non-committal. We chatted for about two minutes before President Trump needed to move on to speaking to the crowd. I thanked them both and returned to the press risers with my videographer.

Based on my brief exchange with Speaker Vos, I thought that maybe he *had* started an audit and was responding to the demands of the people of Wisconsin. Maybe the imaginary audit was *real*?!

Back in Wisconsin

Shortly after returning to Wisconsin, Speaker Vos spoke with local press and detailed how he joined President Trump on his plane to attend the Alabama rally. He shared a picture of himself with President Trump and made sure the press reported his interactions with the most popular president in US history. Then he sat down for a televised interview with Wisconsin's ABC 12 News.

When asked, "Do you believe, as President Trump does, that Wisconsin's election was corrupt?," Vos answered, "I would not use the word corrupt. I don't believe that. Now were some of the practices in individual parts of the state bordering on that? Yeah." He went on to explain that the goal of the legislature's audit was to prevent problems in *future* elections. He was not looking to correct 2020.[1]

President Trump was keenly interested in investigating and correcting the 2020 election. Speaker Robin Vos sounded like he had no intentions of revisiting the past.

President Trump's Response

A day or so later, I spoke with President Trump and told him that I didn't think Vos was being forthright about his efforts. Vos had almost immediately gone to work to sound "reasonable" in Wisconsin and declare they would not be revisiting 2020.

President Trump said, "you were really hard on him."

"What?" I was nervous. "What do you mean? What did I do?" I was scared I had crossed a line and I didn't know how.

"You didn't say anything specific, but man, you were just tough. I mean, the guy's a politician. He says what he needs to say to get out of a difficult spot," Trump said, unconcerned with Vos.

I was surprised that President Trump had picked up on all of Vos's gamesmanship. He knew Vos was tap dancing, and he didn't object. He seemed to know the truth would eventually come out. I was nervous that I needed to correct my own actions.

"I didn't mean to be hard on him. I was trying to be nice," I said, somewhat apologetically.

He laughed. "Ha! If that's you being nice, I don't want to see you being mean. You're tough!" He continued to laugh and talked almost to himself, "who's as tough as you? I don't know. I've negotiated with a lot of people and countries and I can't think of anyone who stands that firm." Then he remembered, "oh yeah! I remember. The Taliban! You're right up there with the Taliban!" He laughed. He explained the Taliban are mission oriented and uncompromising—just like me.

Oh. My. Gosh. President Trump just compared me to the Taliban. I took it as a compliment, but also a note to maybe lighten up a bit. He knew the games being played and rose above them. Just get the truth out. That's all that mattered.

The Imaginary Audit Was Real . . . Kind Of

Wisconsin's Legislative Audit Bureau (LAB) finally released the results of its long-awaited audit on October 19, 2021. The LAB is a government entity within the Wisconsin Legislature that "supports the Legislature in its oversight of Wisconsin government,"[2] according to its website.

The LAB audit focused its attention on the entity responsible for overseeing elections in Wisconsin—the Wisconsin Election Commission (WEC). The WEC was established in 2016 after Wisconsin abolished its predecessor, the Wisconsin Government Accountability Board, which was established in 2008 to replace the Wisconsin Elections Board. It is made up of three Republicans and three Democrats, none of them elected by the people of Wisconsin. Yet they have authority to run elections in the state.

The LAB audit examined WEC's procedures and those of the counties and precincts which fall under WEC's direction.

The report set straight the fact that they *actually did* look into the 2020 election, but was a far cry from the full forensic audit Speaker Vos had promised. The LAB reviewed the election procedures from the 2020 election, including training, maintenance of voter registration records, absentee ballots, ballot processing, electronic voting equipment, post-election audits, complaints filed with the clerks, complaints filed with the Wisconsin Election Commission, and election recount costs.[3]

The most egregious finding in the report was that 44,272 individuals were given absentee ballots and allowed to vote without ever having shown proof of identification. The margin of victory between Joe Biden and President Trump was 20,682 votes. That means thousands of ballots, more than double the margin of victory, came from voters who have never been verified in person by any state official. The report explains it this way:

> According to WEC's data on individuals who voted in the November 2020 General Election and who had not previously voted by methods that required them to provide photo identification or did not have photo identification on file with a municipal clerk.[4]

The rest of the report was a slow trickle of all the laws that were systematically violated all in the name of COVID. However, the auditors refused to say one way or another whether the broken laws had an impact on the outcome of the election, despite the fact that they made several findings that laws were broken.

One of the most shocking findings in Wisconsin was that in 2020, the WEC voted 5–1 to advise county clerks to violate election laws. Yes . . . they actually *voted* to advise breaking the law. To be clear, they openly discussed, on the record, that their recommendations were illegal. One Republican held out voting against breaking the law, but the other five members voted in favor of it. WEC then sent notices to all the counties advising them to break the law, by allowing illegal activity pertaining to mail-in ballots, indefinitely confined voters, and ballots from nursing homes.[5]

One of the recommendations in LAB's report was to "ensure that the absentee ballot certificates made available to municipalities *comply with statutes* by requiring witnesses to print their names."[6] In other words, the group that conducted the audit felt the need to include in their report a recommendation that the WEC follow the law.

LAB's report certainly had good information in it, and the recommendations to follow the law are noteworthy. However, LAB did not look at any of the physical ballots, how they were physically stored, no chain-of-custody examination, no machine inspection, no inspection into the routers or splunk logs to determine unauthorized access, and no forensic examination. Republican Speaker Vos continued to resist calls for a forensic investigation all while saying he supported a full forensic audit. He was speaking out of both sides of his mouth.

Calls to Dissolve WEC

After the LAB report came out detailing the ways the WEC intentionally violated the law in the 2020 election, conservatives around the state started calling to dissolve WEC. Wisconsin is one of the only states in the United States to have created a Commission to run their elections. Typically, state legislatures pass laws governing the procedures of elections, and then the secretaries of state run the elections, under the authority provided by the state legislature. Secretaries of state fall under the executive branch, reporting to the governor, but the laws and procedures of elections are created by the legislature.

In Wisconsin, the state legislature gave authority to a separate commission, which proved to be made of individuals intentionally violating the law. Residents and conservative elected officials started to question whether the WEC should actually have authority over elections, especially since none of the officers are elected officials, but are appointed. Republican Speaker Robin Vos has the authority to hold a vote to dissolve WEC. As of January 2023, nothing has been done to hold WEC accountable.

Speaker Vos Finally Funds Justice Gableman

Meanwhile, after months of delay, Speaker Vos finally gave Justice Gableman the funding he needed to actually pursue his investigation. Perhaps realizing that the LAB audit was woefully inadequate, Vos granted Gableman authority to use approximately $600,000 of state funds to investigate the concerns surrounding the 2020 election.

At the same time, Wisconsin Assembly Election Committee Chairwoman Janel Brandtjen had been working tirelessly with grass-roots efforts around the state to obtain records and information. The subpoenas that she issued in the summer weren't executed exactly right, so she needed to re-do them. Brandtjen relayed to me that Speaker Vos made it clear to her that he would not sign her subpoenas and was not interested in her efforts to further investigate the 2020 election, and was especially not interested in decertifying the 2020 election.

Although Vos would not sign or approve her subpoenas, it did seem possible he would sign subpoenas drafted by Michael Gableman, evidenced by the fact that Gableman told Brandtjen that he would work with her to get subpoenas issued. That's a bit odd, considering Gableman is not an elected official, nor does he have any specific role in government, yet Vos gave Gableman Brandtjen's authority.

It's unclear why Vos wouldn't simply support Brandtjen in her efforts as Election Committee chairwoman, but he didn't. He appointed Gableman instead. Brandtjen was willing to support Gableman's efforts, but she also was determined to continue working with the grassroots efforts in her state—no matter who got the credit, she was dedicated to uncovering the election crimes committed in Wisconsin. She posted her findings on her legislative website, and provided them to Gableman to use in his investigation.

Racine Makes History

In October 2021, the Racine County sheriff's office became the first law enforcement agency in the country to make a finding that election fraud occurred in the 2020 election. Specifically, Racine County Sheriff Christopher Schmaling held a press conference with Lieutenant Michael Luell explaining their investigation into election abuses of the elderly in nursing homes. Lieutenant Luell was responsible for the investigation. He is an attorney and former prosecutor for Racine, so his criminal file is impeccable and matches closely with a tightly formed prosecution case file.

Lieutenant Leull explained that the sheriff's office had received a number of concerns from Racine citizens that their loved ones in nursing homes were abused in order to harvest their ballots. Specifically, elderly residents with dementia who could not remember their children's names cast ballots in 2020. Alzheimer residents who could not remember their loved ones' daily visits, let alone understand what was happening in global politics, voted. Barely cognitive patients that float in and out of lucidity voted. Family members were extremely concerned, and there were enough reports that Lieutenant Leull investigated.

After months of investigation, Luell discovered that the WEC specifically ordered county clerks to violate the law regarding their facilitation of the 2020 election.[7] As it pertains to nursing homes, Wisconsin has specific laws that require designated Special Voting Deputies (SVD) to go in pairs of one Democrat and one Republican to nursing homes and witness residents voting to ensure the elderly are not being abused. In 2020, the county clerks refused to send SVDs to the homes citing COVID as the reason. The nursing homes still allowed the fish tank cleaner, laundry services, family visits, the Orkin service, vending machine service, and even Door Dash deliveries, among others, to visit, but allowing Special Voting Deputies was too dangerous.[8]

According to Wisconsin law, nursing home employees are not allowed to assist the residents with voting. Those duties are reserved for the Special Voting Deputies. However, in 2020, COVID changed the procedures, which violated the law, and employees "assisted" in the voting process. Stories surfaced of employees trying to get residents to vote, but they were staring at the wall incoherent. The employees would wait to find a more lucid moment to harvest the resident's ballot. Ballots, as expected, are required to be kept securely as assigned to each eligible voter. Yet, Lieutenant Leull discovered that stacks of ballots were kept openly on counters at nursing homes throughout Racine County.[9] Although Lieutenant Leull only investigated Racine County, these practices and procedures were implemented statewide. The number of ballots harvested is unknown, but could potentially be in the thousands or even tens of thousands throughout all of Wisconsin. The margin of victory was only 20,682.

WEC made the entire nursing home ballot-harvesting scheme possible by ordering clerks to break the law. At the press conference in October 2021, Lieutenant Luell showed video of Wisconsin Election Commissioners openly discussing the need to break the law and direct other government officials to break the law.[10]

Based on all the evidence gathered during his investigation, including the recorded video meetings conducted via Zoom, the sheriff's office determined that five of the six county commissioners committed election fraud. The sheriff referred charges to Republican District Attorney Patricia Hanson in Racine in November 2021. Hanson responded claiming that as the Racine District Attorney, she did not have jurisdiction to prosecute the election crimes. What?! If the DA can't prosecute, who does she think *can*?!! It was another political hack job. Another Republican shirked her responsibility and refused to hold criminals accountable.

The Legislature Makes a Comeback

It was nearing the end of 2021, and no one in the state seemed willing to pursue the crimes already uncovered or the troubling evidence of fraud that continued to mount.

"What's happening with the Assembly's efforts to subpoena more evidence from Wisconsin election officials?" I asked Janel Brandtjen. "It's been *months* since we first talked about it, and it doesn't look like anything has happened?"

Janel sighed. "I know. I have been in close contact with a handful of grassroots efforts around the state. They are doing really good work through open records requests, getting access to some really shocking information." Janel sounded eager to make progress.

"Anything you can release to the public yet?" I asked, hoping she would either do an interview with me, or issue a press release to allow me to talk about the findings.

I knew that Brandtjen had worked with a number of committed patriots in Wisconsin who had done their own investigations and she had a lot of important information. I had spoken directly with some of the groups and knew the astonishing revelations they had, but weren't quite ready to go public. Janel had consolidated several findings from around the state and posted much of it to her legislative website. The problem was that there was *a lot* of it.

"Well, Gableman is running the official Assembly investigation, so I need to make sure he has a chance to present the evidence as his findings first."

"What are you going to do now?" I asked. Brandtjen had *a lot* of information about election fraud, but it had never really been presented to the public, and Wisconsin residents were eager to see progress.

"Gableman asked to schedule a hearing the first week of December so he could report what he's doing. We'll hold that hearing and see what he's got. I've scheduled one for the following week for myself and will present the findings we've found." Brandtjen said.

When Gableman held his hearing, he simply confirmed that he was appointed and was conducting an investigation. But he wanted to defer sharing any of his findings until he released his final report.

Janel Brandtjen, on the other hand, was ready to dish some dirt.

CHAPTER 12

Exposing the Wisconsin Election Commission

Janel Brandtjen's Committee on Campaigns and Elections held their first evidentiary hearing on December 8, 2021, to discuss some alarming findings concerning the Wisconsin election, including issues arising from the Wisconsin voter roll. Who is in charge of maintenance of the voter roll? Our friends at the Wisconsin Election Commission (WEC).

Legal voters need to be American citizens, over the age of eighteen, generally not convicted felons, and *actually exist*. Every ballot must be tied to a registered voter. Outside groups wanting to cheat and stuff ballots would need to add a lot of fake voters to the roll in order to add fake ballots. The December hearing, chaired by Janel Brandtjen, delved into WEC's management of the voter roll, and took a closer look at the probability of voter roll manipulation.

WEC's Emails with Outside Groups

Beginning in early 2020, and unbeknownst to the people of Wisconsin, the WEC began coordinating with outside groups to manage various aspects of the election.[1] Emails recovered from open records requests show the Wisconsin election officials requested access for a handful of individuals from outside organizations in order to allow them to process voter registration applications.[2] Although a bit concerning that the Director would give these groups access to the applications and voter registration, the early emails seem somewhat innocuous. But when you dig deeper, you can see that the "partnership" between election officials and these groups goes through Election Day and entails much more than processing voter applications.

Vote at Home, the same organization that sponsored Michael Spitzer-Rubenstein, the Democrat operative in Green Bay, sought direct access into WisVote (the state's official voter registration system), and the Director in Milwaukee provided it.[3] Spitzer-Rubenstein updated Milwaukee Director Claire Woodall-Vogg, stating that he was working on four specific aspects of election management: a voter app, drop box siting, voter instruction/marketing materials, and mail ballot processing.[4] WEC directors were using a non-profit funded at least in part by Mark Zuckerberg for advice and influence on operations of the 2020 election.

It became apparent based on the months of communication that election officials at WEC were enabling these liberal-funded groups to gain access to WisVote.[5] WEC officials also assisted these partisan groups in building an app to track voter data real time by tapping directly into WisVote.[6] The series of emails appear to indicate that this group could register new voters into WisVote without having to vet them through the state (to make sure they are *eligible* registered voters).[7]

In one email dated August 28, 2020, a Milwaukee election official explains to the Wisconsin Election Commission how exciting it is that these groups are willing to provide technical assistance on elections *for free*. The email says in part:

> I just wanted to reach out and connect you with Michael
> Spitzer-Rubenstein . . . from the Vote at Home Institute in

case you think other clerks of the WEC staff would find working with them useful. . . .

I have been working with Michael to create inputs and outputs to help us determine staffing needs and staffing responsibilities at Central Count based on actual quantitative data. They have created a tool that is extremely useful in visualizing the time certain processes take. They will also be helping the Election Commission with our voter education communications around absentee voting and the messaging we will use. They have an extremely useful communications toolkit for clerks with zero resources to those that are hiring communications firms. . . .

All in all, they have essentially made my life much easier with the absolutely free technical assistance they are offering.

Why would liberal-funded non-profits offer completely free technical assistance for election operations? Didn't election officials find that suspicious? Why didn't WEC disclose to the citizens of Wisconsin that they were allowing these groups to not only have access, but to direct election officials on how to run their elections? Would the citizens of Wisconsin approve of this access if they had been made aware before the election?

In another email dated September 14, 2020, a member of one of the app development team members working with Vote at Home sent an email to Milwaukee officials requesting access to information not available to the public. He states in part:

The end result of this data will be some formulas, algorithms and reports that cross reference information about ballots and the census data. For example, we want to deliver to Milwaukee and Vote at Home answers to questions like "How many of age residents are also registered to vote?" or "what percentage

of ballots are unreturned in areas with predominately minorities?" To do that we need a clear link address and Census
Tract. We need this for all 300k voters and the 200k+ absentee
ballots, and it needs to be able automatic [sic] as we perform
more inserts. To accomplish this, we were making calls to the
Census API. They allow you to pass in an address and get the
Census Tract. The solution works but it's far too slow. Their
batch solution isn't working either.

So, we are looking for a single file that has all addresses
and Census Tracts. We could then keep those stored in the
application and do the joins. Does that help?

The above-mentioned email shows one of the app developers working
with Milwaukee election officials explaining how they want to develop
an app that *only Wisconsin officials and Vote at Home* can have access to.
That would give Vote at Home, and the liberal activists that support
them, a massive advantage in any election. What was Vote at Home
going to do with this unbridled access? They did not have a contract
with Milwaukee officials, so who was responsible for ensuring this liberal non-profit didn't use the exclusive access for political gain?

Not only did Milwaukee not install safeguards around what Vote
at Home could do with the information, the Milwaukee election official actually went out of the way to ask the City of Milwaukee for
census data that is "less than accessible," so that it can be passed on
to the liberal-funded non-profit so they can further develop their app
and overlay voter data with census data. On September 11, 2020, the
Milwaukee official emailed city officials asking:

Hi,
I wasn't sure whether this would be RITS-ticket worthy or
not. I was wondering if the City has any type of database file

that lists the city address with census tract. We are trying to overlay our voting data with census tracts and addresses seems [sic] to be the most efficient way. The group I am working with says that the census data for this info is *less than accessible*. I thought that since Map Milwaukee has census 2010 data, it might exist in a CSV file or something similar. [emphasis added]

Thanks!

The email appears to be a Milwaukee official using government access to secure privileged and private information for a liberal non-profit. Government officials in Wisconsin were giving special access to liberal groups. Other emails show the same senior election official in Milwaukee explaining to the Democrat operatives from the vote-by-mail non-profit how she will get him the voter roll information every day.

Election officials in Milwaukee provided privileged access to voter information to liberal groups funded by Zuckerberg's money. If Republicans wanted access to the voter roll, they needed to pay the $12,500 fee for *every request*.[8] They'd also have to wait a few days for officials to process the request before turning it over. These emails show that Democrats were getting the information every day, for free. The emails appear to show Milwaukee officials giving deference to the liberal non-profits. One election official writes to the liberal app developer:

Hey . . . ,

Yes, I think I understand what you need. I will start working on getting you the files and then ask you to please check and make sure all is good. The files I will provide will be addresses joined with what census tract they are in and give a CSV and shapefile. Does that work for you?[9]

The liberal groups used that access to finally report to Milwaukee officials that they had created their own access without Milwaukee providing it. The email dated October 19, 2020 says:

> Hi . . . question about the map of voting data:
> 1. Through partners, we should be able to access the voter file to update the map without you needing to pull the data from WisVote.
> 2. They'd want to be able to share the map internally.
>
> Is that okay with you or should we create a separate map for them?[10]

Chairwoman Brandtjen presented a number of findings that demonstrate some type of partnership between Milwaukee officials, Wisconsin Election Commission officials, and multiple liberal organizations to provide liberal-funded non-profits direct access to the voter file and real-time data as to who has voted and who has not, and/or absentee application status.

The most disturbing part about the dozens of emails recovered in open records requests surrounding the 2020 election cycle is the participation of government officials.[11] The liberal-funded non-profits were asking for access that Republicans didn't have, and *election officials gave it to them*! Wisconsin Election officials used their positions of authority to benefit one political party over the other.

What makes the United States great and unique among most nations in the world is that we govern ourselves. Our unique freedoms rest upon the idea that we are a nation governed by the people, for the people. Once the people entrusted with protecting our freedoms choose to shirk their responsibility and use their position to benefit one group over another, they put our entire democratic republic at risk.

An Analysis of the Voter Roll

Representative Brandtjen's hearing went on to explain that independent citizens in Wisconsin purchased the voter roll from WEC and conducted their own analysis. Most successful political campaigns will purchase the voter roll to target their advertising. Purchasing the voter roll does not allow access to add to or change the voter roll, but allows the purchaser to see who is on it. Whether voters want their information available for purchase is another issue, but let's look at what this group found on the August 2021 version of the Wisconsin voter roll. The five findings below are some of the highlights presented at the hearing. To be clear, there were more facts presented than just these five. An experienced software engineer presented the findings . . .

Finding #1: 120,000+ voters have been on the voter roll for over one hundred years

The Wisconsin voter roll has approximately 120,000 voters with a birth and registration date of January 1, 1900 and 1918, meaning that at the time of the 2020 election, they would have been 120 years old. Clearly the birth dates and registration dates are inaccurate, and does not properly reflect the identity of the assigned voter. So why would Wisconsin have so many "fake" voters on their voter roll?

The Wisconsin Election Commission responded to this finding and offered an explanation.[12] In 2006, the state merged local election data into a statewide database. Any registration that was missing information was given a placeholder birthday and registration date of January 1, 1900 and 1918.[13]

First, we know that new voters were entered with birth dates and registration dates of January 1, 1900 and 1918, in the registration process for the 2020 election.[14] So, their explanation is not accurate.

Second, taking WEC's response at face value, that would mean that for about fourteen years there have been 120,000 voters whose voting record does not match a true legitimate identity of a Wisconsin citizen. While the voters may or may not be legitimate, it is possible there were errors when consolidating these systems, and the system that they believe to be complete is actually compromised. It's also possible outside groups that have access to the voter roll have taken advantage of this glitch and inserted additional fake voters. There's no way to know, because they never bothered to fix the missing information. They've had fourteen years to fix it, according to their response.[15] This problem highlights why elections need to be conducted *locally* and not consolidated at the state level. Small local elections are harder to compromise.

Another possible problem with this supposed glitch is that January 1, 1900, could become a default date for nefarious groups to input fraudulent votes. WEC may or may not have been doing that, but as we saw from the above emails, other outside groups have access to the voter registration. WEC is allowing voters to vote whose true identification does not match their voter registration. At best, this is sloppy records management which provides an opportunity for bad actors to abuse the voter roll. At worst, this is criminal activity.

One interesting fact to note is that poll workers in Detroit, Michigan, were using the exact same date as a placeholder. Several Republican poll challengers at the Detroit TCF Center, where they conducted their central count, mentioned that poll workers entered the birthday January 1, 1900, if a voter's registration didn't populate correctly and they needed to make a new registration. Poll workers would make a new voter, right there on the spot, using the birthday January 1, 1900.[16]

Maybe that's a coincidence that poll workers in Michigan and Wisconsin are entering the same fake birthdate to add voters to the registration on Election Day. It strikes me as odd that unrelated election officials in separate states give the same instructions to poll workers to use the exact same fake placeholder date.

Election officials would likely claim that they use the same vendors, or training companies, so it makes sense that they would be using the same date. The problem is that *no one* should be registered to vote with a birthday of January 1, 1900, because it's not actually anyone's birthday. At least, not someone voting in 2020.

Hundreds of thousands of voters on the rolls in multiple states with the exact same birthday claiming to be 120 years old? And citizens in the states do not have the opportunity to transparently understand how election officials manage the system, and who they are allowing to vote? But don't worry. It's all fine, they say.

Finding #2: 157,758 voters all had the same voter registration number
How is this even possible? The same voter registration number exists 157,758 times. Whoever managed the voter roll, rather than numbering every single voter sequentially, used a few different sequencing options, including numbers, letters, and symbols, to number registered voters. One option was to simply add a zero to the front of a number.

For example, if one registration number is 11453, they would also use 011453 as a number, and then 0011453, and then 00011453. In American number systems, adding a zero to the front of the number does not change the value of the number. This creates many registered voters, but the value of the registration number is the same. There were 157,758 voters with the same registration number.

Having 157,758 voters with the same registration number is significant. There could be a similar glitch as WEC claimed for the above scenario. Migrating voter rolls simply created weird number sequences. Maybe. If you reach out to WEC asking for an explanation, the response is a preset list of answers, none of which actually answered the questions.[17]

Rep. Janel Brandtjen and the Republican members of her committee were also concerned and sent formal letters to WEC asking for a response.[18] WEC responded to Rep Brandtjen with a letter that does not directly address any of the concerns.[19] They simply state that there are not 157,758 registered voters with the same number, because machines can differentiate with the preceding zeros. It's unclear, but it appears they've taken the stance that adding a zero in front of the number gives it a different value.

While it's possible that the zeros in front of the number are simply a glitch from the merge (which WEC does not even claim), another possibility exists, and it is much less benign.

Anyone who intends to cheat in the election by ballot stuffing, or casting ballots by fake voters, needs to assign each fake ballot cast to a voter on the voter roll. They can't just use any voter, because if they used a real voter and that voter shows up to vote, it will show that they've already voted when they didn't. If that happens too frequently, people start asking questions. Therefore, ballot stuffers need to be able to identify fake voters on a roll.

It would make sense to have one registration number that the ballot stuffer could remember to know that that voter number is available to use to stuff ballots. Rather than remember 157,758 different voter numbers, the ballot stuffer can simply add a zero to the front and find 157,758 voters on the roll to which they can assign a fake ballot. Of course, there's no way to know whether that type of ballot stuffing occurred without an investigation. What legitimate purpose does it serve to have 157,758 voters with the same registration number, differentiated only by a preceding zero?

We can't confirm whether nefarious actors stuffed ballots without an investigation. What we do know is that anyone trying to cheat had the opportunity to do so by manipulating the voter roll. The voter roll shows clear signs of possible manipulation. Wisconsin needs to correct its voter roll.

Finding #3: Wisconsin has 4.5 million residents over the age of eighteen, but more than 7 million voters on the voter roll

This finding is pretty self-explanatory. Based on the August 2021 version of the Wisconsin voter roll, there are 7,098,448 voters on record.[20] The World Population Review identifies the population of Wisconsin with 5,852,490 residents. WEC's website lists the number of "of age" voters in Wisconsin (those over the age of eighteen) as 4,536,417.[21] There are only 4.5 million residents in Wisconsin who could even possibly be eligible to vote, yet they keep million voters on the voter roll. WEC explains that they minimize the problem by turning voters to "inactive" status if they move out of state, get arrested, or are dead. Only active voters can vote in an election, so problem solved, right? Not exactly.

Legitimate reasons exist to simply change a voter's status to inactive rather than delete them from the list. A voter may move out of state and then return years later. Their voter registration can simply be turned to "active" which would preserve their earlier history. Preserving their history allows the state, political parties, and anyone who purchases the information to know their voting habits.

But is it reasonable to have more inactive voters than active voters? According to the report presented at the legislative hearing, 3.3 million voters are active, leaving 3.7 inactive voters. Election officials can simply change a voter from inactive to active, or vice versa at the request of the voter, or based on circumstances outlined in the law. We would not know, without an audit, whether voters are changed from inactive to active illegally, either by election officials working with outside groups or other bad actors.

Finding #4: 31,872 voters were registered within six months of the election and then moved to inactive following the election

According to the records turned over by WEC, 779,237 voters, or 22 percent of active voters, registered within six months of the November

3, 2020, election.[22] That in itself is weird. When in history have we seen nearly a quarter of the voters suddenly become active just six months before an election? But it gets even more suspicious. Of those new registrations, 31,872 were listed as inactive by the time the report was received in August 2021. On August 4, 2021, Wisconsin Public Radio reported that "the WEC had removed 174,307 voters from the rolls that had not voted in four years."[23] Wisconsin also lists 42,114 voters marked as inactive who voted in the 2020 election. The margin of victory is 20,682. The report states "the number of voters involved would seem to be more than can be explained by any known reason." Investigators reached out to WEC to ask for an explanation in December 2021. Rep Janel Brandtjen and the Republicans on the Election Committee also formally asked for an explanation. WEC provided a written response to the hearing, but did not directly address the glaring problems identified. The response can be read in its entirety on the wisconson.gov website.[24]

To be clear, the number of active voters who were switched to inactive closely following the election was double the margin of victory. The number of voters who registered within six months of the election and then were purged soon after the election is also enough to change the outcome of the election.

The Special Counsel Report

Three months later, Wisconsin voters got another truckload of evidence that their 2020 election was riddled with fraud.

Retired Wisconsin Supreme Court Justice Michael Gableman finally published his report[25] on March 1, 2022, and testified before the Election Committee the same day.[26] His findings confirmed the worst fears of anyone who cares about election security and were consistent with the findings of both the Legislative Audit Bureau and Janel Brandtjen's Election Committee's hearings. Most notably, he found that the private money donations, on their face, violated Wisconsin's bribery laws.

Mark Zuckerberg contributed $419 million dollars to election initiatives around the country.[27] Supposedly, the money was to make elections safer as a result of the COVID-19. However, the money was not primarily used for COVID-19 protection, although some did go for that purpose. For example, in Wisconsin, the money was conditioned upon the five largest counties adopting a Democrat initiative of the Wisconsin Safe Voting Plan (WSVP).[28] The five key counties, Milwaukee, Kenosha, Madison, Racine, and Green Bay, became known as the "Zuckerberg 5."[29]

As noted earlier, Zuckerberg funneled his money through the Center for Tech and Civic Life (CTCL), a liberal non-profit based in Illinois, which received the lion's share of the money, at least $350 million.[30] CTCL is a radical leftist organization filled with Obama Foundation fellows and Obama appointees.[31]

According to the Special Counsel report in Wisconsin:

> [A]nother election purpose existed as evidenced by the documents obtained by the Special Counsel. That other election purpose was to fuse together the CTCL, their allied private corporations, the Zuckerberg 5, and $8.8 million of private funding into joint operations in that group of cities, where the focus would be on facilitating increased in-person and absentee voting, particularly in their "communities of color." See, e.g., App. 7-27 (WSVP). From the beginning, the purpose of the WSVP contract and its private funding was for the Zuckerberg 5 to use CTCL's private money to facilitate greater in-person voting and greater absentee voting, particularly in targeted neighborhoods.[32]

Based on the Special Counsel's report, liberal non-profits funded by Zuckerberg—who was also trying to control the election narrative on his social media platforms—lied to the public about the real use of their money. Why would they need to lie if they weren't doing anything wrong? The obvious answer is that they *were* doing something wrong and they knew it. They knew the money was conditioned upon their ability to control the election process. The Special Counsel further states in his findings:

> **Any Agreement Where a City's Election Officials Receive CTCL or Other's Private Money to Facilitate In-Person and Absentee Voting Within a City Facially Violates Wis. Stat. § 12.11's Prohibition on Election Bribery Under Wis. Stat. § 12.11.**
>
> The CTCL agreement facially violates the election bribery prohibition of Wis. Stat. § 12.11 because the participating cities and public officials received private money to facilitate in-person or absentee voting within such a city. Any similar agreements in the 2022 and 2024 election cycle would also be prohibited election bribery.[33]

According to Wisconsin's Special Counsel, it appears the money was intended to impact in-person and absentee voting, which would have a direct impact on the outcome of the election.[34] Also, according to Wisconsin's Special Counsel—that's bribery.

And it's not just Wisconsin. CTCL provided funds, according to their form 990 they filed with the IRS, to forty-seven of the fifty states, plus Washington, DC.[35] For example, before the 2020 election, the group gave $45 million to Georgia, $38.6 million to Texas, $25 million to Pennsylvania, $25 million to New York, $7.5 million to Ohio, $21 million to New Jersey, $16.8 million to Michigan, $21 million to California, and $5 million to Arizona, among others.[36] Did all the grants to the states have strings attached? Or was it just Wisconsin?

The 136-page report details a number of glaring problems in Wisconsin's elections, each well documented and cited.[37] Most notably, the report addressed these main concerns:

1. Election officials used absentee ballot drop boxes in violation of Wis. Stat. § 6.87(4)(b)1 and § 6.855;
2. The Center for Tech and Civic Life's $8,800,000 Zuckerberg Plan Grants run in the Cities of Milwaukee, Madison, Racine, Kenosha and Green Bay constituted Election Bribery Under Wis. Stat. § 12.11;
3. WEC failed to maintain a sufficiently accurate WisVote voter database, as determined by the Legislative Audit Bureau;
4. The Cities of Milwaukee, Madison, Racine, Kenosha and Green Bay engaging private companies in election administration in unprecedented ways, including tolerating unauthorized users and unauthorized uses of WisVote private voter data under Wisconsin Elections Commission (WEC) policies, such as sharing voter data for free that would have cost the public $12,500;
5. As the Racine County Sheriff's Office has concluded, WEC unlawfully directed the municipal clerks not to send out the legally required special voting deputies to nursing homes, resulting in many nursing homes' registered residents voting at 100 percent rates and many ineligible residents voting, despite a guardianship order or incapacitation;
6. WEC violated the federal Help America Vote Act—WEC allowed unlawful voting by wards-under-guardianship left unchecked by Wisconsin election officials. WEC failed to record that information in the State's WisVote voter database, despite its availability through the circuit courts—all in violation of the federal Help America Vote Act.

7. WEC's failure to record non-citizens in the WisVote voter database allowed non-citizens to vote, even though Wisconsin law requires citizenship to vote—all in violation of the Help America Vote Act. Unlawful voting by non-citizens left unchecked by Wisconsin election officials, with WEC failing to record that information in the State's WisVote voter database; and

8. Wisconsin election officials' and WEC's violation of Federal and Wisconsin Equal Protection Clauses by failing to treat all voters the same in the same election.[38]

What unbelievable findings! Gableman's investigation confirmed the findings previously disclosed in the audits and election hearings, and yet elected officials were silent. Multiple investigations into the election in Wisconsin found egregious activity, very serious signs that the entire election process in Wisconsin is rigged, and very few elected officials were willing to discuss it. Imagine that. Detailed investigations reveal an entire apparatus for rigging elections, and most elected officials refused to acknowledge it. There's only one reason they'd want to hide it.

Justice Gableman was the first official in the country, appointed by a state legislature, to affirmatively find that a state had grounds to decertify its election results from the 2020 election. He states:

Thus it is clear that the Wisconsin Legislature (acting without the concurrence of the Governor, see supra), could decertify the certified electors in the 2020 presidential election.[39]

In additional to Justice Gableman's report, Chairwoman Janel Brandtjen has held at least two more hearings disclosing more radical and infuriating information than the little bit that I had room to disclose here. If you'd like to review the library of abhorrent facts she has uncovered, you can peruse her election findings here: https://legis.wisconsin.gov/assembly/22/brandtjen/election-documents/. Janel Brandtjen is a true American patriot and deserves a medal for all the hard work she has done to make Wisconsin elections more transparent.

Robin Vos's Response and the 2022 Primary

Robin Vos didn't do much with Justice Gableman's report. In fact, it appeared Vos had tried so tirelessly to impede Justice Gableman, that Justice Gableman ended up endorsing Robin Vos's opponent in the Republican 2022 primary![40] Wisconsin Republican voters were angry with Robin Vos's failure to address the glaring problems with elections in Wisconsin, so they found a candidate to challenge Vos in his primary.

Adam Steen lives in the 63rd Assembly District and had a good record as an America First supporter. He was unknown in 63rd Assembly District, the same district that Robin Vos had held since 2004.[41] Vos has deep political ties in Wisconsin, not to mention he was one of the architects of the Wisconsin Election Commission, the woefully corrupt organization that has a habit of breaking election laws.

The 63rd Assembly District is relatively small, especially in a midterm primary. For context, in the 2020 Republican primary in the 63rd District Vos ran unopposed with a total of 3,344 votes cast.[42] In 2018, again, Vos was unopposed and won 5,395 votes.[43] The previous midterm election, in 2014, Vos won the Republican primary with 4,594 votes to his opponent's 540 votes, for a total cast of 5,134.[44] So, if someone wants to win the 63rd Assembly District, they should shoot to find about 5,000 voters. Adam Steen and his grassroots team were on a mission.

Vos had impeded election integrity efforts so forcefully that he caught the attention of President Trump. About a week before the

Republican 2022 primary, Donald Trump endorsed Adam Steen for the 63rd Assembly District and discussed his endorsement at his rally just outside the 63rd District, which easily had 10,000 Wisconsin voters in attendance. Adam Steen held the golden ticket, but would Vos be able to use his ties in Wisconsin to beat Steen?

Adam Steen won 4,824, but somehow Vos managed a miraculous come-from-behind victory to nab 5,084 votes, winning the Republican primary by just 260 votes.[45] That's a record-setting total votes cast in the 63rd District of 9,908 votes! That's triple the number of votes cast in the 2020 primary!

Just to make it interesting, in July 2022, less than one month before the election, on July 31, 2022, the Racine County Municipal Clerk, which is within the 63rd District, received a legal challenge from a grassroots organizer. Specifically, the legal challenge claimed that an analysis of the voter roll from the 63rd Assembly District had 4,643 illegal voters on the roll for the 63rd Assembly District.[46] The legal challenge was complete with spreadsheets of voters that are registered at fake addresses or US Post Office Boxes.

In another instance, before the election, Harry Wait, a Wisconsin voter, wanted to prove one major flaw in the mail-in ballot system. He simply went online and requested through the official website (without showing ID) to receive Robin Vos's ballot sent to his (Harry Wait's) home. Mr. Wait requested ten ballots of prominent Wisconsin politicians, and received most of them, including the mayor of Racine's ballot, about a week later. Wait took the unopened ballots to the sheriff's office and reported a problem with the election system. Rather than acknowledge the obvious problem, Vos criticized Wait.[47]

So what did Vos do once he was declared the winner? He promptly recalled all of the ninety outstanding subpoenas investigating election corruption and canceled the remaining investigation.[48] He shut down any investigation into election corruption.[49]

More Private Money – 2022

For the 2022 election, the city of Milwaukee issued a "private grant to conduct door-to-door canvassing to urge people to vote."[30] The mayor's office stated, "the city is neither receiving nor providing any funds related to the work of 'Milwaukee Votes 2022.' The group is privately funded, not for profit and non-partisan."[31] The mayor may claim the group is non-partisan, but the group selected, GPS Impact, claims on its homepage, "We've helped Democrats, progressive organizations and initiatives, and elected officials win Red states, including Kansas, Michigan, Pennsylvania, Wisconsin, North Carolina, Louisiana and Ohio."[32] So effectively, the mayor of Milwaukee gave this leftist activist group special privileges for the 2022 election by granting them authority to essentially harvest ballots.

CHAPTER 13

Michigan: The RINOs' Alamo

What if some of our state officials fear a report that some of them were not truly elected? I have always said this isn't about Republicans or Democrats. This is about the Constitution and the "purity of elections" clause.

—Matt Deperno, Michigan Lawyer

Michigan Democrat Secretary of State Jocelyn Benson reported a win for Biden on November 4, but the tally had been done secretly, behind closed doors, with the Republicans forcibly removed from the counting room, no website updates, no accountability. We the People simply had to accept the number she published. If anyone disagreed with Benson or questioned how she came up with her numbers, she retorted with name calling and mudslinging. She never addressed the very real concern that windows to the counting room had been boarded up in Michigan to prevent meaningful observation, and challengers had been excluded from the process. Voters had very real questions about the integrity of the election in Michigan, and Michigan wasn't providing answers.

By early December 2020, Pennsylvania, Arizona, and Georgia had already held hearings allowing Rudy Giuliani to present the available evidence of fraud. The Michigan state legislature was under pressure to give Mayor Giuliani the same opportunity to discuss the irregularities, and in some instances, violation of the law. Yet despite its Republican majority, Michigan had been particularly challenging. In the other states, Rudy's team had someone in the state legislature who was willing to challenge the status quo, as well as often times activists on the ground. Michigan's elected Republicans didn't seem to have the desire to fight.

I had spent a couple weeks reaching out to witnesses and working with local counsel in Michigan to try to get authority, either through the courts or legislative subpoena, to further investigate the election in Michigan. Other members of Rudy's team also worked their own contacts, and we were all hitting the same road blocks. Michigan courts were tough, as many of the judges were strong Democrat supporters; they refused to acknowledge the time crunch we were under, and were unlikely to grant any requests to investigate or challenge the 2020 elections. The Republican state legislature was the best option, but they weren't exactly jumping at the chance to clean up the mess of the 2020 election. They finally gave Rudy his hearing on December 2, 2020.

The hearing went like most of the other evidentiary hearings at which Mayor Giuliani presented. December 2 was a long day of witness after witness telling their stories. Republican poll workers were excluded from the election process, made to stand so far away they didn't have the ability to meaningfully observe, and were told if they left to use the bathroom, they would not be allowed to re-enter. Witnesses discussed concerns with the voter rolls and logs, mysterious ballot drops, and obscurity in the counting process.

Some of the witnesses were immigrants who had moved to the United States and built successful businesses and careers. They were grateful for the opportunity to live in the United States and volunteered to work the election, only to discover many irregularities that disadvantaged them. The hearings were televised on OAN and a few other smaller internet platforms in an effort to get the word out about the evidence of fraud. Big corporate media ridiculed the witnesses and empowered radicals to attack them.

As one of the last states to allow a hearing, Michigan was already on notice that Rudy's hearings were highlighting a lot of information they didn't want publicized. After their testimonies, the witnesses were harassed, threatened, and their businesses attacked.[1] What did Michigan's Republican legislature do with the information provided at the hearing? Nothing.

Michigan, like many other states, had a rogue governor and secretary of state who had taken it upon themselves to change election laws in 2020, without the state legislature. Absentee ballot applications were mailed to everyone, whether they were requested or not, despite the fact that Michigan law does not authorize the procedures used in the 2020 election. Secretary of State Benson explained that she felt she needed to provide "alternate voting opportunities."[2] The governor and secretary of state blamed COVID, saying it was for everyone's safety that they *had* to violate the law. They simply pushed the legislature aside, and the Republican legislature let them.

Bailey versus Antrim County

Michigan citizens were not willing to fold.

William Bailey is a voter and Antrim County, Michigan, resident. On November 23, 2020, he sued Antrim County claiming that he had been disenfranchised as a voter. The story goes like this:

On November 4, 2020, Antrim County announced that 16,047 votes had been cast and Joe Biden received 7,769 and Donald Trump received 4,509. In 2016, Donald Trump had received 62 percent of the vote in Antrim, making the 2020 results particularly surprising. Mr.

Bailey made some phone calls and the Antrim County clerk double checked the results, and issued new results.

A closer look showed 18,059 votes cast in Antrim County. Joe Biden received 7,289 votes and Donald Trump received 9,783, meaning Trump won 54 percent of the vote, which is still significantly less than 2016. This also doesn't account for the difference in the number of votes cast. Why were they short, and where did the new votes come from?

Antrim County checked a third time and found 16,044 votes cast and that Joe Biden received 5,960, while Donald Trump received 9,748, winning 60.75 percent. Jocelyn Benson, the Michigan secretary of state, asserted that the error was simply clerical, because the clerk failed to update the Mancelona Township tabulator prior to election night for a down ballot race, and that the correct count was always on the tabulator tape. She insisted that the Antrim County clerk simply made a mistake, and this was not a cause to look closer at every county in Michigan. Benson shut the discussion down, but Bailey continued to fight in court.

Matt Deperno, Bailey's lawyer, aggressively pursued discovery in the case and successfully won a motion to audit the election machines in Antrim County. Deperno hired Allied Security Operations Group, led by Russ Ramsland, to conduct the audit. The initial report released December 13, 2020, found a number of discrepancies, and concluded that Secretary of State Benson's statement that the correct vote count was always reflected on the tabulator tapes "was false." In an extreme finding, the report stated that in Central Lake Township, 1,222 ballots out of 1,491 were reversed, resulting in an 81.96 percent rejection rate.[3] The allowable error rate established by the Federal Election Commission is one out of 250,000 (0.0008 percent).[4]

The report was immediately criticized by the media, and the auditors were barraged with attacks on their character. Critics said the report was biased, but few, if any, directly targeted the substance of their work. The Republican establishment ignored the findings and simply watched as Matt Deperno worked to gain transparency in the 2020 election without help from the Republican legislature. Deperno continued to investigate and release information as it became available.

On April 9, 2021, Deperno released another exhibit in the *Bailey* case, with additional findings from the experts examining the evidence, which found that, despite critics saying otherwise, the voting machines *were* connected to the internet and the vendors knew they were connected. The exhibit produced email communications from election night discussing the terrible internet connection and the decision by the vendors (not election officials) to refuse to save ballot images in an effort to speed up the transmission. State and federal law requires that all election evidence be held for twenty-two months, arguably including the ballot images.

The fact that the machines were connected to the internet does not, in and of itself, prove fraud or manipulation. It does highlight the aggressive disinformation campaign waged immediately following the election to dispel the *belief* that machines were connected to the internet, despite the fact that it was true. Voting machines send the tallies to a central counting facility, *via the internet*, to allow the totals to be counted faster. That's how news networks update their tallies instantaneously on election night. Connecting them to the internet does create some vulnerabilities, but does not mean any malicious activity actually took place. So why all the drama? Why all the hype from election officials across the country trying to convince the public the machines were not connected to the internet when they knew that they were? Why not just say that the machines were connected to the internet, but no security breaches occurred . . . if that was in fact true?

The report included two more alarming discoveries: it identified foreign IP addresses registered to the equipment used in Antrim County's election, and it raised concerns about foreign investment into the machines used. For instance, the British company Telit makes the chips for one brand of voting machine in the US. In June 2020, Telit announced that it had added Yuxiang Yang to its board of directors. According to the press release, "Mr. Yang brings considerable experience from a career in investment and financial markets and is founder and CEO of China Fusion Capital, a Chinese investment management group."[5] An online publication in the U.K., *Financial Mail on Sunday*, published an article on August 15, 2020, raising concerns about Chinese influence in the British government and particularly Telit. Telit declined to comment.

Deperno continued to release exhibit after exhibit detailing technical specifics of anomalies and irregularities from the 2020 election. Corporate media continued to ignore and bury the story, and hurled insults at Deperno and his case. The court eventually dismissed the case, but not based on any of the evidence Deperno had amassed. It dismissed the case on a technicality: the plaintiff was asking for an audit of the election, and Secretary of State Benson told the court she had already conducted an audit. Therefore, the court ruled, the case was moot.

Republicans versus Republicans

In 2020, the Michigan state legislature had 110 Representatives (fifty-eight Republicans, fifty-two Democrats) and thirty-eight senators (twenty Republicans, sixteen Democrats, and two interim). Despite the Republican majority, they did not complete a forensic audit of Michigan's elections. There simply was no demand to do so from the Republican leaders.

William Bailey wasn't the only Michigan voter who disagreed.

Pat Colbeck is an aerospace engineer and former Michigan state senator. Although no longer in the Senate, Colbeck jumped into action shortly after the election and began investigating the fraud with other local teams. He focused his efforts on coordinating multiple grassroots efforts around the state and collecting information in a usable manner. Colbeck believes his role is to "triage the data," and ensure that the various efforts were aware of each other and using the information as it becomes available.

Despite all of the grassroots efforts, the Republican legislature refused to budge. Even a year after the election, the Republican elected leaders took no action. Steve Carra, a freshman legislator, actually proposed legislation to require a partial audit of the 2020 election. His bill only sought 10–20 percent of the ballots and did not go far enough for those seeking a full forensic audit. But, he was the first legislator to stand up and demand action and start the discussion. Legislation wasn't the best vehicle to get an audit, but at least it was something. Carra's bill, however, never made it out of committee.

Jacky Eubanks is a young motivated patriot who initiated her own efforts to investigate the election fraud in Michigan. She began canvassing her home town in Macomb County, a key swing county, and made some interesting findings. Eubanks found that Macomb County has over 170,000 *more* registered voters than people who are of voting age that live in the county. And that number assumes that every person of voting age in Macomb County is a non-felon and a citizen with the legal right to vote. She also found an 18 percent anomaly and irregularity rate between the votes that were recorded, and the affidavits from the residents that lived at the homes. Her findings were more than enough to change the outcome of the 2020 election.

When she presented her findings to the Republican county clerk, she was told she needed more proof. The clerk wanted a bigger sample size from more towns and more counties, but he wasn't willing to investigate the fraud himself. He offered her no assistance or support. So, Eubanks got to work to build a bigger sample size with more communities and continued her investigative efforts.

Republican Senate Targets Republican Constituents

Michigan Senator Ed McBroom, a Republican and chairman of the
Oversight Committee, decided he could end the discussion of election
fraud in Michigan once and for all by conducting his own investigation
into the 2020 election. McBroom refused to meet with attorney Matt
DePerno, who hired the experts and produced most of the available evidence of election fraud. According to DePerno, McBroom also refused
to meet with any of the experts who had conducted the investigation.

On December 16, 2020, DePerno sent an email to the Michigan
state legislature, including Senator McBroom, detailing all of his findings, providing the forensic reports, and inviting the legislature to meet
with him to better understand the evidence of fraud his experts had
found in the State of Michigan. Receiving no response, Deperno sent
follow-up emails in June and August of 2021. None of the legislators
responded. Most of the legislators are Republican.

Instead of engaging in a fact-finding investigation, the Michigan
Senate Oversight Committee, chaired by Republican Ed McBroom,
issued their own report in June 2021.[6] The report targeted conservative Republicans (their own constituents), and recommended that the
Michigan attorney general, a Democrat, investigate those who perpet-
uated the narrative of election fraud. The Republican-led committee
specifically targeted Deperno and his efforts:

> The Committee recommends the attorney general consider
> investigating those who have been utilizing misleading and
> false information about Antrim County to raise money or
> publicity for their own ends. The Committee finds those
> promoting Antrim County as the prime evidence of a
> nationwide conspiracy to steal the election place all other
> statements and actions they make in a position of zero
> credibility.[7]

At that time, 70 percent of Republicans believed the 2020 election was stolen.[8] This means that McBroom's report disregarded the concerns of 70 percent of his voters in an effort to scare or intimidate Matt Deperno and others from continuing the fight for election integrity. Michigan was the only Republican legislature of the five Republican contested states to not make a single effort at taking a closer look at the 2020 election. Pennsylvania, Georgia, Wisconsin, and Arizona all were making varying degrees of efforts to investigate the election. Not Michigan.

Did the Republican leaders of Michigan do anything to protect its constituents from a bizarre Senate report calling for their possible prosecution? Nope. *Some even published the report in their email news blast!* Not only did the establishment fail to reprimand such rogue Republican members, they actually acted as if the report was legitimate information to be reasonably considered. No one seemed concerned that the Republicans they helped get elected to office were using their power to threaten and intimidate the Republican constituents they were supposed to represent.

CHAPTER 14

The Corporate Takeover

Corporations of vast wealth and remorseless staying power have moved into our politics to seize for themselves advantages that can be seized only by control over government.
—Senator Sheldon Whitehouse (D-RI)[1]

Money has always played a role in American elections, and in that sense 2020 was no different from dozens of previous elections. However, the way that money came in—and how it was spent—paints a troubling picture that makes 2020 quite different from anything that had ever happened before. Quite simply, it paved the way for unprecedented manipulation.

As you've read in previous chapters, reports indicate that Facebook CEO Mark Zuckerberg donated between $350 and $410 million to help influence the 2020 election.[2] Conservative voters around the country were outraged at the massive amount of money contributed by one individual and corporation. President Trump has even joked that he's constrained by the personal donation limit of $5,000, yet Zuckerberg can somehow donate hundreds of millions.

So, where does the money go? Does it influence the outcome of elections? Voters around the country complained of "Zuckerbucks" being used to sway an election. If elections are run by the government, cities, and counties, how much influence do special interest groups have over an election?

Big spending in elections usually goes towards media campaigns. Money is spent to create ad campaigns, to buy airtime on TV and radio, and to use digital and social media to promote specific candidates. Joe Biden and Democrat groups spent more than $1 billion in 2020.[3] By comparison, Donald Trump and Republican groups spent $760 million.[4] In an interesting twist, Zuckerberg did not spend his money mostly on media, but instead sent his money to non-profit groups working the elections in key cities and counties. Specifically (and separate from the $1 billion noted above), Zuckerberg sent $350 million to the Center for Tech and Civic Life, based in Chicago.[5]

Center for Tech and Civic Life

It's important to take a closer look at these organizations, including who they were and exactly how they got involved in the 2020 elections. The Center for Tech and Civic Life (CTCL) states its mission is to make elections "more professional, inclusive, and secure."[6] Founder and President Tiana Epps-Johnson was an Obama Foundation Fellow (2018) and Harvard Ash Center Technology and Democracy Fellow (2015). Director Tammy Patrick was the Federal Compliance Officer for Maricopa County (Arizona) Elections Department for eleven years. She was also appointed to the Presidential Commission on Election Administration by President Obama when he launched the Commission in 2013.[7] Director and Secretary for CTCL Christina Sinclaire says that she "served as Director of Client Services at Catalist, providing data and data services to over 200 progressive organizations."[8]

Director Pam Anderson was a former Republican County Clerk in Jefferson County, Colorado. Anderson completed her last term as clerk in 2015, and was remembered for getting "tangled with Republican

Secretary of State Scott Gessler over several issues, including his claims of voter fraud."[9] Apparently, Gessler wanted to investigate election fraud in Colorado, and Anderson resisted his efforts. Both presidential races that Anderson oversaw resulted in an Obama victory in Jefferson County. This is the non-profit through which Mark Zuckerberg funneled his money to impact the 2020 election.[10] We'll see just how that organization used its millions of dollars in a moment.

The National Vote at Home Institute (Vote at Home)

The National Vote at Home Institute is a non-profit that took on an administrative role in elections around the country, and impacted voting in Wisconsin and Georgia. By administrative role, I mean they literally administered the election in several areas: tallying ballots, exchanging vote information with the central count, and manning the machines, among other duties. National Vote at Home Institute (and its lobbying arm, Vote at Home) is the organization that finances Michael Spitzer-Rubenstein, the New York resident who took on an administrative role in Green Bay, Wisconsin, and was given keys, passwords, and access to the machines and ballot counts by the mayor of Green Bay.

The interim executive director of Vote at Home, Xanthe Thomassen, claims in her bio that she aims "to be on the right side of history," by supporting voting rights and "the expansion of vote by mail, absentee, and early voting."[11] She lives in Colorado with her wife, Dana.

The founder and CEO, Amber McReynolds, started working in the Denver Clerk and Recorder's office in 2005, and served as the director of elections for Denver, Colorado, from 2011 to 2018. While in office, she transformed Denver's election system to 100 percent vote-by-mail election system.[12] Since 1920, Denver has voted for the *Republican* presidential candidate in seventeen of the twenty-five presidential elections.

That means Denver has selected the *Democrat* candidate only nine times in the last one hundred years. Four of those nine times were the last four elections since 2008.[13] Only one time in the last one hundred years has Denver voted for the Democrat candidate two years in a row (1932 and 1936). Since 2008, they have voted the Democrat candidate four elections in a row.[14]

Philip Keisling, a Democrat, is the chair and director of the Vote at Home Institute and the National Vote at Home Coalition.[15] Prior to these roles, he served as the Oregon secretary of state from 1991 to 1999, and in the Oregon House of Representatives from 1989 to 1991. "He is known for having championed the state's Vote by Mail system,"[16] which launched in 1981. Since Oregon made vote by mail permanent in 1987, the state has never once voted for a Republican candidate. By 1996, during Keisling's tenure as secretary of state, Oregon became the first state to conduct an entire general election 100 percent by mail.[17] Since Abraham Lincoln was elected in 1860 until the use of mail-in ballots in 1987, Oregon had only voted for the Democrat candidate in seven of the thirty-two elections, and four of those were for FDR.[18] That means Oregon has only voted for four Democrat presidents since Abraham Lincoln—until 1988. After introducing mail-in ballots, Republicans have never won the state.

Vote at Home partners with several far-Left liberal groups, including Democracy Fund, Common Cause, Nonprofit VOTE, Rock the Vote, and Unite America.[19] Board member Stephen Silberstein was a top-twenty donor to Hillary Clinton's super PAC, Priorities USA Action.[20] Vote at Home identifies as a bipartisan group.[21]

The Center for Tech and Civic Life and Vote at Home are only two of many organizations that played a behind-the-scenes role in the 2020 elections, undisclosed on government websites, and only discovered through research. How much influence did these corporations have over the election? A lot.

Who Ran Wisconsin?

The five largest cities in Wisconsin—Milwaukee, Racine, Green Bay, Kenosha, and Madison (The Wisconsin Five)—received a $10.3 million dollar grant from Center for Tech and Civic Life for the 2020 election. In exchange for that money, the cities agreed to allow involvement of "election advisors" from private organizations selected by CTCL, and agreed the money would "be intentional and strategic in reaching our historically disenfranchised residents and communities."

In other words, the cities were required to use the money to benefit Democrat communities. Otherwise, the cities would have to pay back the grant.[22] The Wisconsin Five contracted to allow CTCL to provide personnel from other organizations to come in and "advise" on how to manage the elections on behalf of the municipalities. That's how Michael Spitzer-Rubenstein ended up getting keys to the counting room, access to the machines and ballots, and a city of Green Bay employee ID.

Spitzer-Rubenstein, financed by Vote at Home, was seen on Election Day, at the Green Bay central counting location examining the machine totals and entering them into a spreadsheet on his laptop throughout the day. He also had his cell phone with him and was frequently on the phone at the counting facilities passing information. What makes this particularly remarkable is that the *city officials* allowed this to happen. Using *city* funds to effectively campaign to designated demographics is *expressly illegal*. The city's responsibility is to ensure access to vote for every voter, not to cater to one demographic. But, cater they did.

The private funds in Milwaukee supported a "communications effort . . . focus[ed] on appealing to a variety of communities within Milwaukee, including historically underrepresented communities such as LatinX and African Americans, and would include a specific focus on the re-enfranchisement of voters who are no longer on probation or parole for a felony." The idea that *cities*, and not political parties or campaigns, were engaged in this specific type of activity expressly disenfranchises the other voters in the community, and *it's illegal*. Reaching specific demographics is the responsibility of private organizations, not the government which is supposed to run the election fairly.[23]

Witnesses say that Michael Spitzer-Rubenstein was out of place. Rex Coldagelli, a Republican volunteer observer in Green Bay, had questioned Spitzer-Rubenstein earlier in the day, on Election Day, and couldn't get a clear answer as to who he was. Coldagelli believed Spitzer-Rubenstein had been removed from the counting facility, but saw him back at the tables, with his laptop, later in the day. Coldagelli began asking questions and confronted Spitzer-Rubenstein, wanting to know who he was and where he worked. A city employee named Ahmad Riviera jumped up and stepped between Coldagelli and Spitzer-Rubenstein, demanding that Coldagelli go to a different area of the room and stop confronting Spitzer-Rubenstein.

By this time, it was 11 p.m., and Coldagelli hadn't even learned Spitzer-Rubenstein's name. Coldagelli demanded that Spitzer-Rubenstein sign in, just like every other volunteer was required to do. Eventually, after a heated exchange, Spitzer-Rubenstein signed the logbook. It was due to that one courageous act by Coldagelli, to demand that he follow the rules, that we were even able to identify who Spitzer-Rubenstein was and that he was at the Green Bay central counting facility with a city employee ID.

Another volunteer, Elizabeth Rankin, also demanded to know who Spitzer-Rubenstein was and what he was doing there. Spitzer-Rubenstein told her that he was an observer. Rankin asked him why he was wearing a city employee ID if he was just an observer. Spitzer-Rubenstein didn't answer her. He also refused to answer her when she asked why he was allowed to have his laptop and cell phone in the facility when all of the Republican observers were not allowed to bring them in, and why did he have his own work station? Again, no answer.

The City's Response

After several complaints about the way the Wisconsin election was run, the City attorney for Green Bay responded in a nineteen-page memorandum on April 20, 2021. City Attorney Vanessa Chavez acknowledged the non-city employees engaged in working the election and wrote:

> Among these were Dayna Causby from the Elections Group, Mr. Spitzer-Rubenstein and Sarah Lynn Flynn from the National Vote at Home Institute, Whitney May from the Center for Tech and Civic Life, Erika Reinhardt from US Digital Response, Liz Howard at the Brennan Center, and Ashish Sinha from the Center for Secure and Modern Elections, to name just a few.[24]

In a bizarre admission, Chavez stated, concerning Spitzer-Rubenstein's involvement:

> The City was under no contract with [National Vote at Home Institute], exchanged no funds with the group, nor was it obligated to utilize NVAHI's services.

So then why did Spitzer-Rubenstein get City of Green Bay credentials and have unbridled access to all of the election equipment and infrastructure? Chavez's report confirms the account of several city workers, including Kris Teske, the City of Green Bay Clerk. Teske objected to Spitzer-Rubenstein's involvement and raised concerns to many election officials at the Wisconsin Election Commission.[25] Teske stated she went so far as to question the legality of his involvement, and that she was unwilling to break the law.[26] After months of battle and unresolved complaints, Teske eventually resigned, and Spitzer-Rubenstein was given all of the access to which Teske had been objecting. Chavez, the

City attorney, claims that she investigated and found that the City did nothing wrong.

Mailing In Georgia

In October 2020, *Time* magazine heralded National Vote at Home Institute CEO Amber Reynolds as the woman who wrote "[the vote by mail] plan for the entire country."[27] After her stint in the Denver Recorder's office, she proved that she was capable of scaling a mail-in ballot plan. She helped convert Colorado to a system that has proven to favor Democrats, and COVID launched her into a place to convert the entire country. Like other far-Left liberal groups, Vote at Home targeted key Republican states, including Georgia.

Throughout the run up to the 2020 election, McReynolds was in frequent contact with Brad Raffensperger, Georgia's Secretary of State.[28] Georgia struggled with its primary elections in 2020 for a number of reasons. The State had a difficult time managing new technology and the large influx of mail-in ballots.[29] Governor Kemp and Secretary of State Brad Raffensperger also incorporated voting procedures, like drop boxes, that had not been approved by the legislature, and had not been previously used in elections. The combination of new procedures, unlawful voting practices, mail-in ballots, and COVID made the Peach State's election ripe for the picking.

Election officials and corporate organizations used COVID as a reason to disregard the law, scuttle election security measures, and implement new procedures that had the effect of making voter fraud child's play. McReynolds's national plan, which Georgia adopted, championed the effort to make voting easy and comfortable for everyone. *Time* magazine wrote:

> According to Vote at Home's national plan, states' best option was simple: send ballots, along with return envelopes

with pre-paid postage, directly to all registered voters'
homes—and then allow people to return them in as many
ways as possible.[30]

One glaring problem that has come to light is the negligent management of the voter rolls. If every "voter" on the rolls gets a ballot, whether
they ask for it or not, states end up with hundreds of thousands of ballots without real voters assigned. Grassroots in Wisconsin have found
230,854 voters on the rolls in Waukesha County that are dead, have
moved, have birthdays listed as 1/1/1918, are felons, or are not eligible
to vote for a variety of reasons. Under McReynold's plan, they all got
ballots. That's only one county in one state. Copying this plan in every
county in dozens of states equates to millions of fraudulent ballots.

Ultimately, Georgia adopted several of Vote at Home's recommendations, including which vendors to use, how many drop boxes
to use and where they should be located, and changing the election process to begin processing absentee ballots fifteen days before
Election Day.[31] I reached out to the Georgia Secretary of State's
Office to learn if Vote at Home had the same access to Georgia's
elections as they did in Wisconsin. They have not responded to my
request for comment.

Georgia Deputy Secretary of State Jordan Fuchs has publicly
stated, "[McReynolds] uniquely is aware of the pitfalls that can occur
when [the election] isn't rolled out properly," and McReynolds was a
"strong resource to [Fuchs] personally."[32] Fuchs is also the same staffer
in the secretary of state's office who leaked the phone call between
President Trump and Brad Raffensperger. Fuchs did not respond to
my request for comment. It's unclear if Fuchs was simply unaware of
the massive fraud that could occur through the un-scrubbed voter rolls
and drop boxes, or if she was part of the problem. Like so many other
Republicans, perhaps she got blindsided.

No legislatures in any of the contested states authorized election officials to take money in exchange for access and authority to manage the 2020 election. Elected officials who take money in exchange for influence over the elections have taken a bribe and broken the law. Government officials who allowed unauthorized access by groups to influence the election, whether they took money or not, are complicit in election fraud.

Our nation is suffering under the weight of public attorneys too scared or unwilling to enforce the law. Attorneys general or district attorneys should be enforcing the rule of law, regardless of political party. Political party should not matter in a society that values the law. The district attorney in Green Bay, David Lasee, is a Republican. He has taken no steps to enforce election laws in Green Bay. The attorney general in Georgia, Christopher Carr, is a Republican. He has taken no steps to enforce election laws in Georgia. The district attorney in Racine, Patricia Hanson, is a Republican. Not only has she has taken no steps to enforce election laws in Racine, but she refused to prosecute election crimes referred to her office by the Racine Sheriff. We have elected these public servants to protect and enforce our laws. They aren't doing their jobs. Their conduct threatens our sacred liberty to elect our own leaders.

CHAPTER 15

Blue States, Red States: What Happened in Nevada, New Mexico, and Texas

Nevada and New Mexico play a crucial, but often overlooked, role in the 2020 election. Both showed clear signs of illegal election activity. But as Democrat-run states with very liberal legislatures, courts, and governors, there was little expectation of any objectivity from their elected or appointed officials.

We've all taken for granted that places like California are "Democrat states," guaranteed to produce Democrat wins. What happened in 2020 in Nevada and New Mexico suggested that maybe some "Blue" states aren't as liberal as the swamp would like us to believe. Is it possible that Democrats have been cheating for so long, we've been believing a lie? Like most liberal "successes," maybe it's all an illusion.

Trending Now—Trump States Flip for Biden

Like many states where President Trump was leading on election night, Nevada experienced some mysterious problem that prevented them from completing their count that night. They were able to count millions of votes on Election Day, but needed an extra *three* days to complete the last few hundred thousand.[1] While most other states in the country were able to complete their counting on November 3, Nevada couldn't finish their counting until November 7.

It's interesting to note that every single state that paused their counting when President Trump was leading by hundreds of thousands of votes ultimately went to Biden. When the counts were paused, Trump was ahead. Three days later, Democrat secretaries of state found enough ballots to create a Biden victory. And no one is allowed to question the results. Democrats awarded Nevada to Joe Biden on November 7, 2020.[2] Arizona, Michigan, Wisconsin, Georgia, and Pennsylvania all flipped from a decisive Trump victory to a questionable Biden victory after they paused their vote count and kicked all the Republicans out of the process.

The media wanted you to believe Florida and North Carolina were a toss-up and might go to Biden, despite President Trump's clear lead. Both states continued their count and never stopped. President Trump maintained his lead, and won both states *on election night.* Liberals spew racism claims at anyone who dares to state the obvious: Democrats needed three extra days to learn the results on election night and then manufacture enough votes to overcome the Biden loss and claim a Biden victory.

Notice how the states that stopped counting flipped from Trump to Biden? Not one of them remained a Trump win, yet he had the lead in all of them on election night. Not one of them flipped from Biden to Trump. Only Nevada claimed a Biden lead on election night and remained a Biden win. We're talking about five states. *Five states* needed to pause their counting, remove all of the Republicans from the process, and then magically they switch from a Trump win to a Biden win, changing the outcome of the presidential election. That's a feat of improbability.

Democrats want you to believe that Trump won eighteen out of the nineteen bellwether counties.[3] Ohio, Florida, Iowa, and North Carolina have voted for the winning presidential candidate since 1896, and President Trump won all four.[4] President Trump gained 11.2 million votes, was winning in the five states that stopped counting on election night (all states that flipped for Biden after Republicans had been removed from the process for three days)—and then Joe Biden won the election.

If there truly was some sort of abnormality on election night that legitimately caused states to need to stop counting, there would have been a variety of different scenarios. Not a single state where Biden was winning stopped counting and flipped to Trump. More likely than not, if the five states had not stopped counting, none of them would have flipped, and President Trump would have officially won all five states and the presidential election. It's not a coincidence, it's a tactic.

Signs of Fraud in Nevada

Mail-in ballot fraud is one of the easiest ways to cheat in an election, because ballot stuffing becomes so much easier. Clark County, home to Las Vegas, mailed 81,000 ballots to voters that they knew were inactive, and allowed the US Postal Service to forward ballots to known bad addresses, all in the name of COVID.[5] Election security went out the window in Nevada.

Like other states, Republicans were excluded from the counting process and denied the chance to observe how votes were being counted, especially in the days following the election when the magic Biden vote spike occurred.[6] Nevada GOP representatives were not invited to review that process.[7]

In the name of COVID, election officials lowered the standards for signature verification on mail-in ballots.[8] Apparently, the threat of COVID causes people to sign their names differently, so they needed to lower the match standards. Nevada officials disregarded the law and common-sense election procedures on tens of thousands of ballots. The Nevada GOP filed eight thousand pages of evidence with Nevada courts to demonstrate election fraud.[9] Remember—the margin of victory in Nevada was supposedly 33,569.[10]

Some of their findings include:[11]

- 42,284 duplicate votes cast by voters with matching name, address, and birthdate
- 15,164 out-of-state votes (non-student, non-military)
- 8,842 votes from commercial addresses
- 3,463 votes from vacant properties
- 3,262 votes cast from non-existent addresses
- 2,468 votes from voters who have permanently changed their residential address to another state
- 1,506 votes from deceased voters
- 3,987 votes from non-US citizens

These are astonishing and shocking facts, yet election officials maintain that this was "the most secure election in US history." Why are our leaders unwilling to acknowledge the obvious problems with this election? If they're so confident in their methodology and process, it shouldn't be a problem to allow the voters to check their work, right? Yet, they do everything possible to block any attempt at verifying what they tell us.

Duplicate Voters[12]

An interesting occurrence in Nevada was the massive number of duplicate voters. How did 42,284 people vote twice? That's more than the margin of victory, and yet no one in Nevada leadership wants to question it? The problem arises from the way Nevada has chosen to conduct its voter registration.[13] Democrats run the state and have decided that everyone who is processed through the Nevada DMV should be registered to vote . . . even if they're *already registered.*

As we've learned from several of the other states, like Wisconsin, voter roll bloat makes cheating easier. So, those who want to cheat look for ways to inflate the voter registration. Democrats passed a law in Nevada requiring automatic voter registration for anyone updating information with the DMV, even if they're already registered to vote.

Anyone who moves and changes their address receives a new voter registration, without canceling the old one.[14] Anyone who gets married and changes a name gets a new voter registration, without canceling the old one. Any clerical error on the part of the DMV, when fixed, would become a new voter registration. For example, someone registering a new vehicle with the DMV who adds their middle initial will receive a new voter registration.

As you can imagine, this causes voter roll bloat, which creates lots of opportunity for fraud. At least 42,284 Nevadans had two ballots cast in their name.[15] Whether they personally cast those ballots twice or whether a bad actor used their extra registrations to ballot stuff is unclear. What we do know is this: there were more illegal votes than the margin of victory in the State of Nevada.

Cash for Votes

Nevada also saw an alarmingly brazen campaign to pay certain demographics for their votes, particularly the Native American community.[16] The Nevada GOP received a number of calls and tips from concerned members of the community, and published a statement saying:

> Under the cover of a supposed non-profit and non-partisan
> get out the vote campaign, Native American voter advocacy
> groups in Nevada handed out gift cards, electronics, and

other items to voters in the tribal areas. There are a number of accounts showing the exchange of ballots for 'prizes' on their own Facebook pages, at times even while wearing official Joe Biden campaign gear.[17]

Due to all of the calls and concerns, the Nevada GOP put together a 120-page report detailing the concerns, including video evidence and photographs of the items offered to Native Americans in exchange for their votes.[18] Federal law expressly prohibits soliciting, accepting, or receiving any type of expenditure in consideration of a vote, or withholding a vote.[19] Yet, there are several pages of documents showing Native Americans receiving gas cards, gift cards, and other items in exchange for their ballots.[20]

Ironically, one of the social media posts from the Nevada Native Vote Project states "voting is sacred," and then explains:

> I have incentives for those who go and vote only a limited supply of T-shirts for those of our native community who vote take a picture of you voting send it to me and then come and see me after you're done voting and also I have coffee very nice native coffee for our elders in our native community who vote please reach out to me either on Facebook or on my phone 775-[xxx-xxxx][sic].

Voting *is* sacred. What an insult to the Native American community that they'd buy the sacred right for a cup of coffee or a t-shirt?! Liberals that scream racism accusations or cry to protect the secret ballot also are the ones who actually commit racist acts and violate secret ballot protocol. They target specific people groups and incentivize voters to take pictures of the voting process *for coffee and a t-shirt!* The hypocrisy is stunning.

Nevada CC's Pakistan

True the Vote, the same non-profit organization that uncovered the unthinkable ballot-harvesting organization using drop boxes (which was dramatized in Dinesh D'Souza's movie, *2,000 Mules)*, investigated the Nevada voter roll.[21] After requesting the updated voter roll information, the Nevada secretary of state provided True the Vote with a downloadable voter file via email. Upon review, True the Vote discovered that Nevada officials had cc'd the email to waqas@kavtech.net, which belongs to Waqas Butt, the CEO of Kavtech Solutions Ltd.[22] "Kavtech is a Pakistani owned company, located in Lahore, Punjab, Pakistan, with ties to Pakistani intelligence, military, and the interior."[23]

Catherine Englebrecht, the president of True the Vote, sent a letter to the Department of Justice alerting them to the national security issue on December 3, 2020. Her letter stated in part:

> The fact that this company was cc'd on an email containing access to the Nevada voter registration database appears to be evidence of a breach within the Nevada Secretary of State's email system.
>
> Obviously, the problems that such a breach may evidence includes access to at least the voter registration information of Nevada residents. At worst, it could reveal a breach that gives a foreign power access to not only the State of Nevada's systems, but also to the email systems of anyone whom the State communicates with via email.[24]

When confronted with the fact that Nevada officials had provided information to a Pakistani company associated with Pakistani intelligence, the Nevada secretary of state's office responded with undocumented accusations. Rather than explain why the Pakistani company was allowed access to Nevada voter information, they accused True the Vote of forging the document, and altering the CC line to include the Pakistani company.[25] They never provided any evidence to support their outrageous claims, but the Department of Justice seemed to simply accepted Nevada's explanation. To date, I'm not aware of any action taken by the Department of Justice to investigate.

Setting aside the fact that the individual cc'd in the email owned a Pakistani company with ties to the intelligence community, this email continues the story of private involvement in government affairs. Even if the company and CEO involved were American, why are Democrat state officials working with private companies on elections? At best, it's sloppy and negligent. At worst, it's criminal and a national security threat.

Election Info on Servers in China

Never ones to shy away from controversy, True the Vote continued to investigate concerning findings in the 2020 election, as well as questionable connections with outside groups. They began asking questions about a Michigan-based company, Konnech, raising concerns about the company's ties to China.

On **October 3, 2022**, the *New York Times* wrote a piece slamming "election deniers" for questioning the connection. The article, written by Stuart A. Thompson, is titled "How a Tiny Elections Company Became a Conspiracy Theory Target."[26] The caption for the article read: "Election deniers catapulted a Michigan firm with just 21 U.S. employees to the center of unfounded voter fraud claims, exposing it to vicious threats."

On **October 4, 2022**, the very next day after the *New York Times* article ridiculed those concerned about Konnech, the Los Angeles district attorney announced that it had arrested the CEO of Konnech for storing election workers' private information on servers in China.[27] According to the Los Angeles district attorney's press release:

Konnech distributes and sells its proprietary PollChief software, which is an election worker management system that was utilized by the county in the last California election. The software assists with poll worker assignments, communications and payroll. PollChief requires that workers submit personal identifying information, which is retained by Konnech.

Under its $2.9 million, five-year contract with the county, Konnech was supposed to securely maintain the data and that only United States citizens and permanent residents have access to it.

District Attorney investigators found that in contradiction to the contract, *information was stored on servers in the People's Republic of China.* [emphasis added]

So, we know that at least some information related to the 2020 election was stored on servers in China. The Los Angeles district attorney arrested the CEO for doing so. What about the rest of the election? Was any other information stored on servers in China? Earlier in the press release the LA district attorney, Democrat George Gascón, stated, "This investigation is concerned solely with the personal identifying information of election workers. In this case, the alleged conduct had no impact on the tabulation of votes and did not alter election results."[28] In other words, they weren't willing to investigate it. They didn't look into it and kept their investigation strictly focused on personal information. How convenient.

Remember that *New York Times* writer who, on October 3, 2022, ridiculed "election deniers" as conspiracy theorists who falsely questioned Konnech? Then the next day the CEO got arrested? Well, on October 4, 2022, the day after his condescending (and inaccurate) article, after the district attorney announced the arrest, the same writer for the *New York Times* published another article. This one is titled "Election Software Executive Arrested on Suspicion of Theft." The caption for the article read: "The executive, Eugene Yu, and his firm, Konnech, have been a focus of attention among election deniers."[29]

No outrage. No concern over the security and integrity of American elections. No admission, at least not in the headlines, that the company was storing sensitive information in China. Whose side is the liberal media on?! Apparently not the side of the American people.

A federal judge in Houston presided over a lawsuit between Konnech and True the Vote. On October 31, 2022, the judge threw Catherine Englebrecht and Gregg Phillips in jail for refusing to state the name of an FBI confidential informant in open court. The name of the confidential informant was already in the possession of the federal government, namely the FBI. But the judge used it as an excuse to throw True the Vote in jail just nine days before the 2022 midterms.

Oddities in New Mexico

Like many other states, New Mexico had several odd occurrences throughout the 2020 election. Republican poll challengers reported being kept 100 feet away from the counting, behind velvet ropes, and told any movement beyond the ropes was illegal.[30] The Republicans were effectively kept from having any meaningful participation in the counting process, and were told they were not allowed to see the ballots.

Poll challengers stated that election officials refused access to the process and said Republicans were not allowed to participate. Republicans swore in affidavits that when they tried to check in for shifts as Republican poll challengers, they were denied access, denied the ability to speak with election officials, and denied any opportunity to participate in the process.

One Republican poll challenger stated that election officials' "actions prevented any oversight by Qualified Challengers from any

part of the Absentee Qualification Process and left the sole responsibility in the hands of the [Dona Ana] County Clerk. This is a clear
violation of election laws. Transparency was gone and voter confidence
undermined during this entire operation."[31]

David Gallus, the Republican candidate for state senate in New
Mexico, also signed an affidavit stating:

> In this election and during the removal of the privacy label of
> the Absentee Ballots (AB), there was no oversight by Qualified
> Challengers. Nor was there an Election Board Convened,
> comprised of a Presiding Judge and two additional Judges
> of Election, the judges being from opposing political par-
> ties. When a duly authorized challenger was attempting to
> observe the County Clerk's Absentee Ballot Certification,
> he was barred from entry. The same challenger was again
> ejected, along with three others from oversight at the county
> warehouse where processing of AB was conducted.

Despite New Mexico having a Democrat legislature, executive branch,
and liberal judiciary, they violated the laws that they themselves had
created by refusing both parties a presence in the counting facility.

Secretary of State Maggie Toulouse Oliver, a Democrat, sent a letter to the Republican Party of New Mexico explaining that the removal
of the Republican challengers was justified because they were causing a
disturbance. Republicans dispute any type of disturbance or behavior
warranting removal from the process, and even had video surveillance
pulled showing there was no disturbance.[32] But, *even if* a disturbance
had occurred, the solution is not to prohibit *any* Republicans from
participating in the process. The solution should have been to remove
those that caused a problem and seek to quickly replace them with new
Republican poll challengers.

That offer was never extended. Democrats simply removed the Republicans from the process and counted the election without any oversight. Oliver states in her letter that she's concerned the Republican Party of New Mexico (RPNM) is training their poll challengers to be violent and belligerent. She takes the approach that Republicans are dangerous and should not be allowed in the facilities. What a preposterous statement! Especially coupled with video surveillance that shows no violence or belligerence whatsoever.[33]

Oliver goes a step further and asks RPNM Chairman Pearce to "confirm that RPNM is not instructing its challengers to disobey election board members or are encouraging willful violations of the election code. . . ." Unbelievable. What brazen hypocrisy. As Democrats are violating election laws, they send a letter to Republicans asking for assurances that *Republicans* aren't violating election laws. No. They sure didn't. Only Democrats violated the law in New Mexico, which Biden supposedly won by 99,720.[34]

Request for an Injunction

On October 26, 2020, the Republican Party of New Mexico filed a complaint in state court asking for an injunction, stopping the secretary of state from using the illegal drop boxes.[35] County clerks had missed the deadline for what the New Mexico Election Code calls "secured containers," which are required to be videotaped and their locations posted ninety days before the election to allow time to challenge them.[36]

After a successful challenge the parties settled the case out of court,[37] which prevented the use of "secured containers" that had missed the statutory deadline. The New Mexico secretary of state then invented "drop boxes," which she claimed are somehow different than "secured containers," and have no requirements under New Mexico law. They have no requirements under the New Mexico law, because they are not expressly legal under New Mexico law. The secretary of state invented "drop boxes" and made up her own rules, without the legislature. The RPNM ended up settling the case with individual counties to agree to certain parameters, and the court dismissed the case a few days later.[38]

Drop Boxes

Despite drop boxes being illegal, the State of New Mexico issued Standards and Guidance for how to utilize drop boxes for the election. Among the requirements:

- Drop boxes must remain under the direct supervision of at least two county staff or election workers at all times (aka "ballot collection team"). A ballot collection team must be bipartisan and meet the requirements of election workers pursuant to [New Mexico law].
- When not in use, all drop boxes, including those used in outdoor locations, shall be placed in an area that is inaccessible to the public and otherwise secured and safeguarded.
- Drop boxes must be secured and locked at all times. Only an election official, messenger, or someone designated to retrieve ballots shall have access to the keys and or combinations of the lock.[39]

Even these procedures were not followed. Witnesses reported the drop boxes being unattended, open, and accessible to anyone wanting to drop off a ballot . . . or two or three, or more.[40] One witness swore, "I observed several individuals dropping off multiple ballots into the drop box, and there was one individual who had a large—I would estimate roughly five-inch high—stack of ballots."[41]

Like going to the poll, one person gets one vote. No one should be placing multiple ballots into the drop boxes. Yet, many did.

To put this into perspective, New Mexico has a Democrat legislature, executive branch, and liberal judiciary. If they wanted to change the laws and loosen election standards, they could have done so. They didn't. Then, after not changing the law to allow drop boxes, they issued guidance for how to use the illegal boxes. And after all that, they didn't even follow their own guidance. With Democrats controlling all three branches of New Mexico's government, they *still* couldn't be bothered to implement appropriate laws and follow them. They just did whatever they wanted, which admittedly is much easier than following the rules.

The 2020 election in New Mexico was an exercise in futility. What's the point of having laws, or guidance, if the executive branch isn't going to follow them and there are no repercussions? Apparently, New Mexico had no consequences for breaking the law. In a state totally controlled by Democrats, they are making up the rules as they go and disregarding them as convenient, and no one can question the outcome.

New Mexico 2021

Despite the blatant hypocrisy and double standards in New Mexico during 2020, New Mexico residents stood up and proved that even in a Democrat-controlled state, voters can make change. The 2021 elections went well for the New Mexico GOP. Conservatives turned out strong, secured their elections, and voted in multiple conservative candidates in their local elections, in some cases flipping Democrat incumbent seats to Republicans.[42]

Undercounting Trump Votes in Texas

President Trump was credited with winning Texas, but he likely won by much more than reported. The official vote tally says Trump won Texas by 631,221.[43] During the year following the 2020 election, many groups made efforts to investigate elections in Texas, and pressured the Republican secretary of state. The voters wanted an audit.

Too much infighting in the state prevented a meaningful transparent investigation. Instead, on December 31, 2021, acting Secretary of State John Scott published a progress report on the state's review of the November 2020 election.[44] The fact that they published it on New Year's Eve strongly suggests they were trying to bury any scrutiny of Texas elections. Most of the eleven pages of the report whitewash potential problems, and even report that one county's manual recount shows a 100 percent perfect match.[45] No discrepancies whatsoever. For some reason, Dallas County had 1,193 non-citizens registered to vote.[46]

The biggest discrepancy that deserved more attention than it got was the fact that Texas had to cancel 449,362 voter registrations across four counties because they were duplicates.[47] Some voters moved within the county, some moved outside the county, and that created duplicate registrations.

The report did not state whether the duplicate registrants *both* voted or not, simply that they existed. Whether the voters voted twice, or whether their old registration was used illegally to cast a fraudulent ballot was not a subject of the investigation, it appears. Texas is also apparently still reviewing whether the 2,327 non-citizens who were registered to vote in the four counties actually cast ballots in the 2020 election.[48]

The governor and secretary of state may not be aggressively pursuing transparency in Texas's elections, but the Texas Attorney General did. Ken Paxton was the first attorney general in the country to challenge the obviously corrupt 2020 election. Once he filed *Texas v. Pennsylvania* at the US Supreme Court challenging the administration of the 2020 election, seventeen other attorneys general filed motions supporting his position.[49]

He led the charge for state leaders to step up and protect their states' elections. Liberals hate him and know they need to control him if they stand a chance at stealing the Lone Star State. When they couldn't deter him, they tried a different tactic.

State of Texas v. Stephens

On December 15, 2021, the Court of Criminal Appeal of Texas, the highest criminal appellate court in the state, ruled that the Texas attorney general is *not* allowed to prosecute election crimes.[50] That's right. The court has now determined that the Texas attorney general does *not* have authority to prosecute election crimes in the State of Texas. On appeal, the court considered the following question and made the following ruling:

> May the Texas Legislature delegate to the Attorney General, a member of the executive department, the prosecution of election-law violations in district and inferior courts? No. Because Texas Election Code section 273.021 delegates to the Attorney General a power more properly assigned to the judicial department, we conclude that the statute is unconstitutional. Therefore, we reverse the decision of the court of appeals and remand the case to the trial court to dismiss the indictment.[51]

What?! It's unconstitutional for the attorney general to prosecute election-law violations?! Texas Election Code section 273.021 states *in its entirety*:

> Sec. 273.021. PROSECUTION BY ATTORNEY GENERAL AUTHORIZED. (a) The attorney general may prosecute a criminal offense prescribed by the election laws of this state.

(b) The attorney general may appear before a grand jury in connection with an offense the attorney general is authorized to prosecute under Subsection (a).

(c) The authority to prosecute prescribed by this subchapter does not affect the authority derived from other law to prosecute the same offenses.

The un-American Criminal Court of Appeals of Texas ruled the above law unconstitutional, finding that *the judicial department* is better positioned to prosecute election crimes. That doesn't even make any sense. Judges are supposed to prosecute election law violations? How is that a credible ruling?! If the attorney general can't prosecute election crimes, then only district attorneys have the authority to prosecute those crimes. We see from Arizona and Wisconsin that even Republican district attorneys have refused to prosecute those cases, meaning election crimes will go unchecked. Texas Attorney General Ken Paxton responded with the following statement:

> The Court's decision to suddenly remove our authority to prosecute election fraud can only empower dishonest campaigns to silence voters across the state. This decision is not only wrong on legal grounds, but it has the effect of giving district and county attorneys virtually unlimited discretion to not bring election law prosecutions. Last year's election cycle shows us that officials in our most problematic counties will simply let election fraud run rampant. I will continue to oppose this decision that diminishes our democracy and misconstrues the Texas Constitution.[52]

Make no mistake about it, the far Left is making a play for Texas. They are working all of their dirty schemes, and doing everything they can to take over the State of Texas. They've just eliminated their biggest threat, the Texas attorney general, by removing his ability to prosecute election crimes.

What's the difference between Defund the Police and refusing to prosecute crimes? There's very little distinction. Refusing to prosecute crimes simply takes a case a little longer to get purged from the justice system, but the result is the same: no accountability and criminals on the street. We've seen district attorneys across the country, Republican and Democrat, refuse to prosecute election crimes. District attorneys who refuse to prosecute election crimes are no different than those that support the Defund the Police movement. They just play a different role with the same result. Lawlessness.

Liberals are turning America into a lawless wasteland, and they're after Texas.

CHAPTER 16

2021 Elections in Virginia and New Jersey—One Year Later

Virginia learned from 2020. New Jersey didn't. The results showed.

Americans were still upset about the 2020 election when the November 2021 election rolled around. Many questioned whether the 2021 election could even be conducted fairly. The Arizona Audit had reported significant fraud, yet state officials still had not acted on it. Pennsylvania had not even started an audit. Georgia had quashed any efforts at transparency. Michigan, Nevada, and New Mexico never even acknowledged a problem. Wisconsin had made great discoveries, but state leadership refused to act on them.

In other words, despite plenty of troubling evidence, state leaders refused to act, likely from fear. Fear of the media, fear of being labeled a conspiracy theorist, fear of what people would think. The American people noticed and took action.

Don't Mess with Our Kids

The first thing that got people's attention was that crazy liberal activists made the curious decision to target children.

The radical Left started making more and more outrageous policies affecting American children, like allowing schools to transition students' genders without parental consent or notification.[1] School boards and courts mandated gender-fluid bathrooms, allowing boys to use the girls' bathroom if they identified as female, and vice versa.[2] The transgender policies, and outright activism, from school officials caught the attention of parents nationwide.

Loudoun County, Virginia, was a hot bed of controversy as parents throughout the county resisted the radical policies. Parents in Loudoun County alleged that school leadership at Stone Bridge High School tried to cover up a sexual assault of one of its female students in the girls' bathroom by a fifteen-year-old male student, who identified as female, in May 2021.[3] The boy was transferred to a different school where he sexually assaulted another fifteen-year-old female student.[4]

Parents were angry that school officials, from their perspective, were endangering their children with woke policies and curriculum choices.[5] Rogue school boards were the number one issue during the 2021 election in Virginia. Hardworking Americans haven't bothered to babysit school boards and state leaders while also working hard to provide for families. But the radical liberal policies alarmed the parents, and they showed up in droves in the 2021 election.

Virginia in 2020

In 2020, Virginia went for Joe Biden, though not without suspicious activity of its own. Fairfax County, which shares a border with Loudoun County, suffered a scandal of absentee ballots.[6] A Washington, DC-based non-profit, supposedly "helping" election officials, mailed almost half a million absentee ballots with the wrong return address, meaning they may not be counted if used.[7] This is just another example of election officials giving too much authority to non-profit organizations that have no accountability to the people. Non-profits should not be running our elections.

More than 450,000 of the 760,000 registered voters in the county received absentee ballots with an incorrect return address, voter information partially filled out, or incorrectly filled out.[8] County officials worked hard to calm voters' concerns, saying it was a mistake that was being corrected, but the damage was done. Fairfax County was flooded with incorrect absentee ballots, and the security of the election was compromised.

The 2020 election results of Fairfax County were: Joe Biden received 419,943 votes;[9] Trump received 168,401; Joe Jorgenson and a write-in candidate received a combined 12,479, making the total number of votes 600,238.[10] 600,238 voters out of 761,573 registered voters was a record 78.8 percent voter turnout for the county.[11] It's amazing how all these liberal victories keep setting records with rapidly skyrocketing voter turnout. There were 450,000 fraudulent ballots injected into the system by the Washington, DC, non-profit, meaning more fraudulent ballots existed than any one candidate received throughout the entire election in Fairfax County. Less than a year of the Biden-Harris administration and the woke agenda of the Left got parents' attention. 2021 would be different.

Virginia 2021

Less than a month before the election, Reuters claimed, "The Nov. 2 contest between Youngkin and his Democratic opponent, former Governor Terry McAuliffe, is widely seen as a bellwether of the 2022 congressional races that will determine which party controls Congress for the second half of Biden's term."[12] They're right. The Republicans won in Virginia.

Voters turned out strong to ensure a Youngkin victory, but it wasn't your typical election. According to the *Washington Post*, "an army of poll watchers" showed up to help protect the integrity of the Virginia election.[13] Citizens had finally gotten the message. They worked as poll watchers, challengers, and volunteered where needed. Most importantly, Republicans worked as sworn election officers, a role that Republicans typically don't bother to fill.[14] Physically securing poll locations, meaning having volunteers watch and make sure the process is fair, was key to Youngkin's win in Virginia. Attorneys were available to answer questions or arrive at a polling location on election night.[15]

Virginia State Senator Amanda Chase described it this way, "I think it's been very, very challenging in certain parts of the state to find [Republican] election workers. But with what happened in 2020, people just realized, there was really a wake-up call that occurred."[16] Senator Chase says that leading up to the 2021 election "we saw an influx of volunteers wanting to get involved in the process."[17]

Thanks to the VA GOP, the Youngkin campaign, and several conservative organizations providing volunteers, Virginia secured its election, which resulted in a final count *on election night*. There was no way for cheaters to claim they needed more time to count ballots, because there were enough Republican challengers at the polling stations to confirm there were no ballots left to count. Cheaters can only stuff ballots when no one is there to question it. That's why they removed Republicans from the counting facilities in 2020. If no one is there to challenge the statement that they are still counting ballots, cheaters can continue to drop off ballots for days! There's no one there to stop them. Without opposition, Democrats can wait until after the election is over and then have several *days* to continue bringing in ballots until they change the outcome of the election. Not in Virginia.

Virginia Senator Chase supported Youngkin's campaign and said they had attorneys available at every single precinct, or within a short drive, to respond to concerns from poll challengers.[18] Groups working with Youngkin's campaign also spent a lot of time and resources training poll workers and conducting classes to make sure Republican election workers knew what to look out for.[19]

In Virginia, people showed up to participate and secure a result on election night. Unfortunately, that's not what happened in New Jersey.

New Jersey 2020

If you believe the 2020 election, Joe Biden won the State of New Jersey by 725,061.[20] New Jersey has supposedly elected a Democrat President every election since 1992, so it was not unusual that Joe Biden would win the state.[21] Like the other states we've discussed, the New Jersey legislature did not pass a law instructing the state to send mail-in ballots to every voter. Not to be deterred, the governor, Phil Murphy, issued an executive order stating that as a result of COVID every registered voter would receive a ballot in the mail.[22] Meaning the 2020 election was largely conducted illegally.[23]

For the primaries in 2020, Bergen County, NJ, received over 100,000 mail-in ballots and drop box ballots.[24] In 2016, the same county received 4,000 mail-in ballots. County officials blame COVID for the difference.[25]

Like the other states we've talked about, New Jersey has a problem with its voter roll. One account from The American Prospect said this in July 2020 . . . months *before* the election:

> There have also been numerous reports about bugs and technical glitches in the state's voter registration system. There were reports of the servers crashing and being inaccessible during business hours and problems integrating information from the Motor Vehicle Commission, where people can register to vote, with the voter database. One election official told the *New Jersey Globe* that it was becoming an obstacle to

preparing for today's election. However, this problem with technology has existed even before the pandemic.[26]

Maintaining a fallible and porous voter roll seems to be an important step to allow cheaters to hack the voting system and stuff ballots. They can't stuff ballots, after all, without a sufficient number of fake or duplicate voters on the voter roll that they can use to assign the additional ballots. Based on what we know now, it looks like New Jersey in 2020 suffered from the same corruption as the other states.

Interestingly, in June 2022, the Public Interest Legal Foundation (PILF) published its research of the New Jersey voter roll. The group found 8,239 voters were registered twice, three times, four, five, or even six times.[27] These duplicate registrations are the same person, with the same birthday, at the same address. The differences in the registration are minor differences in the name, like adding a middle initial, or truncating William to Will, but they still have the same birthday and address.

PILF's research found 33,572 voter records had "placeholder or fictitious dates of birth."[28] These records show "registrants without dates of birth indicating eligibility,"[29] meaning tens of thousands of voters may not even be eligible to vote. 6,863 records exist without any actual registration date.[30] A handful of registered voters have future birthdates, indicating that they will be born in 2028 or 2029.[31] 2,398 registered voters have birthdates in 1917 or earlier, meaning they are over 105 years old.[32] New Jersey's records indicate inept management at best, criminal conduct at worst.

So, what happened in 2021?

New Jersey 2021

On election night, November 2, 2021, Republican candidate Jack Ciatterelli won the race. Ten days later he conceded, after Democrats found more ballots.[33] As of midnight, the morning of November 3,

2021, the day *after* the election, Democrat incumbent Murphy had 49.0 percent of the vote, and Republican candidate Jack Ciatterelli had 50.2 percent of the vote.[34]

Bergen County, NJ, the largest county in the state, reported 100 percent of their ballots counted and Republican Ciatterelli winning the county with 52 percent, leading by 42,000 votes statewide.[35] Minutes later, the results flipped, saying Murphy won with 51 percent of the votes.[36] *They had already reported 100 percent of their ballots!* How did the county flip Democrat?

The final result came *ten days* after Election Day in a miraculous comeback by the Democrat incumbent, Phil Murphy. Republican candidate Jack Ciatterelli conceded on November 12, 2021, after precincts he had won miraculously started flipping for Murphy.[37] It's Democrat magic. Find more ballots and claim a victory ten days after the election.

The official excuse for the delay was that the newly installed voting machines were malfunctioning and having trouble connecting to the internet.[38] Supposedly several technical problems caused delay. Election officials had finally dropped the phony narrative that the machines don't connect to the internet. Now, apparently, they do connect to the internet and were malfunctioning.[39]

Election Day Operations

New Jersey did not change their Election Day operations after lessons learned from 2020. They followed an identical election process, and got identical results. Democrats cheated and took several days to manufacture a Democrat win. The Republican candidate won on Election Day, but Democrats were given an extra ten days to find more ballots. Ultimately, the Democrat was declared the winner.

A Republican Election Day operations worker for a New Jersey Senate campaign, Lauren Casper, worked the election and shared the complaints she received on Election Day:

- Republicans were turned away from the polls
- Machines were out of paper and voters were turned away
- Republicans were told they already voted
- Machines malfunctioned and voters were turned away without a provisional ballot
- There were not enough poll workers to process voters
- One precinct was reported as "general chaos" and it looked like Republicans weren't allowed to vote

"I experienced really, really long lines. I experienced people that have been voting at these polls for ten, twenty, thirty years saying, 'Hey, what's up with this? What's the deal? Why is this taking so long?'"[40] Casper explained. She described the polls as "chaos." Multiple polling locations only had two functioning machines, or sometimes only one functioning machine. Many people starting leaving without having had the chance to vote. Since Republicans typically show up to the polls, Election Day malfunctions at the polling locations disadvantaged Republicans.

New Jersey Republicans did not have enough volunteers as poll workers, challengers, or Election Day officials to ensure they had a fair chance to vote, or a clean election. Casper says her greatest frustration was that there were few if any Republican lawyers on-site at any of the polls to respond to concerns happening at the polling locations, and there were many concerns. If there were lawyers on-site anywhere, she was not aware of them and had trouble getting help. When her phone started blowing up at 5 a.m. on Election Day because there were problems at the polls, Casper was told to leave a voicemail on the hotline and wait for someone to respond. There simply weren't enough Republican officials available to solve the problem.

Not all was lost in New Jersey in 2021. Republicans ousted the Democrat Senate president and replaced him with a truck driver who spent only $153 on his campaign.[41] God bless our truckers! Democrats lost six seats to Republicans in the state General Assembly,[42] and Republicans gained two seats in the state Senate,[43] yet somehow Democrats won the governor's race. That's odd. The state felt strongly enough to replace Democrats across the state, but not the governor?

Casper stated that it almost seemed like Republicans in New Jersey didn't think they could win the race and were not prepared for how close the race actually was.[44] They just weren't prepared, and they did not recruit enough volunteers. It all comes down to people showing up and getting involved. An important lesson for 2024 and beyond.

New Legislation

State legislatures were caught off guard when they were thrust to the front lines of the election integrity battles, but many decided they would get to work securing their states' future elections. By the end of 2021, forty-nine states had introduced more than 440 state legislative bills during the 2021 session,[45] and thirty-four of those bills have already become law.[46] This is the biggest push for election reform the nation has seen in at least the last ten years, likely much longer than that.[47] The push for greater election security signaled that states would not sit idly by while activists and partisans bullied their way into manipulating election results.

Georgia, Florida, Iowa, and Texas each passed omnibus election reform bills that added significant safeguards to their election procedures.[48] Texas Democrats attempted to stop the bill by fleeing the state.[49] Their effort was all for show and had no real impact. The bill was signed into law by the Texas governor in September 2021.[50] The law strengthens voter ID requirements, and prevents the secretary of state from sending mail-in ballots to voters who haven't requested one.[51] The bill also bans drive-through voting and extended hours, a practice that Democrats said was necessary due to COVID.[52]

Georgia was one of the first states to create new legislation strengthening the state's election procedures. Never missing an opportunity to cause chaos where there is none, Democrats and several woke companies criticized the legislation, and Major League Baseball pulled its All-Star game from the state in protest.[53] All the emotional outrage was manufactured to manipulate voters. Here are some of the key points:

- Expanded early voting, giving voters seventeen days to cast their ballots.
- Every voter is required to show ID, whether in person or voting by mail.
- Drop boxes are authorized inside county clerks' offices and voting locations, and must be locked once the early voting period ends.
- Creates a hotline for voters to call if they see suspicious activity.
- State officials cannot send unsolicited ballot request forms to individuals.
- The state election board is no longer chaired by the secretary of state.[54]

Georgia Secretary of State Brad Raffensperger did such a bad job in 2020 that he was stripped of his election board position. While there are a number of other provisions in the ninety-eight-page bill, the key points highlight the fact that the bill aims to make voting easier and cheating harder. The only reason to oppose these reforms is if you know you must rely on cheating to win.

Making Progress

And there are other signs of progress as well. The Wisconsin Supreme Court ruled that drop boxes are illegal in the state,[55] which is a good start. Drop boxes were essential to bad actors in the 2020 election, so eliminating them helps to secure the election.

During the spring election in 2022, the City of Green Bay had an error its public notice, claiming the mistake was a typo. The city's notice said they would begin counting ballots at 4 p.m., which would be when observers from both parties would arrive.[56] However, the city actually began counting its ballots at 7 a.m.[57] The same city employee who acknowledged the mistake and referred to it as a typo is the same employee who ushered in Michael Spitzer-Rubenstein in 2020.[58] Republican observers showed up at 7 a.m. anyway, despite the mistake, concerned they could potentially miss the counting. That's an improvement from 2020 where Republicans lacked significant participation.

Another area that has shown significant improvement since 2020 is the fight to get states to purge their voter rolls. As we saw in Wisconsin, mismanaged voter rolls create room for cheaters to fudge the tally. Judicial Watch filed a lawsuit in April 2020 against North Carolina and the State Board of Elections to force them to clean up their voter rolls. In a press release, the organization stated:

> In June 2019, the US Election Assistance Commission (EAC) released **data** showing that voter registration rates in a significant proportion of North Carolina's 100 counties were close to, at or above 100 percent of their age-eligible citizenry—statistics considered by the courts to be a strong indication that a jurisdiction is not taking the steps required by law to remove ineligible registrants. Judicial Watch's analysis also showed that at the time of the EAC report the entire State of North Carolina had a registration rate close to 100 percent of its age-eligible citizenry.[59]

Voter roll bloat and manipulation is a serious threat to free and transparent elections. Judicial Watch announced that it settled the case with North Carolina after the state agreed to purge 430,000 ineligible voters, those who died or moved away.[60] 430,000 ineligible voters! That's remarkable that the rolls were that bad.

Director of Investigations for Judicial Watch Chris Farrell stated that "Judicial Watch has had victory after victory in Kentucky, Ohio, Indiana, and Los Angeles County where we forced these counties and these states to go in and do a legitimate scrub of their voter rolls."[61] Patriot groups around the country are pushing legislatures to pass strong election security legislation, *and* are going the step further to force states to abide by existing law. Legislative efforts, advocacy groups, and Americans simply getting involved is exactly what this nation needs to secure our elections.

CHAPTER 17

A Fatal Mix of Cowardice and Corruption

In many ways, 2020 was the perfect storm for a stolen election. COVID gave Democrats the perfect cover for all the laws they needed to break, and the world was in so much turmoil that nobody was paying attention to all the potential for cheating. No one knew how mail-in ballots would be used, and they assumed there was at least a basic level of security to ensure that only lawful registered voters voted, right? Well, turns out 2020 was a novel year for election security too. Corrupt Democrats, however, needed help to get away with such a breath-taking scope of law-breaking and fraud. Unfortunately, weak and cowardly Republicans were all too happy to cooperate.

But the foundation for 2020's extraordinary exhibition of cowardice and corruption goes back nearly forty years. In 1982 the Democrat National Committee sued the Republican National Committee in New Jersey, claiming the RNC targeted minorities with threats of violating election security laws.[1] Through negotiations, the DNC and the RNC entered into a settlement agreement known as the New Jersey Consent Decree. The consent decree limited the activities the

RNC was authorized to conduct as it related to election security measures.

As a result, other organizations, mostly state GOP parties, had to pick up the slack while the RNC kept its distance from election security involvement. All that came to an abrupt end in 2018 when a judge issued an order declaring the consent decree terminated.[2] Suddenly, for the first time in thirty-five years, the local GOPs were no longer on the hook for coordinating election security efforts, and most looked to the RNC to take up the issue for the 2020 election. The problem was that the RNC hadn't done so in thirty-five years, but now the state parties felt they didn't need to. The result was that no one on the Republican side took responsibility for election security, which therefore went out the window for 2020—and produced the most corrupt election in American history.

Putting the Puzzle Pieces Together

Democrats have a history of rigging elections. Just ask Bernie Sanders if he thinks his party played fair in the primaries. Even Elizabeth Warren and Donna Brazile, two staples in the radical Left community, have stated they believe Democrats rigged the 2016 primary to ensure Hillary Clinton won.[3] If they rig their own primaries, they certainly have no trouble rigging general elections.

So why is there still so much debate over what happened in 2020? The swamp has done an excellent job of burying, or declaring off-limits, mountains of information and evidence about what really happened in the 2020 election. Meanwhile, their media cohorts have flooded the country with fake news. With so much misinformation and misdirection, it's hard to see the truth.

Not one state has done a comprehensive review of the election, not even Arizona. Arizona has not disclosed the information about the voter roll, splunk logs, and administrative machine access. Why not? If this really was the most secure election in US history, why can't state officials allow their residents to actually see proof that the election was secure? The information that has come out in Wisconsin has given us a very good idea of why Arizona officials are hiding access to the same information in Arizona. It's really damning.

Without any one state being transparent about their elections, we have to piece together what we can see in each of the states to get a complete picture. Thankfully, enough states have made efforts at investigating that we are getting a very clear understanding of *how* they cheated. More importantly, we know exactly how to stop them from doing it again.

Here's a run-down of what they did. We'll unpack each one in a minute, but just look at all the cheating they've done! In order to rig elections, the swamp **inflates the voter rolls** to make room for **ballot stuffing**.[4] True the Vote outed their elaborate **ballot trafficking** scheme in *2000 Mules*. They also **harvest ballots**,[5] legitimate or not, by coercing various groups and demographics to provide their ballots.[6] Racine showed an unconscionable ballot-harvesting scheme targeting nursing homes and the elderly, which could have happened in cities across the country.[7] **Centralizing the count**[8] to key counties is crucial, because fewer people are needed to cheat. If the ballots and totals are counted at each precinct, then thousands of people will need to cheat. However, if the tallying process is centralized, a small number of people can cheat for an entire county, and impact the entire state's elections.

This also allows them to **stop counting**[9] if they need to generate more votes to change the outcome of the election. **Mail-in ballots** are the only way cheaters can manufacture enough votes to overcome a substantial margin. Next, they need to **physically remove opposition**[10] (Republicans) from the counting process.[11] Boarding up windows[12] and excluding Republicans from the process[13] allows officials to cheat as much as they want without any oversight, and then no one can prove what they did, because there are no witnesses. When people complain that the process is illegal, media allies **spread misinformation** about what's taking place, so no one can clearly see the truth. Fake news obscures the cheating and leaves people questioning what actually happened. When challenged in court, simply **run out the clock**. Then, **change The Narrative**.

Voter Roll Manipulation

Padding the voter roll is essential to cheating. You can't cheat without fake votes. Fake votes come from fake voters.

In order to stuff ballots, cheaters need to assign those ballots to voters. If they assign illegal votes to real voters, they run the risk of the real voter showing up to the poll and trying to cast a ballot, only to be told they've already voted. Cheaters don't want *real* voters asking real questions, so it's best to cheat using fake voters, or real voters that you know will not show up to vote, like someone who moved out of state. In 2020, and 2021 for that matter, we know there were several reports of voters getting turned away from polls for having already voted.[14] Officials provide a variety of explanations and chalk it up to error. The fact remains that it's possible, maybe likely, that cheaters voted for them using their registration number.

The more probable, and successful, way cheaters cheat by fudging the voter roll is to bloat the roll with fake voters. The fake voters could be real people who no longer live in the state, dead voters, or totally fraudulent voter registrations. We saw hundreds of thousands of these examples in Wisconsin.[15] Michigan poll challengers also reported poll workers registering voters with a birthdate of 1/1/1900.[16] That's obviously not a real birthday of anyone alive today. So, is the voter a real voter who's lawfully allowed to vote? No one knows, because we don't know who they really are if election officials are using placeholder birthdates and addresses. They may be. They may not be. The information is admittedly fake![17]

Places like Nevada are creating voter roll bloat by automatically re-registering the same people multiple times whenever they transact business with the DMV.[18] Voter roll bloat also causes confusion, because real people are on the voter roll with wrong information. No one wants to delete real people from the voter roll, so we err on the side of inclusion, which includes fake voters, giving the cheaters a buffer.

Many states keep voters on their roles, even if they've died, moved out of state, moved to a different county, or made a number of other changes.[19] They simply mark these voters as "inactive." Each state has its own procedure for how an inactive voter becomes active again, whether by moving back into the state and re-registering with the state, or another way to re-activate a voter registration.

However, the reality is, election officials can simply turn them back on to active. There's nothing magic about the process. Someone with access simply needs to makes the voter active.[20] The more suspicious approach to cheating with inactive voters is to simply cast a ballot on behalf of an inactive voter.[21] Both Wisconsin and Pennsylvania have discovered that inactive voters could have voted in 2020.[22] It's not supposed to happen, but it did.

Rather than question the legitimacy of the votes, Democrats claim anyone asking questions is trying to suppress voting rights. They claim questioning why inactive voters voted infringes upon the sacred right to vote of the inactive voters. These extremists are doing everything in their power to obscure the election process and make sure Americans can't find the fraudulent voters.

Ballot Harvesting

About half of US states permit some level of ballot harvesting, meaning someone other than the voter is allowed to turn in the voter's ballot.[23]

The other states either don't specify who is allowed to return a ballot, or specifically identify who may return a ballot for a voter.[24] Alabama is the only state that affirmatively says only the voter may cast their own ballot.[25]

Setting aside the concerns about mail-in ballots, most Americans probably don't care if a spouse or family member drops off their ballot at the mailbox. That is not the concern of ballot harvesting. The concern of ballot harvesting is radical groups using coercion and payment to manufacture votes that would not otherwise exist. This is exactly what Project Veritas uncovered in September 2020, before the election.[26] People in Minnesota were caught on camera with a "cash-for-ballots" scheme.[27] They were paying people for their ballots, would fill them out and turn them in. It's cheating, and it almost certainly helped the Democrats win.

In 2020, many groups conducted ballot harvesting, and a few court cases have actually held people accountable.[28] Ballot harvesters will tell you that suppressing ballot harvesting is racists and seeks to suppress minority votes. The exact opposite is true. Allowing ballot harvesting disadvantages minority voters, because they're more likely to become victims. Ballot harvesters don't go to wealthy neighborhoods to try to buy votes. They target the lower income neighborhoods. Preventing ballot harvesting actually protects minorities.

Mail-In Ballots

Early on in the COVID pandemic, President Trump predicted exactly how Democrats would cheat. They'd manufacture a crisis, force everyone to stay home, and flood the election with millions of mail-in ballots, many of them duplicates, and make it nearly impossible to check their work. The more we investigate, the more evidence we uncover, the more audits we hold, the more it looks like that is exactly what they did.

Mail-in ballots, and the lax policies surrounding them, made it possible for election workers to print ballots on-site.[29] Polling locations could print as many ballots as they needed. Once they removed Republicans from the process, there was no oversight and no Republicans to watch how many ballots were being printed.[30] If they couldn't print fast enough, they could truck ballots in and drop them off in the middle of the night.[31]

Flooding the election with mail-in ballots makes the entire election harder to secure. Rather than ballots stored securely in a controlled environment, we have them strewn about post offices and mailboxes. Rather than ballots controlled by the polling location and only given once the voter arrives and shows ID, ballots were freely printed and given to anyone who showed up to the polls, even those who could not prove citizenship.[32] It's no surprise that the election with the "most votes in history" occurred by mass mail-in ballots.[33] In order for Democrats to beat President Trump and remove him from the White House, they had to inject thousands, perhaps millions, of fake votes into the system. To do that, they needed mail-in ballots.[34]

Ballot Stuffing or Trafficking

Ballot stuffing is the good old-fashioned way to cheat. To ballot stuff, someone adds additional illegitimate votes to be counted. These can be fake ballots, manufactured for the purpose of cheating (counterfeit), or, more likely, these can be fraudulent ballots, meaning real ballots or a real vote cast by someone other than the sworn voter.

President Trump was beating Joe Biden by over 700,000 votes in Pennsylvania on election night. And yet somehow, after they kicked all the Republicans out of the counting facility, boarded up the windows, and continued counting for three more days, Biden made a comeback. How'd he do it? Ballot stuffing. The only way Biden could have had such a miraculous comeback in a state that he was losing so badly was to ballot stuff. The mathematical probability that this comeback occurred naturally is statistically impossible.

Joe Biden's numbers violate Benford's Law, a clear sign of fraudulent activity![35] Benford's Law is a mathematical concept that can be used to detect fraud in natural numbers, and says that the leading number in a set is likely to be small.[36] When people cheat, or commit fraud, they tend to cheat using larger numbers.[37] If those numbers don't fit the probabilities identified in Benford's Law, the indication is that they are likely fraudulent and not naturally occurring.[38] In order to make up for how far behind Biden was, the swamp had to violate Benford's Law[39] and flood the polls with anomalously large numbers for Biden. He cheated. They stuffed the ballot box.

The swamp dropped hundreds of thousands of ballots off in the middle of the night across the country on November 3 and early morning of November 4. They also abused the drop boxes strewn about Democrat cities, allowing Democrat operatives to stuff tens of thousands of ballots into the drop boxes in key cities and counties. As we saw in Georgia, drop box ballot stuffing was essential for a Democrat victory.

Dinesh D'Souza's movie, *2000 Mules,* highlights the work of True the Vote founder Catherine Engelbrecht, showing the liberal operation to traffic ballots through a ballot-trafficking scheme. The results of the investigation conclusively show that the ballot-trafficking efforts of paid liberal operatives was enough to change the outcome of the election, and likely did change the outcome. The media's unabashed attempt to divert attention from the movie shows a disgusting disregard for honest elections. Cheaters are caught on camera to an alarming degree and the media covers it up.

Centralizing the Count

Centralizing the count makes cheating easier, because you need fewer people to do it. States have thousands of precincts, but only need a few counties to flip the state. If the count is de-centralized, meaning counted and recorded at the precinct level, then thousands of precincts would need to cheat. However, if the larger county has the final power to tally the votes, a county could cheat by obscuring which precincts votes came from. In fact, Joe Biden only won 16.7 percent of the counties in the entire country, yet supposedly won more votes than any president in US history.[40]

The Brookings Institution, a liberal think tank, researched the county results and published a report on November 10, 2020, showing that Biden had only won 477 counties, while President Trump won 2,497 counties.[41] Once the rest of the counties completed their tallies, Trump's margin of victory grew, and Biden only won 16 percent of American counties.[42] Yet, he's supposedly the most popular president in US history.

How could it be that the supposedly most popular president in US history, who supposedly won 81 million votes, only won 16 percent of American counties? Centralized vote counting. Centralized vote counting in key counties like Philadelphia County, Wayne County (Detroit), Fulton County (Atlanta), and Milwaukee County were enough to change the outcome of the election in their states, and ultimately nationwide.

Remember that Wisconsin claims their birthdate and registration dates of 1/1/1900 occurred when the state moved towards centralized counting? It's just another example of how centralizing vote counting provides room for manipulation and obscuring the process.

When vote counting occurs in precincts and lower levels than county leadership, people recognize each other, because they live in the same neighborhood. Neighbors know the couple that runs the polling location out of their garage two cul-de-sacs away. They likely don't know the county clerk, or election workers at the county level. They also are likely to recognize people who don't belong in the neighborhood.

Pushing voters and the count to a centralized location obscures the process and creates less accountability and more opportunity to cheat with fewer people.

Stop Counting

When you don't like the way an election count is shaping up, another great way to cheat is to stop counting. As we've seen in five critical states, Democrats stopped counting when the current count would have resulted in a Trump victory. They needed time to manufacture more Biden ballots. Every single state that stopped counting was a state that Trump won on election night and the days to follow. Miraculously, days later, they all flipped to Biden. They did not finalize their count until they had enough votes to change the outcome. Every single state where Trump was leading that stopped counting changed the results of the election from President Trump to Biden. Every. Single. One.

Physically Remove Republicans

Republicans in Philadelphia, Atlanta, Detroit, Milwaukee, Green Bay, Santa Fe, Las Vegas, and Phoenix all complained that they were forcibly removed from polling and counting places, and were denied meaningful participation. We watched in Detroit and Philadelphia as they put pizza boxes and boards in the window to prevent observers from watching what they were doing in the counting facility. Some places like Detroit and Philadelphia even had the police help escort Republicans out of the room!

Systematically synchronized in these mostly Democrat-run cities, the election workers all got the same spontaneous ideas? They all decided, supposedly without coordination, to start restricting Republican access? They tried to keep them 6 feet away, then 100 feet away, then behind ropes, then on the other side of the room, then they held them in pens, behind fencing. Finally, they just removed

Republicans all together. Why? And how did the same illegal and undemocratic procedures take place in cities across the country? It was coordinated. They coordinated to remove Republicans from the process so that they could cheat. You can't stuff fake ballots or duplicate ballots through the machines with Republicans standing there watching, so they had to remove them.

And they did it across the country.

Spread Misinformation

The swamp, in coordination with the mainstream media, are waging an information war against the American people. They started the disinformation campaign before the election by suppressing the truth about Hunter Biden's laptop.[43] In fact, less than one month after the election, one out of six Biden voters say they would have changed their vote if they had known the truth about Hunter Biden's laptop, Kamala Harris's liberal voting record, and other issues.[44] The media deliberately squelched negative stories about the Democrat presidential and vice presidential candidates to ensure the American voters were ignorant of the truth.

Even before the election, the swamp started spreading the story that President Trump would prevent a "peaceful transition of power."[45] This was a curious idea, since it sure looked like Trump was on his way to a big victory, yet we started seeing numerous stories in the media echoing this "concern" that he would prevent "a peaceful transition of power."[46] Clearly, they were trying to convince the public that Biden would be the obvious winner and Donald Trump would refuse to leave the White House.

On election night and the days following, The Narrative was that "there's no evidence of fraud,"[47] which was never true. There was evidence of fraud on Election Day, after Election Day, and every day since. But over and over again, the media repeated the lie, dismissing any storyline that raised instances of irregularities, and attacking anyone who dared question the election. It wasn't enough to shut down the real stories of fraud or to insert the words "discredited" and "debunked" in front of every single report of cheating; they systematically attacked the honest citizens seeking to find out what had truly happened.

There was a lot of evidence of foul play. But anyone who did question election integrity was labeled a racist, conspiracy theorist, or insurrectionist.

Then they changed The Narrative to call it "the most secure election in US history."[48] Once they realized people were seeing the evidence, The Narrative changed to "there's no credible evidence of fraud,"[49] which also was complete bologna. Said another way: there's evidence of fraud, but we don't want you to believe any of it.

Confuse enough Americans or spew enough lies, and people will have a difficult time seeing the truth. The media doesn't have to persuade everyone, they just need to introduce enough doubt to make some people question the facts in front of them.

The Crimes of 2020

For some reason, some Republicans would like to believe that Democrats won the election "fair and square." Those with limited intestinal fortitude shy away from the truth, which is that serious crimes were committed in 2020, and if we hadn't gotten to work immediately to clean up the corruption, Americans would have had no hope of free and fair elections again. There's still work to be done, but a lot of progress has been made. For those questioning whether any crimes occurred for which people could be prosecuted, Appendix A has a memorandum from within Obama's Department of Justice explaining all the election crimes the Department of Justice has authority to prosecute.[50]

Almost all of the laws itemized in the DOJ memo in Appendix A were broken by Democrats in the 2020 election. Yet, the swamp wants America to believe that Democrats won fair and square. They didn't. They cheated and committed crimes in the process. Sadly, while many Democrats in office proved to be corrupt, many of our elected Republican officials were cowards, too weak to fight and far too willing to succumb to the temptation. They all need to go. It doesn't matter if they are Democrats or Republicans. If they participated, or looked the other way, in the crimes of the 2020 election, they need to be removed from office. America must clean out the corruption and hold these crooked politicians accountable.

Run out the Clock

The media and the Left insist that there were *no crimes* committed, and they love to point to the courts, claiming that all charges of criminal activity have been proven wrong. The real story, however, is quite different. Most states have laws dictating when and how elections can be challenged. For practical purposes, states put limitations on election challenges, because the government needs to move forward and actually function. Arizona, for example, requires all election challenges to occur within five days of the canvass.[51] That makes investigating and proving a case quite difficult, and does not give enough time for discovery. The swamp knew President Trump's lawyers wouldn't have enough time to unravel their scheme before the deadlines.

Another challenge was the courts clearly did not want to be involved in what was largely portrayed as a political dispute. Every court punted and refused to hear the case. Not one single court was willing to allow evidence to be presented. The media lied to the public, telling the public that there was no evidence. That wasn't true. The truth was the courts didn't want to hear it. Not one single court allowed a witness to take the stand to testify.

The worst case of all was in Georgia. Georgia had litigated for ten months when the judge finally threw the case out on standing. After ten months! How does that even happen? They had standing to sue for ten months but then suddenly lost their standing when the plaintiffs were making progress? The swamp ran out the clock, and the courts let them do it. All they had left to do to get away with their election heist was to change the narrative.

CHAPTER 18

Changing the Narrative

The media has spent years attacking President Trump, trying to distract voters from the incredible progress he made on the economy, the border, international security, energy independence—pretty much everything he did to help the American people be more prosperous, safer, and freer. But when that didn't slow his popularity, the so-called journalists sunk to a whole new level and started attacking his supporters.

After November 2020, as evidence leaked out about all the suspicious anomalies, strange new rules and broken laws surrounding the election, more and more Americans refused to stay quiet. The media had worked hard to bury the evidence and silence Republicans, claiming it was all a case of unfounded conspiracy theories.

But attacking the evidence wasn't working so well. So the press turned their attention on the 70 million Americans who had voted for Donald Trump, and began a vicious campaign to demonize them.

Trump supporters had organized a January 6 protest to peacefully march to the Capitol after his speech and make their petition known to members of Congress—they did not believe the election was conducted lawfully. President Trump even acknowledged the planned protest, saying:[1]

"I know that everyone here will soon be marching over to the Capitol building to peacefully and patriotically make your voices heard."

The crowd with him at the Ellipse on January 6, 2021, was, from President Trump's perspective, the largest crowd to which he'd ever spoken. President Trump estimated it could be over a million people. The media refused to show the large crowd, and instead showed pictures of much smaller areas of the city. They had their cameras stationed at the Capitol to watch as ANTIFA and others tried to stir up a riot and blame it on America-loving patriots.

The liberal media got busy telling stories about how Trump supporters started a riot and assaulted the Capitol; they even tried to claim patriots killed a police officer.[2] Fake news. According to the autopsy report, one officer died of natural causes on January 7. The autopsy report does not mention anything about a head wound, or show any physical trauma that could have led to his death.[3] While his death is tragic, there's no medical link to the events of January 6.[4]

The other two individuals who were killed that day were Ashli Babbitt and Rosanne Boyland. Babbitt is an Air Force veteran who loyally served her country and was callously, or negligently, shot by a Capitol Police officer as she was unarmed and non-threatening. Babbitt should never have been shot, and the Capitol Police should be held accountable for her murder. The police officer who shot her had a history of poor weapons handling, and many experts believe her murder was the result of a negligent discharge.[5]

Boyland was a peaceful protester who was trampled to death in a stampede caused by Capitol Police.[6] As Boyland lay on the ground suffocating under the weight of the people on top of her, police officers continued to beat and push others on top of her, which ultimately led to her death.[7] She was unarmed and non-threatening.[8] Boyland and Babbit were the only two lives lost on January 6, 2021, and they lost their lives due to the actions of Capitol Police. Where was the media outrage, or the Defund the Police movement? Nowhere to be found.

The whole point of the January 6 protest was to draw attention to all the signs of election fraud and to encourage our government leaders to do the right thing and reconsider the election. Tragically, after the media's propaganda effort, January 6 is a discussion of political prisoners, FBI informants, and framing Trump supporters. While the Left did not convince everyone to believe their fake insurrection story, they did successfully distract ordinary Americans from the fraudulent election.

While the media sensationalized the events of January 6 in order to distract the country from the story of the stolen election, the swamp seized on this lie to try to make sure Donald Trump never held office again.

Impeachment, Round Two

Incredibly, Democrats tried to impeach President Trump, a second time, for this supposed insurrection.

They claimed President Trump somehow incited an insurrection on January 6, supposedly orchestrating an attack on the US Capitol. No evidence ever existed to suggest that he did such a thing. Actually, just the opposite is true. Evidence existed that he supported protecting the Capitol and securing the city prior to January 6, 2021.[9]

President Trump approved every single request for law enforcement support, fencing, or other measures to protect Washington, DC, before January 6, 2021.[10] When asked for more federal law enforcement support, he approved.[11] More military resources or intelligence support or anything else needed, he approved.[12] He approved everything without exception.[13]

Yet Democrats insisted he was at fault. It looked like cheating him out of an election win wasn't enough—they wanted to make sure he could never run for president again. They were hoping to impeach him, get the Senate to convict, and remove him from office less than two weeks before he would leave office anyway. Quite an ambitious plan, even for the power-crazed Democrats. But it didn't work.

Article of Impeachment: Incitement of Insurrection

On January 11, 2021, just five days after President Trump's speech at the Ellipse, the House of Representatives drafted a resolution for one Article of Impeachment: Incitement of an Insurrection. The Democrat-controlled House of Representatives resolved that "the President shall be removed from office on impeachment for, and conviction of, treason, bribery, or other high crimes and misdemeanors."[14]

How did he commit treason, bribery, or a high crime and misdemeanor? They claimed that he "engaged in insurrection or rebellion against the United States."[15] They said that his speech at the Ellipse had incited an insurrection against the United States. The treasonous statements that supposedly put Congress in danger included: "we won this election, and we won it by a landslide," and "if you don't fight like hell, you're not going to have a country anymore."[16]

That's it. According to Congress, those two statements caused thousands of people to turn towards the Capitol, run the two-mile distance, and immediately try to break into the building surrounded by federal law enforcement. Unprepared and uncoordinated (not to mention unarmed), Trump supporters spontaneously decided to overthrow the United States government based on those two statements. That was their entire case for "inciting an insurrection."

The crux of the impeachment article claimed:

> Thus, incited by President Trump, members of the crowd
> he had addressed, in an attempt to, among other objec-
> tives, interfere with the Joint Session's solemn constitutional

duty to certify the results of the 2020 presidential election, unlawfully breached and vandalized the Capitol, injured and killed law enforcement personnel, menaced Members of Congress, the Vice President, and Congressional personnel, and engaged in other violent, deadly, destructive, and seditious acts.[17]

For most of 2020, leftist political groups like Black Lives Matter and ANTIFA rioted, looted, vandalized, and burned buildings across the United States, including federal buildings.[18] Those riots left several people dead at the hands of the liberal protestors,[19] and caused billions of dollars in damage.[20] Where was the outrage from the Democrats over that wave of violence? Not only did they condone it, Vice President Kamala Harris raised money to get those criminals out of jail![21]

While the events of January 6 should never have happened, they paled in comparison to the damage done just months earlier at the hands of liberals.

Yet Democrat officials condemn the January 6 protest, and Speaker Nancy Pelosi claimed:[22]

"The violent domestic attack on Congress on January 6 was the worst assault on the Capitol since the War of 1812 and the worst domestic assault on American Democracy since the Civil War. We are facing a radically new threat in the kinds of forces that combined to attack our government on January 6. The future of our democracy is on the line. This assault was an attempt to overthrow the government."

On May 31, 2020, just months before January 6, 2021, radical Leftists attacked the White House, with President Trump and the First Family inside, throwing bricks, rocks, and threatening violence on the President of the United States.[23] The riot was so dangerous that the Secret Service moved him to the bunker to ensure his safety from the liberal mob.

Is that somehow better than violence at the Capitol? Once in office, the Biden-Harris administration aggressively prosecuted conservatives and have held many Trump supporters in jail for over a year without trial. It's dystopian. They are using the power of government against their political opponents. The Democrats claiming the Capitol breach was the worst attack on democracy seem to have missed the fact that their political supporters threatened the White House just months earlier.

The most dangerous assault on democracy is not the people rising up to challenge their government, it's the government using its authority to silence and control the people. It's egregious and un-American. It's unconstitutional.

Phone Call with Brad Raffensperger

Another part of the impeachment articles said that President Trump "urged the secretary of state of Georgia, Brad Raffensperger, to 'find' enough votes to overturn the Georgia presidential election results and threatened Secretary Raffensperger if he failed to do so."[24] Interesting that Raffensperger recorded the phone call, yet Congress couldn't quote, in the Articles of Impeachment, President Trump's supposed "threat," nor how he supposedly demanded that Raffensperger "find" votes. They couldn't quote his demand or threat, because they didn't exist. He never said anything on the call remotely close to a threat, nor did he demand Raffensperger manufacture false votes, as the Article implies.

In two days, with zero evidence, the House of Representatives voted to impeach Donald Trump on January 13, 2021, with a vote of 232 to 197.[25] Ten Republicans[26] voted with the Democrats to impeach.[27]

Impeachment Trial

The trial for the second impeachment began on February 9, 2021, nearly three weeks after President Trump had left office. The swamp was so determined to get rid of him, they tried him anyway as a former president. Kentucky Senator Rand Paul moved to dismiss the impeachment charge, because the only remedy for impeachment is removal from office. Since he was no longer in office, there really wasn't anything that could be done even if he were convicted. In other words, the whole second impeachment was pointless.

Not to be deterred, the swamp pressed ahead to remove him from office after he'd already left the White House, clearly determined to prevent him from running again in 2024.

They spent five days making baseless accusations and presenting arguments without any foundation whatsoever. President Trump's lawyers pointed out the obviously partisan attack, and gave the Senate enough sound reasoning to acquit, which they did. On February 13, 2021, the United States Senate acquitted Donald Trump of inciting an insurrection by failing to get the requisite super majority of the Senate to convict. They voted 57–43, falling ten votes short of conviction. Seven Republican senators voted with the Democrats to convict.[28]

Any Story but the Election

The most frustrating aspect of all of this wasn't even the sham show trial the swamp performed, or the threat of impeachment and conviction. The most frustrating part was that, with few exceptions, the media obsessively covered every detail of the baseless impeachment trial, but they weren't willing to talk at all about the obvious signs of cheating that had occurred in the election.

And now, anyone who questioned the final "results" of the election was not just "racist" or "un-American:" they were *insurrectionists*. Rather than discuss the mind-boggling events of November 3, and the historic implications of massive election fraud in a presidential election, The Narrative became: insurrectionists assaulted the Capitol, case closed.

The Narrative isn't true. It wasn't true on January 6, 2021. It's not true today. The truth is that hundreds of thousands of people saw signs of cheating, and many showed up to protest to their government.

The Media's Long-Term Campaign

Of course, the media's attacks on Donald Trump are nothing new. Most of the media has been against him since he announced he was running for president in 2015.

They knew he threatened their cabal, and they were determined to take him out at all costs. From day one of his campaign, his family suffered brutal, baseless attacks.[29] The Left accused him of colluding with Russia to rig the 2016 election.[30] Turns out it was actually the Hillary campaign that colluded with Russia.[31]

They attacked his lawyers and campaign workers, threatening anyone close to him in an effort to sway some to betray and lie about him.[32] Some did lie about him, but even then, there wasn't enough to indicate any wrongdoing on his part.[33] The Obama administration illegally surveilled individuals working on the Trump campaign, and lied to the FISA court[34] about their activity. The media covered for them and barely reported the story.

The Left determined to impeach him before he ever even took office.[35] How can anyone legitimately claim a need to impeach a president before he's even sworn into office?! The swamp, including the media, was so determined to get rid of him that they simply fed the public lies about him in order to get him out of their way. Why was he such a threat to them? Because he determined to return the power of government back to the American people, and they didn't like that.

Trump Derangement Syndrome

When Donald Trump won the 2016 election, the media and the Left all, quite simply, lost their minds. As soon as he took office, they complained his family was a security threat, claiming that maybe, possibly, one day, potentially, they could be bribed by a foreign nation.[36] These same media outlets overlook the fact that Hunter Biden has actually taken bribes from Russia,[37] China, and the Ukraine, and admits on video with a Russian prostitute[38] that Russians stole yet another laptop with private information. Somehow, that's okay.

When they couldn't manufacture any crimes Trump committed, they started attacking his policies. They claimed, for instance, that he was inhumane and cruel to immigrants, stating that he kept kids in cages at the border. Those same outlets overlooked the fact that those "cages" were installed under the Obama-Biden administration, and the Biden-Harris administration has created worse conditions than any previous administration.

They attacked President Trump every way they could think of, and none of it worked. He only grew in popularity[39] as the progressives' woke agenda looked more and more absurd.

The idea that President Trump might empower the American people to create wealth, think for themselves, and hold government leaders accountable terrified the swamp. His promise to drain the swamp threatened their power structure, so they had to get rid of him. And so they conspired to do whatever it took to make sure he did not win the 2020 election, even if that meant committing election fraud on a massive scale.

Guantanamo Bay

In the days, months, and years following January 6, 2022, the radical Left, with their vice grip on power, did everything they could to snuff out any political opposition. They controlled Congress, the DC courts, and the media, and they wanted The Narrative to scare anyone away from opposing their story that the election was secure. The Biden-Harris administration went to war on peace-loving Americans for simply being present at the Capitol on January 6, likely with the intent to instill fear in other Americans. Do not challenge the establishment.

They arrested grandmothers, parents, entire families—anyone who showed patriotic support for President Trump. If these political prisoners were lucky enough to get a trial, it was usually a foregone conclusion by a radicalized DC court. Many were never even given a trial and were held longer than any maximum sentence they could receive, even if convicted. Some were placed in solitary confinement for months. Some were denied specific dietary needs, causing excruciating pain and starvation. Most were not given proper visitations, including denial of attorney visits. Quite simply, they were tortured.

On September 30, 2022, thirty-four political prisoners, being held in the DC Metro jail, handwrote a heartbreaking seven-page letter to the court requesting transfer to Guantanamo Bay, where the treatment is more humane. Their collective experience describes various types of torture, and call DC Metro jail an "evisceration facility of the body mind and soul." The letter states in part:

> [January 6 protestors] are all but slowly murdered every way except for their very soul being ripped from their famished chests on behalf of this mercilessly sinister institution. As prisoners of this jail, we have witnessed the horrendous treatment and have been personally afflicted by the hellacious conditions this jail insists on tormenting its traumatized guests with.
>
> Though words will always fall short of an accurate depiction of the magnitude of pandemonium that every prisoner within these walls has had no choice but to endure. What follows is a collection of repeated offenses this correctional facility habitually submits upon its captives. For if this pale dungeon of Human Rights violations dared to summon any

honesty of ward choice pertaining to the abhorrent atrocities that take place behind these unforgiving doors, they should erect a sign above the front gate that says "Abandon All Hope, Yee Who Enter Here."[40]

The letter continues and then provides three pages of bullet points describing the atrocities. A small sampling of the grievances include:

- Begging for help/water/medical aid/mercy through a four-inch window of cold metal doors
- No visitors
- No religious services
- No attorney access
- Mail delayed 3–4 months before delivery
- Laundry returned with brown stains and pubic hair, reeking of ripe urine
- Worms found in salad of "meals"
- Inadequate calorie count of "meals"
- Complete lack of nourishment in "meals"
- Loss of head hair due to malnourishment of "meals"
- Loss of eyesight due to malnourishment of "meals"
- Suffering from scurvy due to malnourishment of "meals"
- Blatant **extortion** via commissary in order to maintain health and or body weight
- Rust in the water
- Rust on bed areas in cells
- Rust on metal cages near face on small window of cells
- Black mold on walls of cells
- Black mold in vents of cells
- Broken toilets that either won't flush or repeatedly explode in cells

- Cockroaches in cells/cell blocks
- Mice in cells/cell blocks
- Repeatedly mocked and or insulted for our skin color or religious documentation
- Vaccine requirements for religious services
- Vaccine requirements for visitors
- Vaccine requirements for speaking with lawyers in prison
- Solitary confinement for 25.5 hours or more at a time
- Politically mocked by staff with Democrat, Black Lives Matter, Kamala Harris, Joe Biden–related attire
- Sent to "The Hole" if we express political views whatsoever
- Denial of water by guards

This list goes on and on of egregious inhumane abuses—all for having a different political view. The letter concludes:

> We hereby request to spend our precious and limited days, should the government continue to insist on holding us captive unconstitutionally as pre-trial detainees, to be transferred and reside at Guantanamo Bay, a detention facility that actually provides nutritional meals, [sic] sunlight exposure, top notch medical care, is respectful of religious requirements, has centers for exercise/entertainment for its detainees despite the fact that those residents are malicious terrorists, members of the Taliban, and few are actual United States citizens, instead of remaining trapped within the wretched confines of cruel and unusual punishment of the D.C. jail.

Thirty-four men signed their names and prisoner numbers to the letter.

The extent the establishment would go to change The Narrative away from the rigged and stolen election and try to demonize American patriots shocks the conscience. Then they used their media pimps to push the story that the stolen election was a lie, calling it The Big Lie.

The Real "Big Lie"

The ultimate media lie was covering up a stolen election. Despite all the obvious signs of fraud, they pushed The Narrative that "there's no evidence of fraud,"[41] and "this was the most secure election in US history."[42] Neither of those statements has ever been true. And yet they insist that citizens' simple requests to investigate the irregularities of this election are "The Big Lie." It would be funny if it weren't so tragic for our country.

Simple common sense would indicate some type of foul play in the 2020 election. First, the overwhelming increase in mail-in ballots, which sets the stage for fraud and ballot stuffing. Second, the fact that the only states that magically flipped from Trump to Biden needed to stop counting for days on end. Third, the fact that election officials were forced to acknowledge machine "glitches" due to supposedly improper maintenance, which resulted in an inaccurate count, awarding a county to Biden which they had to retract because Trump actually won.[43]

Nothing about this election was normal or passes as legitimate, and the media has had to take more and more radical positions to try to defend their last ridiculous position. The same media who lied to America repeatedly about the Russia Hoax, Ukraine Hoax, both fake impeachments, Hillary Clinton's illegal activity, the Biden Crime Family, and a host of other fake stories is the same media who tells America Donald Trump is bad because they don't like his tweets. If we can't believe them on every other story, why should any American believe what they say about the 2020 election?

Americans, in growing numbers, are tuning out the media, recognizing that the big corporate networks are simply pushing an agenda rather than providing unbiased news. As the public realizes that our media and government have been lying to us for decades, a sleeping giant is awakening.

CHAPTER 19

The Great Awakening

The radical Left claims to be a "woke" movement, which supposedly represents a segment of society that is "awake" and is, for some unexplained reason, more enlightened than the rest of us. It's not true. It's a counterfeit movement. Like everything else the Left pushes, the truth is the opposite of what they say. "Woke" Americans struggle to identify genders, but claim to be smarter than the rest of us;[1] they spew racism in the name of eliminating hate;[2] they demand segregation and call it equality.[3]

Anyone who points out their obvious hypocrisy is immediately labeled a racist, regardless of the race of that person. Black people trying to protect American values are white supremacists.[4] Women fighting to protect women's sports and college athletics are sexist. Parents protecting their children from radical indoctrination are domestic terrorists.[5] The Democrats don't care that their policies are nonsensical and dangerous to America. All they really care about is power.

The Counterfeit Price
America is now paying the price for entertaining wokeness and this dangerous, un-American agenda. Radical extremists have taken over our

government and instituted mandates that seem like a page out of the Soviet Union's playbook, even demanding to see papers in Democrat areas of the country simply to be allowed to live a normal life.

Decades ago, they preached tolerance, and America fell for it. They demanded *our* tolerance, and we gave it to them. We tolerated their irrational bullying, and the Republican Party became the party of cowards. Without conservative leadership fighting for American principles, America largely ignored what the bureaucracy was up to. We lived our lives uninterested in the drudgery of politics. Rather than raise our voices and push back on the idiocy, we kept quiet. We became the Silent Majority.

But did they practice what they preached? Not for a second. They won't tolerate a single dissenting voice, a single difference of opinion, a single step out of line from their forced-march towards total government control of our speech, our thoughts, our religion, our way of life.

Every counterfeit pretends to be something it's not. Counterfeit goods pretend to be more expensive than they are by looking like something they are not. Counterfeit money and art all fake a value they do not really have. The same is true with this crazy woke movement. They are not more "awake" than everyone else—if anything, they are tone deaf to the wishes and dreams and values of most Americans. But they got our attention. They did wake up America to the realization that irrational, power-hungry control fiends are trying to cripple our way of life in order to produce a globalist utopia where America as we know it no longer exists.

Corporations have sold their souls for profit. Notice how so many of the largest corporations in the country have gone woke? Why is that? Because it's an easy virtue signal that won't negatively impact their profit . . . at least not yet. Conservatives do not discriminate. Conservatives will still shop at a woke store or eat at a liberal-leaning restaurant. Liberals, on the other hand, do discriminate. Not only will they boycott stores if they disagree with political views, they may end up vandalizing, robbing, or looting it. So from a business standpoint, if a company wants to virtue signal, catering to the Left is the safest option—except that it is now costing us our freedoms.

The woke movement pretends to represent what's best about America, while actually showing us the ugly face of mob rule. But there is a movement that does embody the best of America. A movement I believe will be the Greatest Awakening this nation has ever experienced. We're on the verge of it.

The Great Awakening

America is waking up to the realization that as a self-governed people, there is no auto-pilot switch. We enjoy more freedoms than any country that's ever existed, but those freedoms require vigilance. Everyday Americans cannot ignore the drudgery of government, at any level, and must make an effort to get involved in school boards, city councils, state House and Senate, or even run for federal office.

As more and more Americans wake up to the idea that a self-governed nation requires participation, we're seeing a re-birth of this nation and a return to our founding principles. Our Declaration of Independence declares that:

" . . . Governments are instituted among Men, deriving their just powers from the consent of the governed . . . "

The 2020 election demonstrates that our current government leaders did not get their power from the consent of the governed, as our founders designed. They cheated. They manipulated the system designed to secure our freedoms and used it to entrap America under their control. Many Americans around the country jumped into action to get involved and restore integrity to our elections. Virginia proved it's possible. New Jersey proved it takes work.

When Americans retake our government and honestly elect leaders representing our interests and constitutional values, America will prosper like no other time in history. Imagine the prosperity America can produce when every American is empowered to fulfill his and her destiny, without the burdensome restrictions of an authoritarian government. This generation has the ability to fulfill America's destiny by rededicating ourselves to Jefferson's vision:

" . . . all men are created equal, . . . endowed by their Creator with certain unalienable Rights, . . . among these are Life, Liberty and the pursuit of Happiness."[6]

America is exceptional because our country is founded on the principle that no man and no government can take away these rights. Yet that's exactly what the radical Left is trying to do. The Great Awakening has woken up to this threat, and understands that the fulfillment of America's promise is only possible by rejecting the woke agenda and intolerant thought-police of the Left. We must reject them actively—not tolerate them politely. Only then can we achieve what Martin Luther King Jr. dreamed:

"That my four little children will one day live in a nation where they will not be judged by the color of their skin but by the content of their character."

I firmly believe we can reach that goal, but only if we do the work to protect our elections.

America the Beautiful

The United States of America is the most exceptional country on the face of the earth. Our landscape is diverse and beautiful. Whether we enjoy the New York City skyline, listen to waves from a Hawaiian beach, or enjoy the mountainous terrain in the West, we are all captivated by the beauty of our great nation. Yet, it's the people that make America great.

Communities coming together for high school sports, celebrating graduations or successes of loved ones, and mourning the loss of those dear to us are all brush strokes in the masterpiece that earns this amazing nation its nickname of America the Beautiful. America is beautiful. Beauty, through excellence, has a unique way of healing, restoring, and enriching what's broken—even a nation.

America holds the solution to all of our current problems. Nothing we're currently facing is insurmountable, so long as the government gets out of the way. The American people have what it takes to recover from this totalitarian takeover. In order to do so, we've got to clear out the corruption.

Make America Great Again is about freeing the American people to live to their fullest potential, without interference from the government. It's not a movement about Donald Trump. President Trump just represents what the American people want most of all: Freedom. Freedom from burdensome mandates, taxes, regulations, and legislation. Freedom from limits on our free speech, free thought, and free exercise of our religious beliefs. Our Founding Fathers didn't cement our fundamental freedoms in the Bill of Rights just so we could voluntarily surrender them to anyone who may be offended by our opinions.

Don't Believe Your Lying Eyes

The Biden-Harris administration and the cabal pulling the strings around them think Americans are stupid. They believe they can say whatever they want and we'll just believe them, even if their actions directly contradict their words. Never before in history has an administration taken so many detrimental actions to hurt this country than the Biden-Harris administration has done in its first two years. Are they simply incompetent? Or are their motives more sinister? It's possible we would have better leadership under incompetence.

Leaving Americans and allies behind in Afghanistan, encouraging and enabling an invasion of this nation through our southern border, shutting down the economy with burdensome mandates, allowing crime to run rampant in our streets, paving a way for Russia to invade Ukraine, and trying to federalize elections to ensure states cannot protect themselves is un-American. Not only does it violate any sense of integrity of this great nation, but it violates each and every American citizen working hard to create the best life possible for themselves and their family.

Is that really what we voted for in 2020?

America's Choice

We have a president in the White House who may not even have been elected fairly, and an administration that appears intent on destroying this country. Where do we go from here? We must continue to work to correct the crimes of 2020, but we can't ignore the fact that every year has elections and the years keep coming. We have to commit our efforts to preventing election fraud from ever happening again.

It's tempting to bury our heads in the sand, to continue to allow the media to twist reality, to pretend everything is fine, to shirk our responsibilities, allow fascism to take over America, and kiss our liberty goodbye. Under this scenario, wars will continue, the supply-chain crisis will get worse. Grocery store shelves will run empty, gas prices will continue to rise, and mandates will prevent employment while Biden blames COVID, or Russia, or Trump—anyone but himself. But there's another option.

We can get involved and return this nation to the principles on which we were founded. As a self-governed republic, the American people can choose to re-engage and once again self-govern. We have the option to oust the corrupt and the cowardly from our leadership, re-establish our freedoms, and break the oppressive restrictions from our lives. To do so requires that we all get involved.

President Trump's first term proved that he can take on the swamp and dramatically help this nation. His second election proved he can't drain the swamp alone. It takes all of us. While his first administration had many great achievements, I believe his greatest contribution to this nation thus far may be exposing the swamp for the dirty cheaters that they are. They have a stranglehold on the power centers of this nation and are using it to strangle the life out of every corner of American freedoms. The media's been covering for them for decades, but we can see them clearly now. What are we prepared to do about it?

Can America be Saved?

Many Americans fear that it's too late, that our elections are too compromised. Some don't want to vote, believing there's no longer any chance for honest and fair elections. Can America be saved?

I believe America is not lost, but she hangs in the balance. As we've discussed, there is an elaborate system of voter fraud in place. However, it's so elaborate that it's extremely fragile. They need every area of their scheme to work, or they will not be successful. They must discard ballots from Republican neighborhoods, block Republicans from voting, harass Republican poll challengers, exclude them from the process, block the windows, refuse to accept their challenges, add fake voters to the roll, ballot stuff, ballot harvest, ballot traffic, pay for votes, centralize the vote count, manufacture a crisis to promote mail-in ballots . . . the list goes on and on. If they fail in any of these efforts, they cannot successfully rig an election.

While Republicans have made substantial progress securing elections at the state level, Democrat states have worked to loosen restrictions, but with much less success. Fifteen Blue states legislated to make mail-in voting easier.[7]

Closing loopholes in election operations is one important piece to securing future elections, and many state leaders have done a great job shoring up those weak points. But, that's only half the battle. To truly ensure fair and honest elections, the American people need to show up and get involved.

Some patriots argue that we can't move forward until we clean up 2020, and I certainly understand that idea. However, I don't think we can clean up the crimes of 2020 until we get rid of the corrupt politicians who cheated and the cowardly politicians who let them get away with it. That won't be easy, but it's the only way to truly protect our freedoms and our Republic.

As Ronald Reagan said in his inaugural address as California's governor:

"Freedom is a fragile thing and it's never more than one generation away from extinction. It is not ours by way of inheritance; it must be fought for and defended constantly by each generation, for it comes only once to a people. And those in world history who have known freedom and then lost it have never known it again."[8]

Then-governor Reagan is exactly right. Right now is our time in history to decide for our generation, and for every generation that comes after us, whether we remain free or fall to a government that gets bigger and bigger until it swallows up democracy itself.

Americans have stepped up in record numbers over the last two years to get involved in local government and grassroots efforts to save elections. One example is the Precinct Strategy, which enlists America First patriots to committee positions at the precinct level, which Republicans all too often leave vacant.[9] The easiest thing patriots can do to secure their elections is to volunteer to sit on the committee of your precinct.

A huge advantage the cheaters had in 2020 is that we weren't paying attention. Cheating is easier when no one is watching. But now they have our attention. They won't be able to find as many people willing to cheat when they're under a microscope. Virginia showed us how to secure our elections in 2021, and every state should copy their model.

If we collectively make the decision to get involved in our government and local elections, and take the steps necessary to ensure that we remain self-governed, America will emerge better and more prosperous than we've ever been. Why? Because it's the American people who Make America Great, and the more people get involved, the greater America becomes. America prospers best when people from all walks of life collectively self-govern this amazing nation.

Certainly, we can't expect to clean up all of the corruption and get rid of all of the dirty politicians in 2022, right? But it's a start. Remember that many of those we need to get rid of weren't up for election in 2022. Some of the district attorneys who have refused to prosecute crime are up for election in 2023. Another round of US senators will be on deck in 2024. We can't forget that Mitch McConnell is up for re-election, if he decides to run again, in 2026. That means that the American people must stay focused and intentional about cleaning out corruption until, at the very least, 2026. If Americans stay as engaged as they are now and continue to recruit their friends, I expect we'll see the final flush of draining the swamp in November 2026.

The End and the Beginning

Courage is contagious—more contagious than a virus. As Americans continue to raise their voices and get involved, we're already beginning to see breakthroughs as patriots claim victories in state and local elections. The Save America movement gains more and more momentum as Americans choose to shake off the oppression of big-government mandates.

The rapid rise of the Save America wave rolling across the country shines a light on the corruption that is still hiding in dark places. As Americans get involved to protect their local elections, America First candidates will re-take state, local, and federal offices. With all of us involved to protect our elections, we can take on the swamp and win.

In 2016, Democrats were surprised by Donald Trump's popularity, and were caught unprepared. In 2020, Republicans were surprised by Democrats' efforts to cheat, and were caught unprepared. In 2024, there are no surprises and no excuses. America is ours for the re-taking, if enough people care enough to get involved.

APPENDIX A

DOJ Federal Election Fraud Fact Sheet

Memorandum from within Obama's Department of Justice explaining all the election crimes the Department of Justice has authority to prosecute.

Department of Justice
U.S. Attorney's Office
District of New Hampshire

FOR IMMEDIATE RELEASE
Tuesday, February 2, 2016

Federal Election Fraud Fact Sheet

Most issues concerning the administration and conduct of elections are governed and regulated by state law and are best addressed by state and local election officials. Federal law enforcement and prosecutorial authorities have jurisdiction to investigate and, when appropriate, prosecute election fraud in the following circumstances:

I. Federal Criminal Jurisdiction

Federal criminal jurisdiction over the activities described below can generally be obtained when those activities take place:

- In elections where a federal candidate's name is on the ballot.
- In any election (federal or nonfederal), when the fraud involves the necessary participation of an election official acting "under color of law."
- In connection with voter registration. The fact that voter registration is "unitary" in all 50 States (a citizen registers once to become eligible to vote for both federal and nonfederal candidates) confers federal jurisdiction regardless of the type of election.
- In connection with the misuse, or unauthorized trespass, involving a computer system used in connection with an election, to the extent that the misuse or trespass is conducted "under color of law."

II. Conduct Actionable as Federal Election Fraud, Intimidation, or Suppression

The following activities provide a basis for federal prosecution under the statutes referenced in each category:

- Paying voters to register to vote, or to vote in elections where a federal candidate's name is on the ballot (52 U.S.C. § 10307, 18 U.S.C. § 597), or through the use of the mails in those States where vote buying is a "bribery" offense (18 U.S.C. § 1952), or in federal elections in those States where purchased votes or registrations are voidable under state law (52 U.S.C. § 20511).
- Multiple voting in a federal election, voting for individuals in a federal election who do not personally participate in the voting

act attributed to them, or impersonating voters (52 U.S.C. §§ 10307, 20511).

- Intimidating voters through physical duress in any election (18 U.S.C. § 245(b)(1)(A)); or through physical or economic intimidation in connection with registration to vote or voting in a federal election (52 U.S.C. § 20511, 18 U.S.C. § 594). If the victim is a federal employee, intimidation in connection with all elections is prohibited (18 U.S.C. § 610).

- Malfeasance by election officials, acting "under color of law," such as diluting valid ballots with invalid ones (so-called "ballot box stuffing"), rendering false vote tabulations, or preventing valid voter registrations or votes from being given effect in any election (18 U.S.C. §§ 241, 242), as well as in elections where federal candidates are on the ballot (52 U.S.C. §§ 10307, 20511).

- Qualifying fictitious individuals to vote in federal elections by placing fictitious names on voter registration rolls (52 U.S.C. §§ 10307, 20511); or through "color of law" in any election (18 U.S.C. §§ 241, 242).

- Preventing or impeding qualified voters from participating in an election where a federal candidate's name is on the ballot through such tactics as disseminating false information as to the date, timing, or location of federal voting activity (18 U.S.C. §§ 241, 242).

- Registering to vote, or voting in a federal election, by persons who are not entitled to vote under applicable state law, most notably persons who have committed serious crimes, and persons who are not United States citizens (18 U.S.C. §§ 1015(f), 611, and 52 U.S.C. § 20511).

- Falsely claiming United States citizenship in connection with registering to vote or voting in any election (18 U.S.C. §§ 911, 1015(f)).
- Voting in a federal election by anyone who is not a United States citizen in those States where citizenship is a requisite for the franchise (currently all 50 States) (18 U.S.C. § 611).
- Providing false information concerning a voter's name, address, or period of residence in order to register to vote, or to vote in a federal election (52 U.S.C. §§ 10307, 20511).
- Causing the submission of voter registrations in any election, or of ballots in federal elections, that are materially defective under applicable state law (52 U.S.C. § 20511).
- Ordering, keeping, or having under one's control any troops or armed men at any polling place in a general or special election, if one is a civil or military officer or employee of the United States government (18 U.S.C. § 592).
- To report federal election fraud, intimidation, or suppression contact the United States Attorney's Office Election Day Hotline at **(603) 230–2503**. Inquiries and complaints may also be submitted through the United States Attorney's website at www.usdoj.gov/usao/nh by clicking on the "email us" link.

Complaints about ballot access problems or discrimination can be made directly to the Civil Rights Division's Voting Section in Washington, D.C. at 1-800-253-3931 or by TTY at 1-877-267-8971.

Notes

Chapter 1

1 Loosely defined as political creatures from both parties serving their own financial and personal interests above the interests of those who voted them into power.
2 https://www.nytimes.com/interactive/2020/11/03/us/elections/results-president .html; https://www.nytimes.com/elections/2016/results/president.
3 https://twitter.com/chanelrion/status/1325816990636904449?s=10; https://2001–2009.state.gov/p/eur/rls/rm/39542.htm.
4 Ibid.
5 https://twitter.com/Nancy15660268/status/1325904360048570368?ref_src =twsrc%5Etfw.
6 https://www.forbes.com/sites/alisondurkee/2020/11/16/trump-campaign-lawyers -quit-pennsylvania-lawsuit-again/?sh=33b5f32c443b.

Chapter 2

1 https://www.tmz.com/2021/01/19/capitol-rioter-screams-at-cops-asking-where -backup-is-denounces-siege/.
2 https://abcnews.go.com/US/defense-dozens-capitol-rioters-law-enforcement-us -building/story?id=75976466.
3 Eastman clerked for Supreme Court Justice Clarence Thomas, served as a dean at Chapman University School of Law, and has been cited numerous times in Supreme Court cases as a Constitutional Law scholar.
4 Michigan, Nevada, and New Mexico were also contested, but did not send letters to the president of the Senate for reconsideration.
5 https://en.wikipedia.org/wiki/Electoral_Count_Act.
6 https://scholarship.law.unc.edu/cgi/viewcontent.cgi?article=4003&context=nclr (pg 1660 —the USSC had to reach "antecedent determination" that ECA is constitutional, but it was never argued.)
7 Ibid.
8 Ibid.

9   https://www.pbs.org/newshour/politics/read-pences-full-letter-saying-he-cant-claim
     -unilateral-authority-to-reject-electoral-votes.
10 David Fontana & Bruce Ackerman, *Thomas Jefferson Counts Himself into the Presidency*,
     90 Va. L. Rev. 551 (2004).
11 *Id.*
12 https://thefederalist.com/2021/08/27/flashback-capitol-police-officer-who-shot
     -ashli-babbitt-left-his-gun-unattended-in-a-bathroom-in-2019/.

Chapter 3

1   https://www.youtube.com/watch?v=v_liXxu0XL8.
2   https://www.npr.org/transcripts/943242106.
3   https://www.cisa.gov/news/2020/11/12/joint-statement-elections-infrastructure
     -government-coordinating-council-election.

Chapter 4

1   See Arizona Senate Subpoena.
2   Jack Sellers (R), Bill Gates (R), Clint Hickman (R), Steve Chucri (R), and Steve
     Gallardo (D).
3   https://www.usatoday.com/story/news/factcheck/2021/04/27/fact-check-dominion
     -lawyers-did-not-try-stop-arizona-audit/7357488002/.
4   https://www.abc15.com/news/election-2020/democratic-party-campaigns-to-oust
     -judge.
5   https://www.azmirror.com/2021/04/23/dems-wont-post-1m-bond-so-election
     -audit-wont-be-paused/.

Chapter 6

1   https://intellipaat.com/blog/what-is-splunk/.
2   https://www.washingtonpost.com/context/dominion-response-to-arizona-senate
     -subpoena/dca33a7d-5bf0-4d58-9fd1-2777c2a8f5e0/.
3   https://www.azcentral.com/story/news/politics/elections/2021/08/02/maricopa-co
     -and-dominion-face-monday-deadline-ariz-senate-election-subpoenas/5434136001/.
4   https://www.nytimes.com/interactive/2022/08/02/us/elections/results-arizona-us
     -senate.html.
5   https://www.thegatewaypundit.com/2021/09/exclusive-maricopa-county-supervisor
     -steve-chucri-caught-leaked-recording-maricopa-county-voting-machine-company
     -audit-recount-pretty-bullsht-way-audio/.
6   Ibid.
7   Ibid.
8   Ibid.

Chapter 7

1   https://www.youtube.com/watch?v=hRCXUNOwOjw.
2   Ibid.

3   https://www.youtube.com/watch?v=hRCXUNOwOjw (1:02:53).
4   https://www.statefarmarena.com/news/detail/statement-regarding-absentee-ballot
    -tabulation-at-state-farm-arena.
5   https://www.cnbc.com/2018/11/08/brian-kemp-resigns-as-georgia-secretary-of
    -state-as-he-faces-stacey-abrams.html.
6   https://gov.georgia.gov/about-us/about-governor-brian-p-kemp.
7   https://drive.google.com/file/d/1Cz1etDP8yKDyo05r1SeQPT9UD_-B6Mmt/view
    complaint paragraph 29.
8   https://drive.google.com/file/d/1Cz1etDP8yKDyo05r1SeQPT9UD_-B6Mmt/view
    complain pg 22 allegation C.
9   https://thehill.com/regulation/court-battles/3670303-judge-rules-against-stacey
    -abrams-organization-in-georgia-voting-rights-lawsuit/.
10 https://thefederalist.com/2021/07/16/georgia-secretary-of-state-explains-why-hes
    -just-now-discovering-more-than-10000-illegal-votes-cast-in-2020/.
11 https://www.ajc.com/politics/drop-box-use-soared-in-democratic-areas-before
    -georgia-voting-law/N4ZTGHLWD5BRBOUKBHTUCFVOEU/.
12 https://www.ajc.com/politics/absentee-ballot-rejections-declined-after-georgia
    -installed-drop-boxes/PCWPFF5HEJE5HDG3IE642BO55Y/.
13 https://justthenews.com/sites/default/files/2021-06/Unabridged%20Notes.pdf
    Carter Jones memo.
14 https://justthenews.com/sites/default/files/2021-06/Unabridged%20Notes.pdf
    Carter Jones memo. Pg 1 Monday 11/2, first bullet.
15 https://justthenews.com/sites/default/files/2021-06/Unabridged%20Notes.pdf
    Carter Jones memo. Pg 1 Monday 11/2.
16 https://statisticalatlas.com/county/Georgia/Fulton-County/Race-and-Ethnicity
17 Ibid.
18 https://justthenews.com/sites/default/files/2021-06/Unabridged%20Notes.pdf
    Carter Jones memo. Pg 7.
19 https://www.youtube.com/watch?v=TTtY_ZpS6eY.
20 https://justthenews.com/sites/default/files/2021-06/Unabridged%20Notes.pdf
    Carter Jones memo.
21 https://justthenews.com/sites/default/files/2021-06/Unabridged%20Notes.pdf
    Carter Jones memo. Pg 1.
22 Ibid.
23 https://justthenews.com/sites/default/files/2021-06/Unabridged%20Notes.pdf
    Carter Jones memo. Pg 2.
24 Ibid.
25 https://justthenews.com/sites/default/files/2021-06/Unabridged%20Notes.pdf
    Carter Jones memo.
26 https://justthenews.com/sites/default/files/2021-06/Unabridged%20Notes.pdf
    Carter Jones memo. Pg 13
27 Ibid.
28 Bryan Geels affidavit.

Chapter 8

1   https://www.youtube.com/watch?v=vfBD0JpeKEw (at 18:00).

2   Ibid.
3   https://www.youtube.com/watch?v=vfBD0JpeKEw (testimony begins 17:40).
4   Ibid.
5   https://www.youtube.com/watch?v=vfBD0JpeKEw.
6   https://www.youtube.com/watch?v=vfBD0JpeKEw (18:30).
7   https://www.phillymag.com/news/2020/11/05/election-watchers-philadelphia-vote-count/.
8   https://www.youtube.com/watch?v=vfBD0JpeKEw (testimony begins 17:40).
9   https://www.usatoday.com/story/news/politics/2020/11/04/1-4-million-ballots-still-being-counted-pennsylvania/6158717002/.
10 https://www.c-span.org/video/?477826–1/trump-campaign-court-rules-observe-mail-ballot-counting-philadelphia.
11 https://www.dos.pa.gov/VotingElections/OtherServicesEvents/Documents/Polling-Places-During-COVID-Guidance.pdf.
12 Ibid.
13 https://www.c-span.org/video/?477826–1/trump-campaign-court-rules-observe-mail-ballot-counting-philadelphia.
14 Ibid.
15 https://www.pacourts.us/Storage/media/pdfs/20210604/022305-file-10384.pdf; https://www.youtube.com/watch?v=u8-TahzO7CQ; https://www.phillymag.com/news/2020/11/05/election-watchers-philadelphia-vote-count/;https://www.tampabay.com/news/florida-politics/2020/11/05/pam-bondi-throws-herself-into-trump-effort-to-stop-counting-votes/.
16 https://www.c-span.org/video/?477826–1/trump-campaign-court-rules-observe-mail-ballot-counting-philadelphia (1:44).
17 https://www.youtube.com/watch?v=vfBD0JpeKEw (witness at 17:50) https://www.phillymag.com/news/2020/11/05/election-watchers-philadelphia-vote-count/; https://www.c-span.org/video/?477826–1/trump-campaign-court-rules-observe-mail-ballot-counting-philadelphia.
18 https://codes.findlaw.com/pa/title-25-ps-elections-electoral-districts/pa-st-sect-25-2687.html.
19 https://www.c-span.org/video/?477826–1/trump-campaign-court-rules-observe-mail-ballot-counting-philadelphia.
20 Ibid.
21 Ibid.
22 Ibid.
23 https://www.c-span.org/video/?477856–1/trump-campaign-seeks-court-injunction-stop-pennsylvania-vote-count.
24 Ibid.
25 Ibid.
26 https://www.c-span.org/video/?477875–1/philadelphia-mayor-dismisses-claims-voter-fraud-president-concede.
27 Ibid.
28 Ibid.
29 https://www.legis.state.pa.us/cfdocs/Legis/CSM/showMemoPublic.cfm?chamber=S&SPick=20190&cosponId=28056.; https://www.supremecourt.gov/DocketPDF

/20/20–810/162573/20201203162739451_Final_Emergency%20Application%20
for%20Writ%20of%20Injunction.pdf.

30 Ibid.

31 https://www.supremecourt.gov/DocketPDF/20/20–810/162573
/20201203162739451_Final_Emergency%20Application%20for%20Writ%20
of%20Injunction.pdf (pg 8 paragraph A).

32 https://www.legis.state.pa.us/cfdocs/billinfo/billinfo.cfm?syear=2019&sind
=0&body=S&type=B&bn=411.

33 https://www.supremecourt.gov/DocketPDF/20/20–810/162573/20201
203162739451_Final_Emergency%20Application%20for%20Writ%20of%20
Injunction.pdf (pg 7).

34 Ibid.

35 https://www.supremecourt.gov/DocketPDF/20/20–810/162573
/20201203162739451_Final_Emergency%20Application%20for%20Writ%20
of%20Injunction.pdf (pg 9).

36 https://www.supremecourt.gov/DocketPDF/20/20–810/162573
/20201203162739451_Final_Emergency%20Application%20for%20Writ%20
of%20Injunction.pdf (pg 10).

37 https://www.supremecourt.gov/DocketPDF/20/20–810/162573
/20201203162739451_Final_Emergency%20Application%20for%20Writ%20
of%20Injunction.pdf (pg 12).

38 https://www.usatoday.com/story/news/politics/2020/11/04/1-4-million-ballots-still
-being-counted-pennsylvania/6158717002/.

39 https://www.forbes.com/sites/alisondurkee/2020/11/25/pennsylvania
-court-temporarily-blocks-state-from-certifying-votes-in-response-to-gop
-challenge/?sh=e01f62859074.

40 https://www.usatoday.com/story/news/politics/2020/11/04/1-4-million-ballots-still
-being-counted-pennsylvania/6158717002/.

41 https://www.supremecourt.gov/DocketPDF/20/20–810/162573
/20201203162739451_Final_Emergency%20Application%20for%20Writ%20
of%20Injunction.pdf.

42 https://www.pacourts.us/Storage/media/pdfs/20210603/221938-file-10761
.pdf; https://www.post-gazette.com/news/crime-courts/2020/11/25/pennsylvania-vote
-election-certification-sean-parnell-mike-kelly-commonwealth-court-appeal
/stories/202011250159.

43 Ibid.

44 https://www.marklevinshow.com/wp-content/uploads/sites/301/2020/11
/Memorandum-Opinion-Filed.pdf.

45 https://www.pacourts.us/Storage/media/pdfs/20210603/221938-file-10761.pdf.

46 https://pittsburgh.cbslocal.com/2020/11/28/pennsylvania-supreme-court-dismisses
-mike-kelly-and-sean-parnell-request/.

47 https://www.usatoday.com/story/news/politics/2020/11/04/1-4-million-ballots-still
-being-counted-pennsylvania/6158717002/.

48 https://local21news.com/news/local/commonwealth-court-act-77-unconstitutional
-strikes-down-expansive-mail-in-ballot-law.

49 https://www.mcall.com/news/breaking/mc-pa-mail-in-voting-pennsylvania
    -20220301-fzpi5qm2d5g7lcxmkqpam2ezci-story.html.
50 Ibid.
51 https://www.inquirer.com/politics/pennsylvania/spl/kathy-boockvar-resign
    -pennsylvania-election-official-constitutional-amendment-20210201.html.
52 Ibid.
53 Ibid.
54 https://www.spotlightpa.org/news/2021/02/kathy-boockvar-resigns-pennsylvania
    -election-official-constitutional-amendment/.
55 https://www.npr.org/sections/insurrection-at-the-capitol/2021/01/07/954380156/here
    -are-the-republicans-who-objected-to-the-electoral-college-count; https://www.goerie
    .com/story/news/2021/01/07/election-certification-who-objected-pa
    -election/6577937002/.
56 https://www.news-leader.com/story/news/politics/2021/01/05/past-objections
    -electoral-college-vote-counts-president-trump-josh-hawley/4129641001/.
57 https://www.senate.gov/reference/reference_index_subjects/House_of
    _Representatives_vrd.htm.
58 https://www.vox.com/2021/1/6/22218058/republicans-objections-election-results
59 https://thehill.com/homenews/campaign/524401-key-pa-county-suspends-vote
    -counting-until-10-am-wednesday.
60 https://www.usatoday.com/story/news/politics/2020/11/04/1-4-million-ballots-still
    -being-counted-pennsylvania/6158717002/.
61 https://www.cnn.com/2020/11/06/politics/presidential-election-biden-trump-2020
    /index.html.
62 https://www.politico.com/2020-election/results/pennsylvania/.
63 Ibid.
64 https://www.einpresswire.com/article/562120246/audit-the-vote-pa-lancaster
    -county-canvassing-results.
65 https://www.auditthevotepa.com/allegheny-county.
66 https://www.politico.com/2020-election/results/pennsylvania/.
67 Ibid.
68 https://www.auditthevotepa.com/montgomery-county.
69 https://www.einpresswire.com/article/562120246/audit-the-vote-pa-lancaster
    -county-canvassing-results.
70 https://www.politico.com/2020-election/results/pennsylvania/.
71 https://www.auditthevotepa.com/.
72 https://www.auditthevotepa.com/canvassing-results.

Chapter 9

1   Referred to as secretary of state in other states. It is the same position, but because
    legally Pennsylvania is a Commonwealth, not a state, the title is different.
2   https://www.dos.pa.gov/VotingElections/OtherServicesEvents/Documents/Directive-1
    -of-2021_Access-to-Electronic-Voting-Systems_7-8-2021.pdf.
3   https://www.penncapital-star.com/government-politics/what-we-know-about-the
    -2020-fulton-county-election-review-through-open-records/.

4   https://www.senatorcorman.com/2021/08/20/corman-issues-statement-on-forensic
     -investigation-of-recent-elections-mastriano-obstruction/.
5   https://www.attorneygeneral.gov/taking-action/press-releases/ag-shapiro-sues-senate
     -republicans-on-behalf-of-commonwealth-dos-over-plan-to-subpoena-voters-private
     -data/.
6   https://www.nytimes.com/2022/11/01/us/politics/pennsylvania-supreme-court
     -mail-in-ballots.html.
7   https://www.electionreturns.pa.gov/.
8   Ibid.

Chapter 10

1   https://will-law.org/will-issues-review-of-2020-election-recommendations-for
     -reform/.
2   Ibid.
3   Ibid.
4   Ibid.

Chapter 11

1   https://www.wisn.com/article/vos-former-president-trump-wants-answers-about
     -wisconsins-2020-election/37388466#.
2   https://legis.wisconsin.gov/lab.
3   https://legis.wisconsin.gov/lab/media/3288/21-19full.pdf (Appendix 10).
4   Ibid.
5   https://rumble.com/vpevd4-wisconsin-assembly-committee-on-campaigns-and-
     elections-nov-10-2021.html.
6   https://legis.wisconsin.gov/lab/media/3288/21-19full.pdf (Appendix 7) [Emphasis added].
7   https://rumble.com/vpevd4-wisconsin-assembly-committee-on-campaigns-and
     -elections-nov-10-2021.html.
8   https://www.youtube.com/watch?v=Xb5gQdiVGbk (25:21).
9   https://www.youtube.com/watch?v=Xb5gQdiVGbk.
10   Ibid.

Chapter 12

1   https://legis.wisconsin.gov/assembly/22/brandtjen/media/1534/presentation
     -combined.pdf; https://legis.wisconsin.gov/assembly/22/brandtjen/media/1466/hearing
     -packet-3-31-21.pdf.
2   https://legis.wisconsin.gov/assembly/22/brandtjen/media/1534/presentation
     -combined.pdf; https://www.maciverinstitute.com/2022/02/wec-receives-election-bribery
     -complaint-about-racine-city-officials/; https://legis.wisconsin.gov/assembly/22/brandtjen
     /media/1459/green-bay-3-10-21.pdf.
3   https://legis.wisconsin.gov/assembly/22/brandtjen/media/1534/presentation
     -combined.pdf; https://legis.wisconsin.gov/assembly/22/brandtjen/media/1466/hearing
     -packet-3-31-21.pdf.
4   Ibid.

5   https://legis.wisconsin.gov/assembly/22/brandtjen/media/1534/presentation
     -combined.pdf; https://legis.wisconsin.gov/assembly/22/brandtjen/media/1466/hearing
     -packet-3-31-21.pdf.
6   Ibid.
7   Ibid.
8   https://urbanmilwaukee.com/pressrelease/elections-commission-chair-responds-to
     -federal-request-for-wisconsin-voter-information/.
9   Email from Hannah Bubacz to Harrison at https://legis.wisconsin.gov/assembly/22
     /brandtjen/media/1534/presentation-combined.pdf.
10   Email from Michael Spitzer-Rubenstein to Claire Woodall Vogg October 19, 2020 https://
     legis.wisconsin.gov/assembly/22/brandtjen/media/1534/presentation-combined
     .pdf.
11   https://legis.wisconsin.gov/assembly/22/brandtjen/media/1466/hearing
     -packet-3-31-21.pdf.
12   https://sports.yahoo.com/fact-checkers-blast-donald-trump-190145727.html;
     https://www.washingtonpost.com/politics/2021/12/10/wisconsin-voter-registration
     -conspiracy-debunked/.
13   https://sports.yahoo.com/fact-checkers-blast-donald-trump-190145727.html;
     https://www.washingtonpost.com/politics/2021/12/10/wisconsin-voter-registration
     -conspiracy-debunked/.
14   https://rumble.com/vv6bow-wis.-investigates-voter-roll-maintenance.html
15   https://www.washingtonpost.com/politics/2021/12/10/wisconsin-voter-registration
     -conspiracy-debunked/.
16   https://rumble.com/vv6bow-wis.-investigates-voter-roll-maintenance.html
17   The email exchange is available at https://legis.wisconsin.gov/assembly/22/brandtjen
     /election-documents/.
18   The communication is available at https://legis.wisconsin.gov/assembly/22/brandtjen
     /election-documents/.
19   https://legis.wisconsin.gov/assembly/22/brandtjen/media/1541/wec-response
     -12-30-21.pdf.
20   Jeff O'Donnell's report, pg 1 see link: https://legis.wisconsin.gov/assembly/22
     /brandtjen/media/1534/presentation-combined.pdf.
21   Ibid.
22   Wisconsin Voter File Analysis, Jeff O'Donnell, 12/4/21, pg 5.
23   Ibid.
24   https://legis.wisconsin.gov/assembly/22/brandtjen/media/1541/wec-response
     -12-30-21.pdf.
25   https://fox11digital.com/news/PDFs/Gableman%20report.pdf.
26   https://fox11online.com/news/state/michael-gableman-releases-report-on-wisconsin
     -2020-election.
27   https://nypost.com/2021/10/13/mark-zuckerberg-spent-419m-on-nonprofits-ahead
     -of-2020-election-and-got-out-the-dem-vote/.
28   https://legis.wisconsin.gov/assembly/22/brandtjen/media/1552/osc-second-interim
     -report.pdf (pg 22).
29   https://legis.wisconsin.gov/assembly/22/brandtjen/media/1552/osc-second-interim
     -report.pdf (pg 23).

30 https://www.npr.org/2020/12/08/943242106/how-private-money-from-facebooks-ceo-saved-the-2020-election.
31 https://www.techandciviclife.org/board-of-directors/.
32 https://legis.wisconsin.gov/assembly/22/brandtjen/media/1552/osc-second-interim-report.pdf (pg 17).
33 Ibid.
34 Id.
35 https://ballotpedia.org/Center_for_Tech_and_Civic_Life%27s_(CTCL)_grants_to_election_agencies,_2020.
36 Ibid.
37 https://fox11digital.com/news/PDFs/Gableman%20report.pdf.
38 https://fox11digital.com/news/PDFs/Gableman%20report.pdf (pg 7–8).
39 https://fox11digital.com/news/PDFs/Gableman%20report.pdf (pg 136).
40 https://www.jsonline.com/story/news/politics/elections/2022/08/06/michael-gableman-endorses-robin-vos-opponent-adam-steen/10255706002/.
41 https://legis.wisconsin.gov/assembly/63/vos/.
42 https://ballotpedia.org/Wisconsin_State_Assembly_District_63.
43 Ibid.
44 https://ballotpedia.org/Robin_Vos.
45 https://www.nytimes.com/interactive/2022/08/09/us/elections/results-wisconsin-assembly-district-63.html.
46 https://legis.wisconsin.gov/assembly/22/brandtjen/election-documents/.
47 https://www.washingtonpost.com/politics/2022/07/28/wisconsin-voter-fraud/; https://captimes.com/news/government/activist-charged-with-election-fraud-for-requesting-absentee-ballot-for-robin-vos/article_82e7229a-d9cc-5bf5-9bcc-ea26c994c0cd.html.
48 https://madison.com/news/local/govt-and-politics/robin-vos-withdraws-subpoenas-issued-by-michael-gablemans-election-review/article_4e98cc44-e3f9-5c32-8110-ff30088240ab.html.
49 Ibid.
50 https://twitter.com/JasonCalvi/status/1569361318666436614.
51 https://twitter.com/JasonCalvi/status/1569430104039645185.
52 https://gpsimpact.com/.

Chapter 13

1 https://himaforcongress.com/.
2 https://wwmt.com/news/election/more-than-27-million-michigan-voters-request-absentee-ballots-for-nov-3-election.
3 Antrim Michigan Forensic Report pg 2.
4 Ibid.
5 Antrim Michigan Forensic Report pg. 7, Figure 8.
6 https://misenategopcdn.s3.us-east-1.amazonaws.com/99/doccuments/20210623/SMPO_2020ElectionReport_2.pdf.
7 https://misenategopcdn.s3.us-east-1.amazonaws.com/99/doccuments/20210623/SMPO_2020ElectionReport_2.pdf (pg 19).
8 https://www.politico.com/news/2020/11/09/republicans-free-fair-elections-435488.

Chapter 14

[1] https://www.americanprogress.org/issues/democracy/news/2017/03/29/429442/corporate-capture-threatens-democratic-government/.

[2] https://www.npr.org/2020/12/08/943242106/how-private-money-from-facebooks-ceo-saved-the-2020-election.

[3] https://adage.com/article/campaign-trail/political-ad-spending-year-reached-whopping-85-billion/2295646.

[4] Ibid.

[5] https://www.npr.org/2020/12/08/943242106/how-private-money-from-facebooks-ceo-saved-the-2020-election.

[6] https://www.techandciviclife.org/our-story/.

[7] https://www.techandciviclife.org/board-of-directors/#.

[8] Ibid.

[9] https://www.coloradopolitics.com/news/bartels-celebrating-a-true-public-servant/article_37e3cd98-2cfb-11eb-a8e8-af9a4e0527c9.html.

[10] https://www.npr.org/2020/12/08/943242106/how-private-money-from-facebooks-ceo-saved-the-2020-election.

[11] https://voteathome.org/staff/xanthe-thomassen/.

[12] https://en.wikipedia.org/wiki/Amber_McReynolds#cite_note-:2–3.

[13] https://www.270towin.com/states/Colorado.

[14] Ibid.

[15] https://www.influencewatch.org/non-profit/national-vote-at-home-institute/.

[16] https://en.wikipedia.org/wiki/Phil_Keisling.

[17] https://www.multco.us/elections/brief-history-vote-mail-oregon.

[18] https://www.statista.com/statistics/1130754/oregon-electoral-votes-since-1860/.

[19] https://www.influencewatch.org/non-profit/national-vote-at-home-institute/.

[20] Ibid.

[21] https://voteathome.org/.

[22] Pg 20 of Erick Kaardal's memo.

[23] Pg 8 of Erick Kaardals report.

[24] Pg 9 of the city attorney's report.

[25] https://wisconsinspotlight.com/clerk-i-will-not-break-the-law/.

[26] Ibid.

[27] https://time.com/5901694/amber-mcreynolds-vote-by-mail-2020-election/.

[28] Ibid.

[29] Ibid.

[30] Ibid.

[31] https://time.com/5901694/amber-mcreynolds-vote-by-mail-2020-election/; https://www.influencewatch.org/non-profit/national-vote-at-home-institute/.

[32] https://time.com/5901694/amber-mcreynolds-vote-by-mail-2020-election/.

Chapter 15

[1] https://www.npr.org/sections/live-updates-2020-election-results/2020/11/07/932481031/ap-calls-nevada-for-joe-biden (shows he did not win until Nov 7).

2   https://www.npr.org/sections/live-updates-2020-election-results/2020/11/07
    /932481031/ap-calls-nevada-for-joe-biden.
3   https://www.cnn.com/factsfirst/politics/factcheck_38192161-1b4b-4d96-a057-
    ee0726691742.
4   https://twitter.com/realLizUSA/status/1425599157859913730.
5   https://nevadagop.org/united-states-postal-service-whistleblower-testimony-on
    -election/.
6   https://nevadagop.org/poll-workers-observers-experiences-with-the-2020-election/.
7   Ibid.
8   https://www.reviewjournal.com/opinion/opinion-columns/victor-joecks/victor
    -joecks-county-lowers-confidence-level-for-ballot-signatures-2156478/.
9   https://twitter.com/nvgop/status/1334609079516348416.
10 https://www.politico.com/2020-election/results/nevada/.
11 https://nevadagop.org/cash-for-votes-in-nevada/; https://nevadagop.org/double-voting
    -in-nevada/; https://nevadagop.org/illegal-voters/; https://nevadagop.org/out-of-state
    -voters/; https://nevadagop.org/united-states-postal-service-whistleblower-testimony-on
    -election/; https://nevadagop.org/poll-workers-observers-experiences-with-the-2020
    -election/.
12 https://nevadagop.org/double-voting-in-nevada/.
13 Ibid.
14 Ibid.
15 Ibid.
16 Ibid.
17 Ibid.
18 https://nevadagop.org/wp-content/uploads/2020/12/Money-for-Votes.pdf.
19 18 USC section 597; https://nevadagop.org/wp-content/uploads/2020/12/Money-for
    -Votes.pdf.
20 https://nevadagop.org/wp-content/uploads/2020/12/Money-for-Votes.pdf.
21 https://www.truethevote.org/true-the-vote-sends-letter-to-doj-reporting-serious
    -national-security-matter-and-breach-within-nevada-secretary-of-states-email-system/.
22 Ibid.
23 True the Vote letter to DOJ: https://www.truethevote.org/true-the-vote-sends-letter
    -to-doj-reporting-serious-national-security-matter-and-breach-within-nevada-secretary
    -of-states-email-system/.
24 https://www.truethevote.org/true-the-vote-sends-letter-to-doj-reporting-serious
    -national-security-matter-and-breach-within-nevada-secretary-of-states-email-system/.
25 https://thenevadaindependent.com/article/secretary-of-state-no-voter-info-sent-to
    -pakistani-government-state-election-system-has-not-been-hacked.
26 https://www.instagram.com/p/CjUVzFNN1qB/?utm_source=ig_web_copy_link.
27 https://da.lacounty.gov/media/news/head-election-worker-management-company
    -arrested-connection-theft-personal-data.
28 Ibid.
29 https://www.instagram.com/p/CjUVzFNN1qB/?utm_source=ig_web_copy_link.
30 NV GOP affidavit.
31 NV GOP Affidavit.

32 https://www.lcsun-news.com/story/news/politics/elections/2020/11/02/video -shows-moments-leading-gop-challengers-ejection-dona-ana-county/6127042002/.

33 Ibid.

34 https://www.politico.com/2020-election/results/new-mexico/.

35 Complaint 10/26.

36 Complaint.

37 https://www.lcsun-news.com/story/news/2020/10/29/nm-gops-absentee-ballot -drop-box-lawsuit-gets-resolution/6076532002/.

38 Ibid.

39 Exhibit 1 to the Complaint filed 10/26/2020.

40 NV GOP Affidavit.

41 Ibid.

42 https://www.krqe.com/news/politics-government/elections/city-council-races -leaning-more-conservative/.

43 https://www.politico.com/2020-election/results/texas/.

44 https://www.sos.texas.gov/elections/forms/phase1-progress-report.pdf.

45 https://www.sos.texas.gov/elections/forms/phase1-progress-report.pdf (pg. 4 - Tarrant County).

46 https://www.sos.texas.gov/elections/forms/phase1-progress-report.pdf (pg.8).

47 https://www.sos.texas.gov/elections/forms/phase1-progress-report.pdf (pg 9).

48 Ibid.

49 https://www.reuters.com/article/us-usa-election-court-brief/several-u-s-states-back -texas-bid-to-upend-biden-election-win-at-supreme-court-idUSKBN28J2WE.

50 https://search.txcourts.gov/SearchMedia.aspx?MediaVersionID=7dbdaca3-3a6d -4a75-925f-883fa825acae&coa=coscca&DT=OPINION&MediaID=8976a0aa -8fa8-4814-91bb-f0d79f1108fc.

51 Ibid.

52 https://www.texasattorneygeneral.gov/news/releases/paxton-asks-court-criminal -appeals-reverse-its-decision-stripping-oag-authority-stop-election-fraud.

Chapter 16

1 https://www.heritage.org/gender/commentary/school-districts-are-hiding -information-about-gender-transitioning-children-their.

2 https://www.cbsnews.com/news/federal-court-rules-that-transgender-students-must -be-allowed-to-use-bathrooms-that-match-their-gender/.

3 https://nypost.com/2021/10/27/loudoun-county-parents-demand-resignations-over -sexual-assault/.

4 https://nypost.com/2021/10/26/virginia-teen-found-guilty-of-sexual-assault-that -sparked-volatile-school-board-meeting/.

5 https://www.foxnews.com/media/loudoun-county-parents-demand-school-officials -resign-friends-first.

6 https://dcist.com/story/20/08/06/fairfax-county-absentee-ballot-applications- virginia-department-of-elections/.

7 Ibid.

8 https://dcist.com/story/20/08/06/fairfax-county-absentee-ballot-applications -virginia-department-of-elections/.

9   https://results.elections.virginia.gov/vaelections/2020%20November%20General
     /Site/Locality/FAIRFAX_COUNTY/Index.html.
10   Ibid.
11   https://www.tysonsreporter.com/2020/11/09/fairfax-county-sets-record-turnout-for
     -2020-election/.
12   https://www.reuters.com/world/us/virginia-republican-tries-thread-needle-election
     -fraud-claims-2021-10-12/.
13   https://www.washingtonpost.com/dc-md-va/2021/10/27/virginia-poll-watchers
     -election/.
14   Private interview.
15   Ibid.
16   Ibid.
17   Ibid.
18   Ibid.
19   Ibid.
20   https://en.wikipedia.org/wiki/2020_United_States_presidential_election_in_New
     _Jersey.
21   https://www.270towin.com/states/New_Jersey.
22   https://www.nj.gov/governor/news/news/562020/20200814b.shtml; https://prospect
     .org/civil-rights/how-new-jersey-became-a-vote-by-mail-state/.
23   https://www.nj.gov/governor/news/news/562020/20200814b.shtml.
24   https://prospect.org/civil-rights/how-new-jersey-became-a-vote-by-mail-state/.
25   Ibid.
26   Ibid.
27   https://publicinterestlegal.org/wp-content/uploads/2022/06/NJ-Data-Review-2022
     -1P-FINAL-4.pdf.
28   https://publicinterestlegal.org/wp-content/uploads/2022/06/NJ-Data-Review-2022
     -1P-FINAL-4.pdf (pg 3).
29   Ibid.
30   Ibid.
31   Ibid.
32   https://publicinterestlegal.org/wp-content/uploads/2022/06/NJ-Data-Review-2022
     -1P-FINAL-4.pdf (pg 2).
33   https://www.thegatewaypundit.com/2021/11/developing-new-jersey-governors-race
     -much-closer-expected-dem-murphy-49-3-gop-ciattarelli-49-9/; NY Times Edison Data.
34   Ibid.
35   https://www.thegatewaypundit.com/2021/11/breaking-democrat-tricks-new-jersey
     -governors-race-republican-winning-largest-county-100-votes-counted-vote-flips
     -democrat-miraculously-wins-county/.
36   Ibid.
37   Ibid.
38   https://en.wikipedia.org/wiki/2021_New_Jersey_gubernatorial_election#cite_note-9.
39   https://en.wikipedia.org/wiki/2021_New_Jersey_gubernatorial_election#cite_note-9.
40   Private interview.
41   https://www.nbcnewyork.com/news/local/after-spending-just-153-on-campaign
     -truck-driver-beats-nj-senate-president/3378682/.

42 https://en.wikipedia.org/wiki/2021_New_Jersey_General_Assembly_election.
43 https://en.wikipedia.org/wiki/2021_New_Jersey_State_Senate_election.
44 Private interview.
45 https://www.brennancenter.org/our-work/research-reports/voting-laws-roundup
    -december-2021.
46 https://www.nbcnews.com/politics/elections/19-states-enacted-voting-restrictions
    -2021-rcna8342.
47 https://www.brennancenter.org/our-work/research-reports/voting-laws-roundup
    -december-2021.
48 https://www.nbcnews.com/politics/elections/19-states-enacted-voting-restrictions
    -2021-rcna8342.
49 Ibid.
50 Ibid.
51 https://www.npr.org/2021/07/09/1014579306/texas-republicans-have-a-new
    -voting-bill-heres-whats-in-it.
52 Ibid.
53 https://www.cbsnews.com/news/georgia-voting-law-9-facts/.
54 Ibid.
55 https://www.npr.org/2022/07/08/1100696685/wisconsin-supreme-court-ballot
    -drop-boxes-disability-assistance; https://www.politico.com/news/2022/02/11/wisconsin
    -state-supreme-court-drop-boxes-ban-spring-election-00008377.
56 https://www.greenbaypressgazette.com/story/news/politics/elections/2022/02/15
    /republicans-object-error-green-bay-ballot-count-time/6807262001/.
57 Ibid.
58 https://www.greenbaypressgazette.com/news/; https://fox11online.com/news/local/green
    -bay/green-bay-mayor-talks-about-calls-for-his-resignation-election-investigation.
59 https://www.judicialwatch.org/north-carolina-voter-rolls-lawsuit/.
60 Ibid.
61 https://rumble.com/vvkgzw-n.c.-removes-430k-inactive-voters-from-rolls.html.

Chapter 17

1 https://www.politico.com/story/2018/01/09/rnc-ballot-security-consent-decree
   -328995.
2 https://www.politico.com/f/?id=00000160-db8a-dcd4-a96b-ffabe0680001.
3 https://www.washingtonpost.com/news/the-fix/wp/2017/11/02/ex-dnc-chair-goes
   -at-the-clintons-alleging-hillarys-campaign-hijacked-dnc-during-primary-with
   -bernie-sanders/.
4 https://www.maciverinstitute.com/2022/02/shocking-evidence-of-widespread-fraud
   -in-wisconsins-voter-database/.
5 https://justthenews.com/politics-policy/elections/georgia-opens-investigation
   -possible-illegal-ballot-harvesting-2020; https://katv.com/news/nation-world/georgia
   -opens-investigation-into-ballot-harvesting-claims.
6 https://nypost.com/2020/09/27/project-veritas-uncovers-ballot-harvesting-fraud-in
   -minnesota/.

7   https://journaltimes.com/news/local/govt-and-politics/eight-cases-of-election-fraud
     -at-racine-county-nursing-home-sheriff-schmaling-says/article_1722e503-a13b
     -5f3d-bd7e-c72a68962e4d.html.
8   https://urbanmilwaukee.com/2020/11/03/look-inside-milwaukees-central-count
     -facility/.
9   https://thehill.com/homenews/campaign/524401-key-pa-county-suspends-vote
     -counting-until-10-am-wednesday.
10   https://mc4ei.com/testimony-of-fraud-in-the-2020-michigan-election-listening-to
     -those-who-were-there/.
11   https://rumble.com/vpokri-republican-workers-blocked-from-participating-in-2020
     -election.html.
12   https://www.cnn.com/2020/11/05/media/detroit-windows-covered-ballots-vote
     -center/index.html.
13   https://mc4ei.com/testimony-of-fraud-in-the-2020-michigan-election-listening-to
     -those-who-were-there/.
14   https://www.khou.com/article/news/investigations/houston-woman-turned
     -away-at-polls-after-being-told-she-already-voted/285-23ff25d7-49ea-4ee8-95ec
     -38ddb83a0ac5; https://abc11.com/nc-vote-provisional-ballot-voter-already-voted-what
     -is-a/7588117/; https://www.newsleader.com/story/news/politics/elections/2020/11
     /03/voting-old-way-didnt-work-out-staunton-man-provisional-ballot-voter-id
     -election-2020/6144019002/.
15   Janel Brandtjen's hearing 12/8 and Jeff O'Donnell's report.
16   Christina's interviews on OAN in Detroit.
17   https://www.washingtonpost.com/politics/2021/12/10/wisconsin-voter-registration
     -conspiracy-debunked/.
18   https://nevadagop.org/double-voting-in-nevada/.
19   Janel Brandtjen's hearing 12/8.
20   https://rumble.com/vv0f62-wisc.-elections-commission-hearing-offers-more-clarity
     -on-election-security.html.
21   Ibid.
22   https://rumble.com/vv0f62-wisc.-elections-commission-hearing-offers-more-clarity
     -on-election-security.html; Janel Brandtjen's hearing 12/8, Jeff O'Donnell report &
     Audit the Vote PA report.
23   https://ballotpedia.org/Ballot_harvesting_laws_by_state.
24   Ibid.
25   Ibid.
26   https://www.projectveritas.com/news/ilhan-omar-connected-cash-for-ballots-voter
     -fraud-scheme-corrupts-elections/; https://nypost.com/2020/09/27/project-veritas
     -uncovers-ballot-harvesting-fraud-in-minnesota/.
27   https://www.projectveritas.com/news/ilhan-omar-connected-cash-for-ballots-voter
     -fraud-scheme-corrupts-elections/.
28   https://www.azcentral.com/story/news/local/arizona/2020/12/23/two-yuma-women
     -indicted-ballot-harvesting/4033370001/; https://www.texasattorneygeneral.gov/news
     /releases/ag-paxton-san-antonio-election-fraudster-arrested-widespread-vote
     -harvesting-and-fraud.
29   Arizona Audit.

30 Arizona Audit revealed that ballots were printed on-site.
31 https://www.thegatewaypundit.com/2021/02/exclusive-tcf-center-election-fraud
    -newly-recovered-video-shows-late-night-deliveries-tens-thousands-illegal-ballots
    -michigan-arena/.
32 Arizona Audit.
33 https://www.cbsnews.com/news/joe-biden-popular-vote-record-barack-obama-us
    -presidential-election-donald-trump/.
34 https://republicans-cha.house.gov/threat-ballot-harvesting;   https://www.bloomberg
    .com/news/articles/2020-05-29/election-lawyer-s-vote-by-mail-crusade-meets-gop
    -resistance?leadSource=uverify%20wall.
35 https://gnews.org/534248/.
36 https://www.acfeinsights.com/acfe-insights/what-is-benfords-law; https://en.wikipedia
    .org/wiki/Benford%27s_law.
37 https://www.acfeinsights.com/acfe-insights/what-is-benfords-law.
38 Ibid.
39 https://gnews.org/534248/.
40 https://www.usatoday.com/story/news/factcheck/2020/12/09/fact-check-joe-biden
    -won-most-votes-ever-and-fewest-counties/3865097001/.
41 Ibid.
42 Ibid.
43 https://thefederalist.com/2020/11/24/poll-one-in-six-biden-voters-would-have
    -changed-their-vote-if-they-had-known-about-scandals-suppressed-by-media/.
44 Ibid.
45 https://www.politico.com/news/2020/09/23/trump-peaceful-transition-of
    -power-420791.
46 Ibid.
47 https://www.nytimes.com/2020/11/10/us/politics/voting-fraud.html.
48 https://www.cbsnews.com/live-updates/2020-election-most-secure-history-dhs/.
49 https://www.washingtonpost.com/politics/2020/12/14/there-is-not-has-not-been
    -any-credible-evidence-significant-fraud-2020-election/.
50 https://www.justice.gov/usao-nh/pr/federal-election-fraud-fact-sheet.
51 https://www.azleg.gov/viewdocument/?docName=https%3A%2F%2Fwww.azleg
    .gov%2Fars%2F16%2F00673.htm.

Chapter 18

1   https://www.npr.org/2021/02/10/966396848/read-trumps-jan-6-speech-a-key-part
    -of-impeachment-trial.
2   https://www.nytimes.com/2021/01/08/us/politics/police-officer-killed-capitol.html.
3   https://www.judicialwatch.org/jw-sicknick-documents/; https://www.uscp.gov/media
    -center/press-releases/medical-examiner-finds-uscp-officer-brian-sicknick-died
    -natural-causes; https://www.judicialwatch.org/jw-sicknick-documents/.
4   https://www.judicialwatch.org/jw-sicknick-documents/; In the eight months following
    January 6, four Capitol police officers died by suicide https://www.cnbc.com/2021
    /08/02/3rd-police-officer-gunther-hashida-kills-himself-after-capitol-riot-by
    -trump-mob.html.

5   https://rollcall.com/2019/02/27/capitol-police-weapon-left-unattended-in-capitol
    -bathroom-again/; https://thefederalist.com/2021/08/27/flashback-capitol-police-officer
    -who-shot-ashli-babbitt-left-his-gun-unattended-in-a-bathroom-in-2019/.
6   https://rumble.com/vqhs4y-jan.-6-witness-says-police-caused-stampede-and-killed
    -rosanne-boyland.html; https://rumble.com/vv63b0-new-jan-6-footage-reveals-officer
    -assaulted-rosanne-boyland.html; https://rumble.com/vs6he3-videos-shed-light-on
    -death-of-rosanne-boyland-at-us-capitol-on-jan.-6.html.
7   https://www.thegatewaypundit.com/2021/12/riveting-oan-interview-jan-6-witness
    -philip-anderson-knocked-unconscious-next-rosanne-boyland-died-says-police
    -caused-stampede-killed/.
8   https://www.thegatewaypundit.com/2021/12/riveting-oan-interview-jan-6-witness
    -philip-anderson-knocked-unconscious-next-rosanne-boyland-died-says-police
    -caused-stampede-killed/.
9   https://www.youtube.com/watch?v=dNuYYHOvmd4.
10 https://www.youtube.com/watch?v=dNuYYHOvmd4 https://s3.documentcloud.org
    /documents/21113253/dod-ig-jan-6.pdf.
11 https://www.youtube.com/watch?v=dNuYYHOvmd4.
12 https://s3.documentcloud.org/documents/21113253/dod-ig-jan-6.pdf.
13 Ibid.
14 https://www.congress.gov/117/bills/hres24/BILLS-117hres24ih.pdf (pg 2, line 12).
15 https://www.congress.gov/117/bills/hres24/BILLS-117hres24ih.pdf (pg 3, line 4).
16 https://www.congress.gov/117/bills/hres24/BILLS-117hres24ih.pdf.
17 https://www.congress.gov/117/bills/hres24/BILLS-117hres24ih.pdf (pg 4, line 8).
18 https://www.nytimes.com/article/george-floyd-protests-timeline.html.
19 *Id.*
20 https://www.axios.com/riots-cost-property-damage-276c9bcc-a455-4067-b06a
    -66f9db4cea9c.html.
21 https://twitter.com/kamalaharris/status/1267555018128965643?lang=en.
22 https://www.speaker.gov/newsroom/72121-2.
23 https://apnews.com/article/donald-trump-ap-top-news-george-floyd-politics
    -a2326518da6b25b4509bef1ec85f5d7f.
24 https://www.congress.gov/117/bills/hres24/BILLS-117hres24ih.pdf (pg 4, line 23).
25 https://www.cnn.com/2021/02/13/politics/republican-votes-trump-guilty-convict
    -impeachment/index.html; https://en.wikipedia.org/wiki/Second_impeachment_trial_of
    _Donald_Trump.
26 Liz Cheney (R-WY); Tom Rice (R-SC); Dan Newhouse (R-WA); Adam Kinzinger (R-
    IL); Anthony Gonzalez (R-OH); Fred Upton (R-MI); Jaime Herrera Beutler (R-WA);
    Peter Meijer (R-MI); John Katko (R-NY); David Valadoa (R-CA).
27 https://www.npr.org/2021/01/14/956621191/these-are-the-10-republicans-who-
    voted-to-impeach-trump.
28 https://www.cnbc.com/2021/02/13/the-7-republicans-who-voted-to-convict-trump.
    html Richard Burr (R-NC); Bill Cassidy (R-LA); Susan Collins (R-ME); Lisa
    Murkowski (R-AK); Mitt Romney (R-UT); Ben Sasse (R-NE); and Pat Toomey (R-
    PA) voted with the Democrats.
29 https://www.theatlantic.com/politics/archive/2017/11/the-secret-correspondence
    -between-donald-trump-jr-and-wikileaks/545738/.

30 https://www.cnn.com/2018/01/05/politics/trump-russia-investigation
    -documentary/index.html.
31 https://www.cnn.com/2017/10/24/politics/fusion-gps-clinton-campaign/index.html;
    https://www.baltimoresun.com/opinion/editorial/bs-ed-1027-alt-fact-russia-dossier
    -20171025-story.html; https://www.voanews.com/a/discredited-steele-dossier-flags
    -important-lessons-for-media/6342968.html.
32 https://www.npr.org/2019/03/07/701045248/paul-manafort-former-trump
    -campaign-chairman-sentenced-to-just-under-4-years.
33 https://www.politico.com/news/2021/11/28/cohen-trump-grifting-american
    -people-523419.
34 https://www.justice.gov/usao-ct/pr/fbi-attorney-admits-altering-email-used-fisa
    -application-during-crossfire-hurricane.
35 https://www.politico.com/magazine/story/2016/04/donald-trump-2016
    -impeachment-213817/.
36 https://www.nbcnews.com/politics/donald-trump/officials-rejected-jared-kushner
    -top-secret-security-clearance-were-overruled-n962221.
37 https://www.hsgac.senate.gov/media/majority-media/johnson-grassley-release-report
    -on-conflicts-of-interest-investigation.
38 https://www.dailymail.co.uk/news/article-9881213/Unearthed-video-shows-naked
    -Hunter-Biden-claiming-Russian-drug-dealers-stole-laptop.html.
39 https://www.cnn.com/2019/05/06/politics/donald-trump-approval-rating-strong
    -economy/index.html.
40 https://www.scribd.com/document/598106810/34-US-Political-Prisoners-Demand-
    Transfer-to-Guantanomo-Bay-to-Escape-Intolerable-Conditions-and-Receive
    -Same-Rights-as-Violent-Foreign-Terrorists#download&from_embed; https://www
    .thegatewaypundit.com/2022/10/breaking-34-us-political-prisoners-dc-gulag
    -demand-transfer-guantanamo-bay-escape-intolerable-conditions-receive-rights
    -violent-foreign-terrorists/.
41 https://www.nytimes.com/2020/11/10/us/politics/voting-fraud.html.
42 https://www.vox.com/2020/11/13/21563825/2020-elections-most-secure-dhs-cisa
    -krebs.
43 https://www.freep.com/story/news/politics/elections/2020/11/06/antrim-county
    -vote-glitch-software-update/6194745002/.

Chapter 19

1 https://www.womenshealthmag.com/relationships/a36395721/gender-identity-list/.
2 https://www.cnn.com/2021/09/04/us/census-browning-of-america-myth-blake
   /index.html.
3 https://www.nas.org/blogs/article/harvard_prepares_to_host_all_black_graduation.
4 https://www.washingtonpost.com/opinions/2021/01/15/understand-trumps
   -support-we-must-think-terms-multiracial-whiteness/ Donna Jackson on Weekly; https:
   //www.npr.org/2021/01/24/960060957/understanding-multiracial-whiteness-and
   -trump-supporters.
5 https://www.wsj.com/articles/about-those-domestic-terrorists-national-school
   -boards-association-merrick-garland-memo-fbi-11635285900.
6 https://www.archives.gov/founding-docs/declaration-transcript Declaration of Independence

7   https://www.nbcnews.com/politics/elections/19-states-enacted-voting-restrictions
    -2021-rcna8342.
8   https://www.reaganlibrary.gov/archives/speech/january-5-1967-inaugural-address
    -public-ceremony Jan. 5, 1967 Governor Inaugural Address.
9   Statement from President Donald J. Trump, February 27, 2022 www.precinctstrategy
    .com.

Index

Acknowledgments

This book would not have been possible without the help and support of many people who worked tirelessly, often at their own expense, to investigate the 2020 election. To everyone who has volunteered, donated, and given resources to take a closer look at who is pulling the strings in our elections, you are American heroes. Over the course of two years, I've interviewed dozens, possibly hundreds, of people who have spent their own time and money to collect a piece of the puzzle. You are why America will be great again.

The book itself would never have come into being without the guidance and mentorship of my editor, agent, and friend, Marji Ross. Thank you for teaching me how to put a project like this together, and for your expertise and knowledge of what matters to readers and what doesn't. When I thought this book would never get completed, your vision saved it, and I'm forever grateful.

Thank you One America News, and the entire Herring family. Robert "Mr. H," Charles, Bobby, and the whole One America News team gave me the room to run after this story. Your dedication to America, free speech, and real news empowered me to investigate how our elections have gone so far off the rails. Thank you for everything you have done for me and this great nation. You are patriots.

Thank you to the brave elected officials willing to honor their constituents and take a closer look at the integrity of elections. Many elected officials were too scared to touch the subject. Some even feared for their own seats. But, there were some who did it anyway. The Arizona Senate, led by Karen Fann, made history when they were willing to conduct an audit. Arizona senators Sonny Borrelli, Wendy Rogers, and each senator who voted for the audit, thank you. In the Arizona House of Representatives, Mark Finchem and Leo Biassucci stood up to the mainstream media and supported the Arizona Senate. Wisconsin State Representative Janel Brandtjen was the megaphone in Wisconsin calling for transparency. Pennsylvania's Senator Doug Mastriano and Representative Rob Kauffman brought the issue to Pennsylvania. Thank you.

Even in the face of the Defund the Police movement, many patriot sheriffs stood up in their communities to try to hold criminals accountable. Sheriff Christopher Schmaling and Lieutenant Michael Luell in Racine followed the law and did their jobs, despite the Racine district attorney refusing to prosecute. Thank you to all the sheriffs holding the line.

My family was incredibly supportive of me throughout this whole process. My parents, my sister, Carrie, and my brother-in-law, Matt, were the lifeblood for my efforts. Thank you for always being there for me and encouraging me to do whatever crazy idea came to mind. I'm so grateful for you and couldn't have picked a better family.

My greatest appreciation to Steve Bannon for continuing to discuss this important topic, inform his viewers of the concerns, and lend his voice by writing the introduction. I am forever grateful for Steve's fight and willingness to sound the alarm.

Thank you Skyhorse Publishing for agreeing to work on this project and having the courage to publish this book. Your team has been so kind and gracious throughout the project. Thank you Hector Carosso and Tony Lyons for all of your work to make this happen.

Thank you Amber Colleran for a great cover design! You took the heart of the book and put it on the cover. I'm very grateful.

Lastly, thank you to my readers. Thank you for taking the time to learn this issue. If you're not already, please find a local grassroots organization in your area and get involved. We will restore America to the land of the free, but it requires each of us to first be brave. We must boldly exercise our rights, and hold the government accountable, before we lose it all. We have a choice: to be the last generation to know America as a free country, or to be the first generation to re-establish our constitutional rights and usher in the greatest era of prosperity this nation has known. History will determine if we make the sacrifice now, or later.